# The Cross-Border Connection

# The Cross-Border Connection

*Immigrants, Emigrants, and Their Homelands*

ROGER WALDINGER

Harvard University Press

Cambridge, Massachusetts
London, England

First Harvard University Press paperback edition, 2017
First Printing

*Library of Congress Cataloging-in-Publication Data*

Waldinger, Roger David.
The cross-border connection : immigrants, emigrants, and their homelands / Roger Waldinger.
pages cm
Includes bibliographical references and index.
ISBN 978-0-674-73673-3 (cloth : alk. paper)
ISBN 978-0-674-97550-7 (pbk.)
1. Emigration and immigration.   2. Immigrants.   I. Title.
JV6033.W35 2015
305.9'0691—dc23
2014011216

# Contents

# The Cross-Border Connection

# CHAPTER ONE

# Immigrants, Emigrants, and Their Homelands

IMMIGRANTS ARE the people who leave one country behind to settle down somewhere else. Or so the dictionary contends. While citizens and sometimes even the scholars see the phenomenon in just this way, close observers of the immigrant experience in the United States have long known better. Though the huge transatlantic movements of the last century of migration generated millions of settlers, they also produced a continuous flow of people moving in the other direction. As discovered more than a century ago by the team that the US Immigration Commission sent to Europe, the results of the homeward bound flow were difficult to miss:

> The investigators . . . were impressed by the number of men in Italy and various Slavic communities who speak English and who exhibit a distinct affection for the United States. The unwillingness of such men to work in the fields at 25 to 30 cents a day; their tendency to acquire property; their general initiative; and most concretely, the money they can show, make a vivid impression. They are dispensers of information and inspiration, and are often willing to follow up the inspiration by loans to prospective migrants. (Wyman 1993: 6)

As the commissioners unintentionally pointed out, the very same migrations that peopled America was a way of knitting old and new worlds together. Return migration belonged to a broader complex of social ties, facilitating migration while also channeling ideas, information, experiences, and capital back to the places from which the immigrants had originally come. Though separated by thousands of miles and an ocean that took days, not hours, to cross, the migrants and stay-at-homes maintained the connection. Millions of letters crossed the Atlantic to be read, sometimes by the individual recipients, sometimes by one of the literate villagers, in a public event that disseminated the news to a far wider audience. While the letters were designed to keep relatives and friends informed of the latest developments in the migrant's life, they had other, deeper effects—namely, that of reporting on the advantages to be gained from life in the new world, thereby encouraging even greater numbers to engage in the migrant flow. The envelopes didn't contain news only: looking inside, one found cash. That money should flow from one side of the Atlantic to another was no accident; rather, this was the very idea that impelled migrants to leave home. Earning money in places where wages were high but spending money where the cost of living was low, the poor exploited the rich, using their access to the resources of a wealthier country to make life better back home. Migration didn't just generate social change back home; it was also often the lever for political transformation. Nationalist movements found fertile soil in the United States. With agitators freely plying their trade without fear of government repression, and a population base doing well enough to provide material assistance, the immigrants provided valuable support for the movements seeking to take apart the multiethnic empires that prevailed during the last era of mass migration.[1]

One never wants to say that the more things change, the more they stay the same. But the careful student of contemporary immigration to the United States can't help but notice the similarities. Yes, America's foreign-born population has grown rapidly over the past four decades: ever since 1970, when the foreign-born population fell to its historic nadir of 4.7 percent, the foreign-born presence has been continuously rising. The forty million foreign-born persons now living in the United States make up 13 percent of the population; numbers are growing so rapidly that the immigration rate—measured as the annual flow of persons as a percentage of total population—is approaching levels seen during the last century of migration, when the country's population was less than one-third its current size.

If there is plenty of migration for settlement, evidence of connections linking "here" and "there" is no less striking than it was a hundred years ago. Of course, the places of origin are no longer the same. Although there is a continuing flow of migrants from Eastern Europe, transatlantic migration now takes on very modest proportions. Instead, the new immigrants come mainly from elsewhere in the Western Hemisphere, with sizable and growing numbers arriving from Asia and still small but expanding populations coming from Africa.

Regardless of origins, the immigrants of the current era of mass migration are maintaining home country connections, doing so in ways that remind one of the past but also look quite different, as changes in technology, communication, as well as the social environment would lead one to expect. Yesterday, the simple letter did an excellent job of bridging here and there, even though the passage from one side to another was far from speedy. Today communication between migrants and their relatives and friends can be instantaneous. A huge, near-constant flow of telephone traffic moves between the United States and the countries from which its immigrants come. While telephone lines might not extend to some of the small, isolated villages from which the immigrants come, the rapid diffusion of cell phones allows almost everyone, everywhere, to be connected. Telecommunication may not be free, but it's not terribly expensive: competition within the telecommunications industry is constantly driving prices down. While the best prices are to be found on the Internet, cheap telephone cards are sold in just about every other store in the immigrant neighborhoods of Los Angeles, New York, Miami, and increasingly every other major US city. Access is also growing at the other end: the migrants' friends and relatives at home may be too poor to own a phone, in which case the purchase can be made by the migrant abroad.

As in the past, people and money are moving back and forth. At Christmastime, airplanes headed for El Salvador or Jamaica or Port-au-Prince are packed with immigrants, many equipped with US passports, on the way to spend the holidays with relatives still living at home. As with communication, the ethnic tourism of immigrants and those of their relatives lucky enough to enter the United States with a visa is a good business, attracting investors eager to serve this market and help it grow. Even more attractive, perhaps, is the business of sending the dollars earned by the immigrants in the United States back to the countries from which they have come. The flow of remittances has burgeoned to impressive proportions. Remittances received by developing countries are large (the second largest source of development finance after direct foreign investment); rising (up by almost fivefold between 1989 and 2011); stable (with less volatility than other sources, such as capital market flows or development assistance, and much less severely hit by the financial crisis that began in 2008); and free, requiring neither interest nor repayment of capital (Sirkeci, Cohen, and Ratha 2012). With so much money leaving a rich country and heading toward a wide variety of poor countries, there is no shortage of actors seeking to facilitate what the immigrants want to do on their own accord. Remittances rank as a top priority for the World Bank, the International Monetary Fund, and the American Development Bank, to name just a few. For the private sector, the remittance business is an opportunity to be exploited, which is why large American banks are taking over Mexican chains, Central American banks are opening branches in Los Angeles's immigrant neighborhoods, and all of the banks, whether US or foreign, are opening their doors for undocumented immigrants.

In the past, the emigrants' efforts to get ahead on their own won them the contempt of the compatriots and states that they left behind. As depicted by the famous Mexican writer and former diplomat Octavio Paz, in his book *The Labyrinth of Solitude,* written in the middle of the last century, the emigrants who looked for fortune across the border did so at the price of their souls:

> [The *pachuco's*] whole being is sheer negative impulse . . . he has lost his whole inheritance: language, religion, customs, beliefs. He is left without a body and a soul with which to confront the elements, defenseless against the stares of everyone. (1950 [1994 ed.]: 14–15)

While Paz looked down from Olympian heights, popular culture spread the same view, with most Mexican movies, for example, portraying migration to the United States and Mexican American life in *el norte* in a negative light (Maciel 2000).

But that was then, and this is now. Yesterday's traitors have become today's heroes, as today's sending countries realize that emigration of so many nationals is a stroke of good luck, provided that the emigrants don't cut their ties to their old homes. Consequently, sending countries are reaching out to their expatriates, providing them with services, trying to solve the problems encountered in the United States, intervening with US authorities and policy makers, doing what they can to ensure that the flow of remittances doesn't stop, and converting the migrants and their descendants into ethnic lobbyists. The very same Mexican government that long ignored the nationals living north of the Rio Grande now embraces them. Mexico's consular infrastructure mirrors the size and dispersion of its emigrants: from Alaska to Arkansas and from Minnesota to Florida, Mexico's fifty-one consulates are spread across the United States, with mobile units regularly connecting with emigrants in more far-flung locations. While the consuls' job description includes resolution of everyday problems, the Institute for Mexicans in the Exterior focuses on the longer term, providing programs designed to build diasporic awareness and loyalty, while also providing an institutional framework linking migrant leaders and Mexican officials (González Gutierrez 2006a; Laglagaron

2010). The Salvadoran government has done the same on a smaller scale, making special efforts to ensure that the many Salvadorans living in the United States without full legal status take advantage of opportunities to gain permission that will allow them to live legally in the United States on a temporary basis, without any guarantee of long-term, permanent residence (Popkin 2003; Nosthas 2006).

Although immigrants' "here-there" connections are the subject of burgeoning scholarly interest, the results are disappointing. Committed to theories of globalization, proof of which they find in immigrants' extensive cross-border ties, most researchers have ignored the ways in which contemporary nation-states (especially the most powerful among them) circumscribe the immigrants' social connections while transforming their identities. Methodologically, too much of the research has focused on concerted cross-border activities rather than on the more common and routine sort, and paid little attention to the processes that bind the immigrants to their new homes. Remittances and their consequences have been the subject of extensive, sophisticated quantitative research, telling us much about this one side of a multifaceted phenomenon, but little, if anything, about other myriad connections extending from receiving to sending state and then back again.

This book seeks to do better. Rather than restricting the focus to either the sending or the receiving side, it encompasses both. By analyzing the factors that both promote *and* supplant cross-border involvements, this book goes beyond the usual polarities, highlighting the impact of globalization while showing how it stands in tension with the continuing force of the nation-state. The book uses multiple methodologies, intersecting with the full range of relevant disciplines: anthropology, history, political science, and sociology. I draw on an abundance of sources: fieldwork; documents; newspaper accounts from the US mainstream and ethnic media, as well as the foreign press; a broad range of large-scale, representative surveys conducted in the United States and the countries from which today's migrants come; as well as a vast secondary literature.

The next chapter will set the intellectual context, explaining how scholars have sought to understand the connections between immigrants and their homelands. This chapter critically assesses the sprawling and ever-expanding scholarship on the phenomenon known as "immigrant transnationalism." As I will show, this literature has produced a new way of looking at migration, demonstrating that connections between place of reception and place of origin are an inherent, enduring component of the long-distance migrations of the modern world. The problem, however, is that connectivity between sending and receiving societies is cause *and* effect of international migration. Hence, discovering that migrants engage in cross-border activities begs the question, sidestepping the challenge of understanding the sources and types of variations in these connections that migration almost always produces: Why might these linkages persist, attenuate, or simply fade away? What different patterns characterize the many forms of cross-border involvement—whether occurring in political, economic, or cultural spheres, or involving concerted action or everyday, uncoordinated activities of ordinary immigrants? And what happens as the experiences and resources acquired through migration filter back to the home country?

Chapter 3 begins the job of answering these questions. I start with the premise that the people opting for life in another state are not just *immigrants* but also *emigrants,* retaining ties to people and places left behind. Few international migrants come as lonely adventurers; instead, they move by making use of the one resource on which they can almost always count—namely, support from one another—which is why social connections between veterans and newcomers lubricate the migration process. But the chains of mutual help extend across borders as well since the cross-border progression of families takes place at a much slower rate, in more erratic, incomplete fashion, with both migrants and stay-at-homes depending on one another for survival. Thus, in moving to another country, the migrants pull one society onto the territory of another state, creating a *zone of intersocietal convergence,* linking "here" and "there." Still *of* the sending state, even though no longer *in* it, the immigrants transplant the home country society onto the receiving-state ground. In the process, *alien* territory becomes a *familiar* environment, yielding the infrastructure needed to keep up here–there connections and providing the means by which migrants can sustain identities as *home* community members while living on *foreign* soil.

The migrants cross borders in order to access resources that do not spill out from the territories of the rich states where they are contained. As the newcomers settle down and acquire competencies that the new environment values and rewards, the migrants gain ever-greater capacity to help out relatives and communities left behind. But then, the paradox of international migration kicks in: the migrants find that their own lives, just like the resources that lured them to a foreign land, get confined to the territory on which they have converged. Physical distance proves a hard constraint on continuing cross-border interchanges, leading almost inevitably to social separation. The new society that they have entered simultaneously transforms and absorbs the migrants, making them increasingly different from the people left behind and reducing the needs and motivation to keep the ties. Over time, an increasingly large share of the core familial network changes location; as the center of social gravity moves from "there" to "here," the costs and benefits of maintaining the cross-border connection prove increasingly unfavorable. Hence, the migrants increasingly find themselves not just *in* the receiving state but increasingly *of* it, leading intersocietal *convergence* to give way to intersocietal *divergence.*

Moreover, the fact that international migration is not just a social but a political phenomenon structures the ties between "here" and "there." Though territorial boundaries have become more heavily guarded, they prove to be protective once they are traversed, insulating migrants from the pressures of the home state and providing them with political freedoms previously unavailable. The material and the political combine: the receiving country's wealth generates resources used for leverage back home; further weight comes from the skills, allies, ideas, and experiences acquired in a new political system. Consequently, some migrants maintain long-term engagements across borders, presenting themselves as members of the community they left behind, though they often advance interests distinct from those that have remained in place. These many cross-border migrant involvements—whether short- or long-term, whether maintained by individuals calling home or traveling or by organized groups seeking to influence policy—galvanize responses from sending states that seek to influence and embrace emigrants and a diaspora found in the territory of another state. In the process, the boundaries of the homeland polity become the object of conflict. The migrants, wanting full citizenship rights, seek a cross-border extension of the polity, one that corresponds to the intersocietal convergence produced by migration. Government elites and many of the stay-at-homes prove resistant, opposed to the costs imposed by extending political entitlements to those who voted with their feet for life in a foreign state and who increasingly behave like the foreigners among whom they live. But neither homeland, grassroots politics, nor state efforts at diaspora engagement interests the mass of the migrant rank and file. *Intersocietal divergence* becomes the dominant trend because most immigrants and immigrant offspring become progressively disconnected, reorienting concerns and commitments to the place where they actually live. Starting out as strangers, the migrants are turned into nationals—a process that also estranges them from the people and places where their journey started.

Chapter 4 shows how migration generates cross-border connections of all types. The typical migrant doesn't turn her back on the place left behind: travel, communication, and material exchanges all bridge kin and communities separated by space, effectively allowing emigrants to be immigrants at the same time. Only an elite group of "transnationals" seems able to live their lives across borders; however, that option proves impractical for almost all. Access to the technology that might shrink distance is highly uneven, with significant disparities *among* immigrants but even greater disparities *between* immigrants and stay-at-homes. And while long-distance communication is easier and cheaper than ever, the brute fact of physical separation still matters. Keeping things moving between "here" and "there" requires scarce resources that are unequally shared, of which money and the capacity to move back and forth freely across borders are the most important. Consequently, relatively few migrants succeed in maintaining high-intensity cross-border contacts of all types. Moreover, the incentives to connect and the resources needed to do so follow opposing tracks: years of residence in the country of reception increase the material capacity to engage in the cross-border circuit, but they paradoxically reduce the motivation to do so.

Cross-border social ties may be dense and relatively persistent, but, as Chapter 5 will show, they don't suffice to maintain immigrants' engagement in the politics of their homelands. Political detachment occurs for a variety of reasons: Prior experience told the migrants that their state could do little to help, which is precisely why they voted with their feet. Homeland political matters also lose salience once the migrants have transitioned to a new polity, where homeland political activity generates only symbolic rewards and the environment lacks the features—namely, party mobilization and the example and influence of politically oriented neighbors and friends—that would spur attention to homeland matters. Hence, while most migrants maintain extensive social ties to the places left behind, political attention starts low and quickly flags. For a minority of immigrants, the experience of migration to a richer, democratic country paradoxically *facilitates* their continuing home country engagement. Living abroad, migrant political activists enjoy protection from home-state officials eager to tamp down dissent. Over time, most migrants, including the disadvantaged, get ahead: the economic resources leveraged as a result of migration gives them clout that homeland officials generally can't afford to ignore. In the case of the United States, political structure and political culture facilitate and encourage homeland-oriented activism and motivate ethnic lobbying. In this context, moreover, a long history of rallying around homeland causes has made homeland-oriented activism a fully acceptable, almost normative path of Americanization.

Chapters 4 and 5 mainly highlight the microlevel, providing ample evidence of cross-border connectedness, but these chapters focus principally on the receiving side and the pressures that weaken home country ties.

The remainder of the book expands the focus to encompass the country of origin, thus swiveling to zero in on the *zone of intersocietal convergence* and linking places of *emigration* with places of *immigration*. Chapter 6 turns to the large canvas and develops a framework for understanding the interactions between emigrants and emigration states. This chapter emphasizes the dualities at the heart of the migration phenomenon: immigrants are also emigrants, aliens are also citizens, foreigners are also nationals, nonmembers are also members. At once *of* the sending state but not *in* it, the migrants are members whose everyday cross-border connections and ongoing needs draw the sending state across borders; residing abroad, however, their claims to belonging are undermined by their presence on foreign soil. At once *in* the receiving state but not *of* it, the migrants can access the economic and political resources available in their new home, using these resources to gain leverage in the home left behind; as outsiders, however, their rights are circumscribed and their acceptance is uncertain, vulnerabilities that can be aggravated if continuing homeland involvement triggers the suspicion of receiving-state nationals. Both conditions activate interventions by home states seeking to influence and protect nationals abroad. While extension to the territory of another state keeps options inherently constrained, even limited engagements can inflame the passions of receiving-state nationals, already anxious about the foreigners in their midst.

Chapter 7 applies the framework developed in Chapter 6 to a specific case—that of Mexico and Mexican emigrants in the United States—via a comparison of two different types of emigration policy: expatriate voting, a relatively new development, and provision of an emigrant identity card, a long-standing component of traditional consular services, though one that has recently been transformed. Focusing on the complex set of interactions linking migrants, sending states, and receiving states, this chapter identifies the key differences and similarities between these two policies. Both policies suffered from a capacity deficit inherent in sending-state efforts to connect with nationals living in a territory that the home country cannot control; both also generated conflict over membership and rights. Nonetheless, Mexico's efforts to resolve the immigrants' identification problems in the receiving society proved useful to millions; by contrast, a tiny proportion of emigrants took advantage of the first opportunity to vote from abroad. These diverging experiences demonstrate that sending states can exercise influence when intervening on the receiving-state side, where the embeddedness of immigration provides a source of leverage. By contrast, the search to reengage the emigrants back home encounters greater difficulties and yields poorer results because the emigrants' extraterritorial status impedes the effort to sustain the connection to the people and places left behind. In the end, the chapter shows that extension to the territory of another state yields far more constraints than those found on home soil as well as unpredictable reactions from receiving states and their peoples, not to speak of nationals who no longer perceive the migrants as full members of the society they left.

Chapter 8 continues to scrutinize the zone of intersocietal convergence, this time tightening the frame to see what happens when immigrants come together to do good for the local communities they left behind. Here the spotlight falls on an immigrant universal: namely, the hometown associations that crop up in countless migrant destinations throughout the world. Though often formed in order to reduce feelings of isolation and create a familiar environment in a strange world, contemporary hometown associations increasingly seek to raise funds in order to assist the very same communities where the migrants originally lived but from which they had to depart. This chapter shows how conflict, both among migrants in the host country, and between migrants in the host country and stay-at-homes in the homeland, is an inherent aspect of hometown association activities and their efforts to create sociability "here" and development "there." The reader will also see that the hometown migrants now living abroad find it difficult to decide what they share in common and that those who do engage in organized efforts to span "here" and "there" represent a select few. Moreover, the issue of how the migrants and their associations relate to the people and institutions left behind is often a dilemma that gets resolved in any number of ways, not all of which render satisfaction for either side.

With this book, I hope to provide both an innovative intellectual perspective and a guide to the immigrant reality unfolding before our eyes. As opposed to the globalists who see immigrants living in two worlds and the nationalists insisting that these same home country connections be cut, I will show that the immigrants are instead between here and there, keeping in touch with and trying to remain true to the people and places that they have left behind while simultaneously shifting loyalties and allegiances to the people and places where they have settled. The pages to follow tell this story in its full complexity, attending to the many, often unanticipated ties linking "here" and "there," as well as the factors that break them apart.

# CHAPTER TWO

# Beyond Transnationalism

FOR THE CONTEMPORARY student of international migration, the central intellectual problem is how to manage two competing methodological temptations—nationalism, on one hand, and transnationalism, on the other. Methodological nationalism is the more common approach because in both scholarly and popular views, nation-states are thought normally to contain societies (as implied by the concept of "American—or Mexican or French—society"); from this perspective, the appearance of foreigners, with their foreign attachments, is seen as a deviant event, disrupting an otherwise integrated whole, only to later melt away and disappear. Consequently, the scholars—like the nationals—stand with their back at the border, looking inward, their focus fixed on the new arrivals. What they see is that the immigrants respond pragmatically to the opportunities that they encounter, searching for a better life and adapting a cultural tool-kit that pays dividends in their new home. Because the receiving environment is dynamic and its institutions open, the new arrivals respond in kind, crossing ethnic boundaries, heading away from others of their own kind and toward the mainstream, whatever that might be.

More recently, however, the alternative approach appears more enticing: as the movements of goods, services, ideas, and people (though the latter to a notably lesser extent) appear to be sweeping across boundaries, the epiphenomenon seems to involve the nation-state. From this standpoint, social relations and activities (if not societies) naturally extend across national boundaries. Looking across borders, the view is one of nation-states that have lost the capacity they once possessed to control the passage of people across frontiers; unable to keep out or extrude unwanted foreigners, they also find it hard to maintain the line between citizens and aliens, which, if not disappearing altogether, is increasingly blurred. Whereas ties to home and host country were previously seen as mutually exclusive, today's political and ideological environment appears more relaxed: the shift from melting pot to multiculturalism legitimates the expression of and organization around home country loyalties. Thus, with stepped-up migration has come the proliferation of activities linking the migrants to the places from which they come, whether of the routine sort, involving remittances, communication, and travel, or the more concerted activities of home country political engagement or immigrant philanthropy. Ours, it appears, is a transnational age, where there are few emigration states without diasporas that they are trying to mobilize and few emigrations where self-conscious diaspora social action cannot be found.

The appeal of the transnational approach is easy to see because it reminds us that to say international migration is to say cross-border connections. Whereas the mythology of the classic countries of immigration assumes that the newcomers are arriving in order to build a life in the new land, in reality, that is often not the case: many migrants instead want to take advantage of the gap between rich and poorer places in order to accumulate resources designed to be used upon their return back home. Some eventually act on these plans; others, whether wanting to or not, end up establishing roots in the country of arrival. Given the uncertain, transitional nature of the migration process, connections linking origin and destination places are ubiquitous. Large flows of remittances, migrant associations raising funds to help hometowns left behind, trains or airplanes filled with immigrants returning home for visits to kin and friends—these features are encountered wherever large numbers of international migrants are found throughout the contemporary world. These same phenomena transform the places from which the emigrants come, providing both the opportunities and the motivations to leave, which is why receiving states find that migrations, once begun, are so difficult to stop. For all these reasons, a transnational approach appropriately points beyond a US-centrism that defines the problem as one of "immigration." Indeed, by successfully directing scholars' interest toward the linkages tying migrants, stay-at-homes, and emigration states, the transnational approach has underscored the *international* dimension of population movements across borders, with the fruitful result of refocusing attention toward the myriad feedbacks and spillovers that pull points of origin and points of destination together.

This new sensitivity has unquestionably generated significant value added; nonetheless, in its implementation, the transnational perspective has left much to be desired, as this chapter will show. While rejecting the conventional view that social relations are normally contained within the boundaries of a state, the students of immigrant transnationalism have unfortunately tended to forget about all the opposing processes that transform foreigners into nationals and cut their ties off at the water's edge. The better view, as will be shown in this chapter, lies beyond the simplistic dichotomies of the two competing methodological temptations, emphasizing instead the *regularity* of international migration and its *inevitable* collision with the mechanisms by which nation-states attempt to keep themselves apart from the world.

## The Career of a Concept

The transnational concept has had an honorable career, though one that most scholars of immigrant transnationalism have curiously ignored. As interest in matters transnational has exploded across the social sciences, scholars have increasingly sought to ask where the concept originated and why. Historian Pierre-Yves Saunier has now identified the German linguist Georg Curtius (1820–1895) as the likely first user of the adjective *transnational* in an 1862 lecture; in this lecture, he insisted that all national languages were connected to families of languages that extended beyond contemporary national frameworks (Saunier 2009). Subsequent American uses around the turn of the twentieth century invoked the term as a synonym for transcontinental when referring to highways.

However, credit for landmark use, as Saunier puts it, belongs to the early twentieth-century American intellectual, Randolph Bourne, whose 1916 essay on "Trans-national America" responded to the jingoism of the times. Calling for a cosmopolitan America that would accept immigrants' dual loyalties and ongoing home country connections, Bourne argued that America could *transcend* nationalism by accepting the contributions of multiple nationalities: "In a world which has dreamed of internationalism, we find that we have all unawares been building up the first international nation" (1916: 93). Yet Bourne was not so much an internationalist as a proponent of a liberal American nationalism, advocating a sort of multiculturalism before multiculturalism, in which "American nationality [would] not entail the suppression of diversity nor of multiple identities" (Hollinger 1995: 95).

While Bourne was then forgotten by all but the historians, phenomena explicitly labeled and understood as "transnational" attracted the attention of a growing scholarly audience well before they gained the preoccupation of immigration scholars. American diplomat turned law professor Phillip Jessup was first both to identify the phenomena that were specifically "transnational" and to explain why this new concept was needed. Writing in the early 1950s, well before the concept of globalization had entered the lexicon, Jessup nonetheless broke the frames "of traditional thinking about inter-state relationships by pointing to the myriad forms of border-crossing relations among state and non-state actors" (Zumbansen 2006: 738). Anticipating the political scientists' later concept of "interdependency," Jessup noted that the "line between the internal and the transnational is rather thin" (1956: 26). What struck this mid-twentieth-century analyst was how the previous few decades had blurred that seemingly sacrosanct distinction. "The growing concern for minorities, human rights, and the genocide convention [marked] the invasion of the domestic realm of the national state. Forty years ago it was unthinkable that a state administering colonies should be called to international account for its management." As of the mid-1950s, noted Jessup, it had already become routine.

Thus, themes that were later to gain prominence—the diminishing importance of territoriality, the constraints on state sovereignty, the role of nonstate actors—were already sounded by Jessup at the very start. Jessup's proposal to separate out a distinctively transnational realm from the international sphere quickly gained traction in law. Responding to similar concerns, though seemingly oblivious to intellectual trends among their colleagues in law, political scientists headed in a like direction. In the early 1960s, Raymond Aron proposed the notion of a "transnational society," encompassing a broad range of activities and beliefs crossing frontiers. In his understanding,

> A transnational society reveals itself by commercial exchange, migration of persons, common beliefs, organizations that cross frontiers, and lastly, ceremonies or competitions open to members of those units. A transnational society flourishes in proportion to the freedom of exchange, migration, or communication, the strength of common beliefs, the number of non-national organizations, and the solemnity of collective ceremonies. (Aron 1966: 93)

While the movement of ideas, people, goods, and organizations across borders had the potential to generate a "transnational" politics reducible neither to the relations between states nor within them, Aron was skeptical that "transnational society" could affect interstate politics, noting that transnational tendencies—the socialist internationals, the gold standard, the Olympic movement—had gained momentum at the turn of the last century but had failed to stop the arrival of World War I.

However, other scholars in the international relations field, most notably, Karl Kaiser (1971) and Joseph Nye and Robert Keohane (1971), picked up Aron's idea and turned it into a weapon for attacking political scientists' traditionally state-centric view. They argued for a focus on "transnational relations"—"contacts, coalitions, and interactions across state boundaries that are not controlled by the central foreign policy organs of governments (Nye and Keohane 1971: xi)—contending that "the reciprocal effects between transnational relations and the interstate system" were "centrally important to the understanding of contemporary world politics." Nye and Keohane never quite clarified whether the growing role of nonstate actors and their enhanced ability to penetrate state boundaries was an add-on to the existing state system or rather the emergence of a new stage altogether. Counterposing transnationalism as the ideology of some of the rich to nationalism as the ideology of the poor suggested the latter, but what indeed transnational*ism,* as such, might entail was never fully fleshed out.

This early interest in matters transnational helped galvanize the field of international political economy; much attention, in particular, was paid to the growth of the entities labeled "transnational corporations," and it was through this particular literature that the transnational concept came to the attention of the anthropologists who then applied it to migration. But the broader, theoretical claims developed by the political scientists interested in transnational relations and their impact made much less progress: in a debate that pitted "state-centered" versus "society-dominated" views of world politics, the transnational perspective proved vulnerable to a demonstration that the state *still* mattered (Risse-Kappen 1995), a view that the persistence of international tensions through the close of the "short twentieth century" (Hobsbawm 1994) made compelling.[1] With the end of the Cold War (Josselin and Wallace 2001) and the tremendous diffusion of transnational nongovernmental organizations, perspectives then changed because interest in a broad array of nonstate actors breathed new life into the transnational concept.

The attention drawn to transnational corporations provided the catalyst needed to move the transnational concept from law and political science to the study of migration. Transmission took place via anthropology for reasons related to the discipline's underlying orientation and its theoretical disputes that erupted during the 1980s. Territory had long defined the division of labor between sociology and anthropology, with the former taking responsibility for societies where the researchers actually lived, and the anthropologists focusing on the foreign places where the "others" resided. In disrupting the "isomorphism of space, place and culture," the international movements of people—whether of elites or workers—blurred the boundaries of the anthropologists' field, displacing it both toward a multiplicity of spaces and the connections extending across "culture," "society," "community," and "nation" (Gupta and Ferguson 1992).

## Stranger through the Gates: The Development of an Intellectual Field

The anthropologists directly responsible for applying a transnational perspective to the study of migration responded to one particular, boundary-blurring phenomenon: the long-term, back-and-forth migrations and persistent home country connections characteristic of the Caribbean. According to Nina Glick Schiller, Linda Basch, and Cristina Blanc-Szanton, the strength and prevalence of these ties, described as "transnational" social fields, demonstrated that neither settlement nor the severing of home country ties was inevitable. In the contemporary age of migration, rather, "transmigrants develop and maintain multiple relations—familial, economic, social, organizational, religious, and political—that span borders" (Glick Schiller et al. 1992: 1: 52). With so fundamental a change, entirely new conceptualizations were needed. *Transnationalism* became the label used for identifying the social connections between receiving and sending countries, and the word *transmigrants* denoted the people who forged those ties and kept them alive.

Not only was the perspective new, so too was the reality it sought to illuminate. The anthropologists were wise enough to see that what they called "transnationalism" characterized the earlier wave of mass migration and that social scientists—not just political actors—had been responsible for extinguishing the memory of this earlier experience. Still, the argument for a historical break proved irresistible: technological changes facilitated here–there connections; a more inhospitable reception context encouraged the newcomers to keep up their home society ties; and sending states more quickly and more avidly sought to retain and influence the transmigrants, in the process constructing "deterritorialized nation-states" (Basch et al. 1995).

A volume of conference proceedings, published in 1992, announced the intellectual program; two years later, a book entitled *Nations Unbound* delivered the results. Neither a monograph nor an edited collection, the book was a pastiche, made up of the different projects that the authors had independently conducted and out of which their new theoretical framework had grown. Though the book incorporated insights from Szanton-Blanc's research on Filipinos, it drew principally from the research that Glick Schiller and Basch had conducted among immigrant organizations of Haitian and Eastern Caribbean migrants in New York City. As the authors' most complete statement on the topic, *Nations Unbound* merits close review.

Seeking to develop a "transnational analytical framework," Basch, Glick Schiller, and Szanton-Blanc defined transnationalism as "the processes by which immigrants forge and sustain multi-stranded social relations that link together their societies of origin and settlement." While never forgetting about the contextual constraints on immigrants' cross-border ties, the theoretical framework emphasized the scope for action:

> Many immigrants today build social fields that cross geographic, cultural, and political borders . . . Transmigrations take actions, make decisions, and develop subjectivities and identities embedded in networks of relationships that connect them simultaneously to two or more nation-states. (Basch et al., 1995: 7)

This perspective, as the authors themselves noted, "made central the agency of transmigrants" (22). Consequently, transnationalism encompassed the activities of the transmigrants: building kinship networks that extended across two (or more) states; starting businesses that either facilitated or were dependent on cross-state connections; forming organizations oriented toward both receiving and sending states; using their influence to affect sending-country policies, whether for reasons connected to self-advancement or political commitments; or pressuring the host society government to secure policies that would advance sending-country goals. For the authors, moreover, action and self-understanding were contingently, not inherently, related; only under certain circumstances, the authors pointed out, would the people who had built up these multistranded, cross-state connections "develop a collective representation that acknowledged *their* transnationalism" (182; emphasis added). As shown by the case studies, that understanding was unlikely to take the form of a "globalized, politicized proletariat" (290). Rather, the awareness that the authors characterized as *trans*nationalist can be more accurately described, following David

Fitzgerald (2004), as "dual nationalist," expressing a commitment to not one, but two distinctive, bounded national communities.

On the other hand, the options available to the transmigrants were circumscribed by the responses taken by the relevant actors located in both sending and receiving states. As the authors wrote, the transmigrants' "identities and practices are configured by hegemonic categories, such as race and ethnicity, that are deeply embedded in the nation building processes of these nation-states" (22). Highlighting a variety of influences, the authors' most original contribution was to underline the ways in which sending-state actors sought to retain emigrants' loyalties, and shape their own attachments in ways that would suit the goals of sending-state leaders. With these policies, sending-state leaders embarked on a new strategy, one that the authors characterized as "deterritorialized nation-state building" (269). Lying behind the strategy was the claim that the nation-state stretched beyond its geographic boundaries; unlike the earlier diasporas, which were made up of dispersed peoples lacking a state, in this situation "there is no longer a diaspora because where its people go, their state goes too" (269).

More than two decades after its publication, *Nations Unbound* is among the most widely cited of the many, growing publications seeking to advance the transnational perspective. Full of rich, careful, empirical detail, tracing out the development of immigrant organizations over an extended historical period, it fully deserves the attention it has received. Theoretically, the authors' greatest contribution was to show that the traditional nation-building approaches that have dominated immigration scholarship badly needed revision in order to take account of both the continuing home country ties and the continuing influence of home country actors. Ironically, however, the authors developed neither a framework nor the conceptual vocabulary for understanding the complex set of interactions to which they drew attention.

Instead, they focused their theoretical contribution on that aspect of the immigrant experience that they labeled "transnationalism." Though transnationalism has since taken on the status of a paradigm, in the authors' formulation it is just a descriptive, context-dependent concept meant to apply to immigrants' cross-state connections. Attaching the suffix -*ism,* meaning "condition of being," to the word *transnational,* and emphasizing the corresponding differences between the so-called transmigrants and the immigrants, understood as those who cut home country ties, the authors emphasized the boundedness of the phenomenon when in fact its boundaries were far more diffuse. As a condition of being, transnational*ism* also implied stability in the here–there ties of the so-called transmigrants, as indeed the authors insisted in their conclusions, even if the case study evidence often indicated otherwise. Moreover, the authors' insistence that transnationalism was a real, existing phenomenon main-tained by the transmigrants conflicted with their own evidence, which instead suggested that it was a claim put forward by persons with very variable degrees of here–there connectedness. And precisely for this reason, as a singular noun, transnationalism was ill-suited to describe the multiple, often conflicting goals, plans, ideas, and beliefs entertained by the so-called transmigrants regarding the uses to which their here–there connections should be put. That the transnationalism of the transmigrants often turned out to be home country nationalism was yet another source of confusion. While provocative, the title of *Nations Unbound* similarly conflicted with the authors' own evidence, in which they skillfully and insightfully showed how not just the so-called transmigrants but also a wide variety of actors in both sending and receiving states engaged in conflict over the relevant social collectivity to which the immigrants were expected to belong. In the end, therefore, rather than enlarging the focus, *Nations Unbound* narrowed it, leading to the development of what scholars now call "transnational migration studies," a new field in search of scholarly recognition devoted to the study of immigrants' here–there connections at the expense of the broader social field in which those con-nections are embedded.

> A close examination of the familial, economic, and organizational practices of immigrants in the United States from the Caribbean and from the Philippines points to the same conclusion: immigrants from St. Vincent, Grenada, Haiti, and the Philippines are developing and elaborating transna-tional practices that allow them to remain incorporated in their country of origin while simultaneously becoming incorporated into the United States. (260)

RECEPTION   Beginning at the margins of a discipline that until then had been marginal to the study of immigration to America, the idea of "immi-grant transnationalism" quickly took off. Since migration is inherently a transitional process, invariably yielding back-and-forth moves and exchanges of myriad types, what the anthropologists called "transnationalism" could almost always be found, at least once one knew what to look for. Framing the new perspective against the publicly dominant but intellectually belea-guered perspective of assimilation lent additional appeal. The twin emphasis on novelty—of both the intellectual perspective *and* the phenomenon—provided the perfect means for launching a new research program, as Ewa Morawska pointed out:

> By setting up immigrants' transnationalism as a new and exciting idea, soci-
> ologists and anthropologists . . . have reinforced each other's success strate-
> gies, removing from their "cognitive sight"' even a suspicion that their novel
> phenomenon may not be so new at all. (2005: 215)[2]

Last, the zeitgeist also helped because the transnational concept provided
immigration scholars with a way of thinking about globalization, of which
the mass migrations of peoples and the spillovers they generate may comprise the most visible, if not leading, edge. With attention focused on so
many other phenomena of a seemingly transnational nature—whether corporations, or human rights activists, or nongovernmental organizations—
the effort to identify a "migratory counterpart" (Kivisto 2001: 549) struck
an obvious chord.

No less important, prominent gatekeepers ushered the newcomer
through the door. The formation of a research center on "transnational
communities" at Oxford University provided instant respectability while
assembling the type of global network for which the transnational perspective seemed to call. Still more decisive was the entry of Alejandro
Portes, the most influential US immigration scholar and a researcher with
a consistent, almost uncanny ability to set trends and whose intervention
gave the study of transnationalism the prominence it had not possessed
before. In a widely read 1997 article, outlining the immigration research
agenda for the new century about to begin, Portes put the study of "transnational communities" at the top of the list; here, he argued that the
homeland connections maintained by contemporary immigrants, while
not unprecedented, possessed qualities that made them distinctive and
therefore demanding of scholarly attention:

> The number of people involved, the nearly instantaneous character of com-
> munications across space, and the fact that the cumulative character of the
> process makes participation "normative" within certain immigrant groups.
> (Portes 1997: 813)

REFINEMENTS   Two years later, Portes announced his own program,
starting with a critique of the very anthropologists and the other qualitative social scientists who had gotten the field started. In their enthusiasm,
he charged, these previous researchers had muddied the waters, finding
transnationalism wherever they looked—an easy error to commit since
most immigrants engage in at least *some* cross-border activity, but one
that deprived the transnational concept of any specific meaning. It was
better, he argued, to focus on those aspects of the phenomenon that were
at once novel and distinctive: "occupations and activities that require

regular and sustained social contacts over time across national borders for their implementation" (Portes, Guarnizo, and Landolt 1999: 219). Conceptually muddled, the earlier work was deficient on methodological grounds as well: Portes charged that the ethnographers had sampled on the dependent variable, looking exclusively at those immigrants who maintained regular, recurrent homeland connections, at the expense of those who broke off or scaled back their ties. Instead, he called for survey research that would establish the prevalence of transnationalism—as *he* defined it—and also identify "the major factors associated with its emergence" (Portes et al. 2002). Results, based on a survey of Colombian, Dominican, and Salvadoran immigrants in the United States, followed soon thereafter. However, the particular question posed by Portes also largely determined the answer that his research would provide: since engaging in regular and sustained cross-border activities entails knowledge, money, and time, not to speak of legal rights, the conclusions—that only a small proportion of immigrants engage in regular cross-border activities and that transnationalism is "mainly the pursuit of solid, family men [who are] educated, well-connected and firmly established in the host country" and not "the recently arrived and the downwardly mobile" (Portes 2003: 887)—were entirely predictable.

While drawing attention to the topic and giving it newfound legitimacy, this intervention generated controversy among the scholarly transnationalists themselves. The ethnographers shot back. Emphasizing the "importance of ongoing observations . . . of what people do" as contrasted to "what they say that they do," Glick Schiller underlined the contextual, situational influences that might lead immigrants to accent host country ties at one time and home country ties at another (for a similar argument, see Smith 2006). But methodological quarrels were actually a sideshow to deeper conceptual differences. On the one hand, while Portes and collaborators used surveys to collect information, they were ultimately engaged in case studies, just like the anthropologists whom they criticized. Insofar as they were valid, their results shed light on patterns among migrants from small, peripheral countries in close proximity to the United States—indeed, just like the small or, in some cases, tiny island societies on which Basch and Glick Schiller had already shined a bright light. But whether the lessons from these studies could be extrapolated to populations of different origins and migrating under different circumstances was a question the surveys could not answer. On the other hand, the anthropologists had always insisted on distinguishing the people they called "the transmigrants" from the rank-and-file immigrants, which was exactly the same argument that Portes and his collaborators advanced. Indeed, years after initiating the transnational perspective, Glick Schiller continued to sound the very same note, contending that "distinguishing transmigrants from migrants who have very different experiences of connection and incorporation has proven useful" (2003: 105); in her view, only the transmigrants "live their lives across borders, participating" simultaneously in social relations that embed them in more than one nation-state" (2003: 105).

Thus, Portes and Glick Schiller stood on the same conceptual side, each emphasizing a kind of hard transnationalism consistent with the concept's etymological roots—meaning a condition of being beyond the nation. Still, insofar as they conceded that only "some" migrants would find themselves "suspended, in effect, between two countries" (Portes and Rumbaut 2006: 131), both took a relatively cautious stance. The more breathtaking view, which is associated with scholars seeking to create the new research field of "transnational migration studies," saw the development of communication and travel technology, combined with the spread of economic and political globalization, as creating a social world that is ontologically transnational. In this light, "transnational phenomena and dynamics are the rule rather than the exception, the central tendencies, rather than the outliers" (Khagram and Levitt 2005: 6).

Not everyone has been willing to go quite so far; depending on the context, the more daring have also been willing to hedge their bets. Thus, statements of a softer transnationalist view concede the "significance or durability of national or state borders" (Levitt and Jaworsky 2007: 134) but portray home and host country ties as mutually compatible (Morawska 2003). These arguments emphasize the relaxation of the demands for national "belonging," so that participation in both sending and receiving states is allowed and sometimes even encouraged. Hence, transnationalism's salient quality involves "simultaneity," with "movement and attachment" to home and host countries "rotating back and forth and changing direction over time," as "persons change or swing one way or the other, depending on the context" (Levitt and Glick Schiller 2004: 1011). An alternative, rather modest claim contends that migrants and their descendants "may continue to participate in the daily life of the society from which they emigrated but which they did not abandon" (Glick Schiller 1999: 94).

Since so few migrants pursue cross-border activities in a coherent, consistent way, scholars adopting a transnational perspective have increasingly opted for a more disaggregated view. Unpacking the notion of "transnational community," Faist (2000) argued that some cross-border activities and exchanges are particularistic, entailing connections between specific families or kinship groups, whereas others work at a higher level of aggregation, involving identification with a trans-border community. Levitt and Waters (2002) took another tack, differentiating between homeland engagements that took a concrete, behavioral form and those entailing a symbolic, identificational component. Glick Schiller (2003) distinguished between transnational "ways of being," or ongoing cross-border activities, and "ways of belonging," practices signaling an identity with another people or place. Similarly, many researchers emphasize transnational *practices,* substituting the fine lines associated with "transnational*ism*" with a continuum in which the regular, sustained trans-state practices of the transmigrants shade off into something more erratic and less intense (Levitt 2001a).

The concept of "transnational social field" more successfully captures this broad range of cross-border activities. Defined as a set of interlocking networks across national boundaries, this concept moves "beyond the direct experience of migration where individuals who do not move themselves maintain social relations across borders through various forms of communication" such that individuals "with direct connections to migrants will connect with those who do not" (Levitt and Glick Schiller 2004: 1009). Although this formulation frames the concept in sending-state terms, it can be easily extended to the receiving-state context as well. Implying that migrants engaged in intense, ongoing cross-border connections will be the neighbors, friends, or acquaintances of migrants engaged in more occasional or even evanescent contacts, it points to the ways in which high densities of migrants with *varying* degrees of home country connectedness can facilitate connections for any and all that might be interested.

## Beyond Transnationalism

A near-quarter century of debate and discussion has generated a proliferation of concepts and an unending disagreement over definitions, both of which suggest that something may be amiss. As indicated by the conceptual jungle that has quickly emerged—of which the terms *transmigrant, transmigration, transterritorialization, transnational social field, transnational social formation,* and *transnational life* are but a sampler— the temptation to apply the prefix *trans-* to one or another aspect of the migrant phenomenon has proven overwhelming but without doing much to illuminate the matter at hand. Since connectivity between sending and receiving states is at once cause and effect of international migration, discovering the cross-border activities of remittance sending or political involvement that migrations almost always produce is no surprise. Consequently, finding, as do Guarnizo, Portes, and Haller (2003: 1213), that there is "such a thing as a class of political transmigrants—immigrants who become involved in their home country polities on a regular basis" is not a "fundamental question," as they suggest, but rather the null hypothesis. Moreover, the empirical results showing that only a few "transmigrants" maintain regular home country connections ironically moves transnationalism to the periphery of the migrant experience. An alternative tack is to provide hypotheses that cannot be falsified, as when scholars find that the second generation retains scant home country connections, to which they counter with the speculation that some immigrant offspring might "become transnational activists if and when they choose to do so during a particular life-cycle stage" (Levitt and Jaworsky 2007: 114).

A better approach is followed by Levitt and Glick Schiller, who advise researchers to make "the relative importance of nationally restricted and transnational social fields" a matter of "empirical analysis" (2004: 1009). However, that agenda has thus far largely been a matter of exhortation, not implementation. More important, it blunts the intellectual challenge, putting the question right back into the traditional "immigration" frame. In focusing on the cross-state experiences of the immigrants, the great majority of whom get captured by the new state where they have come to reside, one loses sight of the feedbacks between sending and receiving sides—precisely the most important contribution that this new literature has generated.

However, the transnational perspective goes no further than noting the limitations of the conventional view because its proponents provide no tools for thinking about how or why home country connections would persist. Simply portraying the "migrant experience as a kind of gauge, which, while anchored, pivots between a new land and transnational incorporation," as do Levitt and Glick Schiller (2004: 1011), yields a purely descriptive statement, lacking a framework to explain which "migrants manage that pivot," how they do so, under which conditions, with what success, and for how long. And in asserting that "some migrants continued to be active in their homelands at the same time that they become part of the countries that received them" (Levitt and Jaworsky 2007: 130), the scholarly transnationalists just point out an empirical anomaly, one easily absorbed by assimilation theory. Even if assimilation theory ignores the prevalence of migrants' home country ties, its straightforward, rational choice explanation can be applied equally well to the reduction of home country connections: the same motivations impelling migration—the search for a better life—encourage a cutting off of home country ties since orientations toward the host country and its expectations yield the greatest rewards.

Indeed, clear statements of mechanisms are difficult to detect, as noted by Itzigsohn and Saucedo, who could find "no theoretical guidelines . . . to generate hypotheses about why people participate in transnational practices" (2002: 771). In reaction, they suggested three possibilities: linear, reactive, and resource-dependent transnationalism. The first, depicting the cross-border connection "as simply the continuation" of pre migration bonds, emphasizes the *geographic* location of key social ties, with territorial boundaries growing in salience if and as those ties shift from home to host society. Reactive transnationalism sees resources as *negatively* associated with cross-border ties: territorial boundaries will be less salient among the less successful and more frustrated, who will seek economic opportunity and social support in the home country. In contrast, resource-dependent transnationalism implies that resources will be *positively* associated with cross-border ties, with territorial boundaries of less salience for political or economic entrepreneurs, who can turn ongoing exchanges between host and home states into a source of advantage.

While plausible, these hypotheses are at best an initial, rough guide. "Linear transnationalism" simply reproduces the assimilation perspective in new garb; "reactive" and "resource-dependent" transnationalism are mutually exclusive. As cross-border connections inherently involve the transmission of resources, frustration with host-state conditions could only be a necessary but not sufficient cause of continued home country engagement. Moreover, the phenomenon is too complex to be treated in such a broad-brush fashion. Rather than looking for a one-size-fits-all approach, the better goal entails explaining variations across the different forms of cross-border involvement—whether occurring in political, economic, or cultural spheres, or whether involving concerted action or the everyday, uncoordinated activities of ordinary immigrants. Likewise, one needs theoretical tools to explain how and why cross-border connections change over time—whether biographical, intergenerational, or historical.

Indeed, temporal change is perhaps the acid test for any approach emphasizing the durability of the cross-border connections that migration puts in place. If cross-state ties are an integral part of the migrant phenomenon, what happens to those attachments as a new generation, raised and/ or born in the country of destination, replaces the migrants? Will home country connections persist, as did the long-distance bonds that knit together the classical diasporas? Or will they instead fade, to be replaced by activities and attachments oriented toward the society of destination?

These questions lie at the heart of a debate about the importance of assimilation as opposed to transnationalism. At the outset, as already noted, transnationalism was posed as an alternative to assimilation, a framing that almost surely contributed to the appeal of this new perspective. Later, scholars of varying methodological and theoretical stripes concluded that assimilation and transnationalism were in fact compatible, yielding combinations of various types, with the most engaged homeland activists likely to be also among the most deeply embedded in the host country.

This now stock response is problematic for a variety of reasons. First, it misses the fundamental tensions produced when international migration moves people from the territory of one state on to the territory of another. As *immigrants* oriented toward the host country, the migrants are a foreign presence; as *emigrants* oriented toward their original home, the migrants have an affiliation with a foreign place and people. Consequently, whether on native or new grounds, the migrants' quest for acceptance and claims for belonging are in question.

Second, it is precisely this conflict that assimilation, which is exclusively focused on the receiving society, *cannot* detect. By emphasizing the *blurring* of social boundaries and the *decline* of an ethnic difference, assimilation misses the ways in which receiving states transform foreigners into nationals, in effect, exchanging one "we-they" distinction for another. Moreover, the preoccupation with differences *internal* to the receiving society leaves unanswered the specific challenge issued by transnationalism, which extends the scope *externally* to the society of origin. However, maintaining those cross-state connections can be harmful to *immigrant* acceptance since public opinion tends to view the political allegiance of hyphenated nationals with suspicion.

The gradual withering away of home country ties *can* be interpreted as evidence of assimilation; however, doing so would miss the fundamental tensions produced when international migration encounters the liberal state and its bounded, political community. What Alba and Nee define as assimilation—"the decline of an ethnic distinction and its corollary cultural and social differences" (2003: 14) looks that way only if one turns one's back to the national border. Something quite different appears if one looks across borders: namely, states excluding the foreigners that they can and transforming the chosen few into nationals, that is, the exchange of one "we-they" collectivity for another. As shown by the experience of Salvadoran migrants to the United States—who regularly remit earnings but, reflecting the large proportion who are undocumented, travel home much less frequently—cross-state ties do not just wither on their own. Rather, the potential to maintain contacts with the home country (and hometown) is impeded by states' vigorous efforts at controlling migratory movements, putting up barriers at the territorial frontier, and creating blockages for those migrants who have crossed into the state's territory but have not yet managed to become a member of the state's people.

Moreover, the relevant boundaries encompass not just the external divides at the geographic frontier but also the formal, internal cleavages distinguishing citizens and aliens. In emphasizing the compatibility of assimilation and transnationalism, this contrast gets ignored, with the ironic result that the transnational perspective ends up mirroring the dominant view and thereby obscuring the inherently political nature of population movements across boundaries. Thus, while the scholars of transnationalism emphasize migrants' ability to gain simultaneous incorporation at both ends of the chain, in turn, providing a conduit for a flow of ideas, resources, and people that brings points of destination and settlement together, they rarely analyze incorporation but rather take it for granted. Luis Guarnizo (2001), for example, constructs his study of Colombian, Dominican, and Salvadoran immigrants in the United States as an investigation into dual citizenship's impact on immigrant political participation, not noting that the question is relevant only to the lucky few who have joined the club of the Americans as opposed to the candidate Americans who have not yet naturalized, not to speak of the undocumented immigrants whose residence on US soil violates the law. Moreover, the vivid, often compelling ethnographic studies generally point to the asymmetry in power relations between migrants and hometowners but *not* the simultaneity in incorporation; they instead show that the relationship between the migrants and host country dominants is one of exclusion. For example, Peggy Levitt's (2001b) case study of Dominican migrants in Boston and their ongoing ties to their sending village in the Dominican Republic provides extensive detail on the ways in which Dominican political organizations have changed their practices in order to facilitate participation by migrants. Thanks to their US earned incomes and the possibility that they could intervene with US politicians to advance Dominican interests, the migrants are a force with which Dominican political leaders must contend. But not so Boston politicians, whom, as Levitt shows, don't pay attention to groups that don't vote—such as her Dominicans—and have every reason *not* to facilitate the incorporation of newcomers whose loyalties and behavior would be hard to predict. Robert Smith's wonderful ethnography of Mexicans in New York (2006) tells a very similar story. Focusing on migrants from a village in the Mexican state of Puebla, he shows how activists in New York have used their ability to raise money from the emigrants in order to overturn the established leadership in the town they left behind. But if migration has given formerly powerless peasants a voice in Mexico, it has yielded no such gains in New York. Though the particular migrants studied by Smith were long settled and thus enjoyed unusually high levels of naturalization, they were *in* the United States, but not *of* it: as Smith explains, their involvement with their place of origin coexisted with "utter disengagement with New York politics" (2006: 66).

Notwithstanding these shortcomings, the students of immigrant transnationalism deserve a good deal of credit, most important for seeing that connections between "here" and "there," between place of reception and place of origin, between homes new and old, are an inherent and enduring component of the long-distance migrations of the modern world. The problem is that the discovery of cross-border connections just begs the question. If international migration is a recurring phenomenon, cross-state social action, whether uncoordinated or concerted, will also reappear. Moreover, the analysis can't be confined to a so-called "transnational social field" linking movers and stay-behinds in distant and disparate locations. That field itself is embedded in a broader field made up of state and civil society actors here and there who respond in various ways to the challenges and opportunities generated by the cross-state flows produced by migration. While aware of these interactions—which, indeed, were foregrounded in Basch et al.'s pioneering *Nations Unbound*—the scholarly transnationalists are too taken with the migrants' cross-border connections to ask systematically about the factors that might weaken or possibly end these ties. Nor are they quite ready to take critical distance from the migrants and their claims to belong to or represent a homeland community where they no longer reside and whose interests and points of view they may no longer share. Consequently, the key questions are those that the literature has yet to pose: Do the processes that cut across borders escape the control of states and their peoples, and if so, for how long and to what extent? Or are cross-state connections mainly circumscribed by state actors and nationalizing forces, with migrant activity and identity increasingly confined to territorial boundaries, whether of receiving or sending states? Which of the various forces involved in the triangular social field encompassing migrants here and there are the most influential, and where—whether on sending or receiving grounds—are those influences to be found? And how does the relative power of the interactants vary across relevant spheres, whether occurring in the cross-state dimension, involving the migrants and the stay-at-homes, or transpiring in the receiving-state dimension, where the migrants encounter the nationals? We will return to these issues in the next chapter; first, however, we will step back and seek further clarity by returning to the intellectual history of the transnational concept itself.

## Transnationalisms in Conflict

Talk of transnationalism is in the air. Unfortunately, there are two definitions in currency, both highlighting cross-state ties but varying as to the identity of the people connected across borders. To some extent, the result has been a boon, with the growth in transnational scholarly talk across disciplines and intellectual contexts encouraging and legitimating further use. On the other hand, regardless of field, clarity and precision seem hard to find, as bemoaned by the historian Patricia Clavin, who writes, "Transnationalism is in danger of becoming a catch-all concept, with almost as many meanings as there are instances of it" (2005: 434).[3] Regardless of how transnationalism is defined, the scholars do seem to generally like it: focusing on transnational *civil* society at the expense of transnational *un*civil society (Price 2003), they run the risk of succumbing to "the romance of the non-state actor" (Halliday 2001) while obscuring how the same border-spanning processes might lead to very different ends.

Still, the contrast to the "transnationalism" of the global historians and the political scientists highlights essential features of the immigrant phenomenon that its students have swept under the rug. First, few of the contemporary migrations called "transnational" actually deserve the appellation, though ironically, the "transnational" label would have been very appropriate were we talking about the *last* great age of migration. At the turn of the twentieth century, no small proportion of the international movers understood themselves to be "workers of the world." So they were also accepted—as shown by the role of migrants in transmitting labor, socialist, or anarchist ideas from one national setting to another, not to speak of their simultaneous or successive participation in several national movements (Hobsbawm 1988).[4] As the solidarities generated by the migration process often provided the underpinning for labor movements of various kinds, labor internationalism and home country allegiances continued to prove compatible well through the first part of the twentieth century (Mormino and Pozzetta 1987; Buhle and Georgakas 1996). But as of the early twenty-first century, the best approximation of transnationalism of this sort is to be found among Islamic internationalists (Dalacoura 2001)—evidence of the ubiquitous triumph of nationalist ideals. Whereas the "transnational capitalist class" (Sklair 2001) is still bound to its country of origin but oriented toward the elimination of economic nationalism, the political behavior described by scholars of contemporary *immigrant* "transnationalism" is altogether different. Instead, the migratory and ethnic phenomena of interest involve long-distance, *cross-state* affiliations of a *particularist* sort. Because the scale may be global but the focus is resolutely local (Lyons and Mandaville 2011), migrant cross-border politics represents a form of social action distinguishable from *transnationalism* in any of its incarnations.

On the other hand, the highly selective groups of migrants animating concerted, homeland-oriented activities do share *some* characteristics with the normative environmental or human rights activists seen by the political scientists as exemplifying the new transnationalism. As Sarah Wayland (2004) has noted, all form networks that extend across state borders, thereby engaging in suprastate relations; all simultaneously engage in domestic *and* international politics. Like their environmental or human rights counterparts, the homeland activists make use of their cross-state networks and their residence in a more open political environment to generate what political scientists Keck and Sikkink (1998) called the "boomerang effect." Home country activists may be blocked in their effort to produce political change; having escaped the home country's jurisdiction, migrants can get around those obstacles by shifting the political venue to a host country or international stage, where they can then mobilize symbolic or material resources to pressure home country authorities. While this same basic pattern applies to the long-distance immigrant activists of the *last* age of migration—whether wanting help for nationalist movements or protection against home country persecution—the contemporary emergence of transnational *political structures*—such as free trade or human rights regimes—furnish leverage points on home country authorities not available before.

Of course, the boomerang effect works precisely because of the unequal distribution of resources in a very unequal world: the migrants have a card to play only because they are trying to pressure a poor, less powerful country based on their perch in a rich, more powerful place. Even so, applying leverage through cross-state migrant or ethnic social action involves a difficult, hard-to-manage dialectic, one that reflects fundamental distinctions among the "transnationalisms" of different type. As cosmopolitans functioning in "a cultural milieu of internationalism" (Keck and Sikkink 1998: 16), host country transnational activists have an affinity for the migrant outsiders from faraway places.

Among the former, cross-border connections reflect a commitment to a common set of values, regardless of ideology or background. Theirs is a "global consciousness" oriented toward (self-proclaimed) principled ideas and values, revolving around a belief in universalistic rights that are shared by members of all states and not just one's own. The migrant outsiders, in contrast, are enmeshed in cross-state linkages that are organized not by principle but rather by kind and seek to maintain connections to homeland others of the same type. Advantage flows to the homeland activists when they invoke the type of issues that resonate with those *host country* social actors or authorities that are oriented toward human rights matters in *both* home *and* host settings. Human rights, minority protection, even sustainable development issues might strike the chord wanted by a certain host country or international audience, but in that case, migrant groups have to refashion their agenda to maintain the desired frame. Other issues—toppling the home government or creating a new national entity altogether—are unlikely to do as well; interethnic fissures produced by opposing national loyalties imported from abroad provide a further source of dissonance. The problem is not one of acceptance of ethnic or religious diversity, which homeland allies are often happy to tolerate or even encourage. The nub of the issue, rather, is the particularistic commitment entailed in homeland loyalty, which threatens to alienate the migrants from other groups that otherwise favor cross-border engagement, not to speak of migrants' rights. In the end, cross-border activism comes in fundamentally different kinds, a distinction that application of a common term—*transnationalism*—only hides.

## Cross-Border Activities:
## Varieties and Sources of Variation

While the advent of the transnational perspective produced an "excited rush to address an interesting area of global activity," it also left "much conceptual muddling" (Vertovec 1999: 448). Indeed, the unending effort to refine concepts and definitions, as well as the quarrels surveyed above, point to deeper problems. One involves a core ambiguity, pointed out in a widely cited article published just when the literature began to take off:

> The "nation" in transnational usually refers to the territorial, social, and cultural aspects of the nations concerned. Implicit in anthropological studies of transnational processes is the work of the "state," as for example, the guardians of national borders, the arbiter of citizenship, and the entity

> responsible for foreign policy. Transnational and global phenomena conflict
> with the jurisdiction and power of states and are what might be called
> "trans-statal." This term has not gained common usage, but the conditions
> suggesting it are reflected in the works of those who write about globaliza-
> tion and transnationalism. (Kearney 1995: 548)

Put differently, the concept of "transnationalism" conflates "state" and
"nation," the first referring to territorial units, the second to social collectivities. By definition, international migration involves connections that
cross the territorial units of the global. However, connectivity and social
collectivity are analytically and practically distinct. Unfortunately, few
scholars have paid much attention to the matter, instead defining transnational "in common sense terms as 'cross-border' (and therefore, technically, 'trans-state')" (Fox 2005: 172).

Substituting a concept referring to territorial organizations with one
referring to putative political communities yields numerous problems.
Connectivity does *not* imply collectivity: masses of migrants communicate with relatives abroad whom they may support and visit; many fewer
engage in activities linking them to a broader, place-of-origin collectivity,
whether at the local or national level. Identification or affiliation with a
collectivity defined in place-of-origin terms does *not* imply connectivity,
as demonstrated by exile communities that frame identity in home country
terms but do so against the home regime, making contact with the émigrés a source of peril for those still at home.

Ironically, the social collectivities studied by the scholars of contemporary *immigrant* "transnationalism" have mainly taken a bilocal form,
linking particular places in sending and receiving countries. Salient examples include Roger Rouse's early work on the "migration circuit" linking
a small community in Mexico's central plateau with Redwood City,
located in California's Silicon Valley (1991; 1995); Peggy Levitt's 2001
book, *The Transnational Villagers,* a study of the ties connecting a small
community in the Dominican Republic and its migrants living in Boston;
Robert Smith's 2006 book on Mexican New Yorkers and the small town
in Puebla from which they came and to which they, and some of their
children, recurrently return; and Michael Smith and Matt Bakker's 2008
*Citizenship across Borders,* which examines the political involvements of
Mexican migrants in the states and communities from which they come.

The analytic problem, however, is that the localistic connections linking
hometowners here and there do not distinguish cross-border movement
from long-distance population movements of any other sort. In many
respects, long-distance migrants are all one of a kind: as Michael Piore
(1979) argued years ago, what matters is not the color of the identity card

or the passport but rather that migrants are social outsiders, evaluating conditions here in light of the standards there. More important, long-distance migrants, whether international or internal, undergo similar experiences, namely, those of displacement and strangeness, which is why they suddenly discover a commonality in people originating from the same place. Finding comfort in the company of a familiar face, gaining pleasure from reminiscing about times gone by, or deriving satisfaction from the effort to make things better for the home and hometowners left behind, migrant hometowners repeatedly come together. Hence, the anthropological literature on third-world migrations, from which the scholarly transnationalists drew their inspiration (e.g., Mayer 1962), is replete with such examples, to which could be added similar, though less commonly noted cases from the historical literature on intra-European migration; migration in China; or, for that matter, rural-to-urban migration in the United States.[5]

Migrant bilocalism featured prominently during the *last* age of mass migration, when most movers were displaced peasants. Coming from multiethnic empires or nation-states established before their peoples had been nationalized—"Italy is made, now we must make Italians," reportedly said the Italian nationalist Massimo D'Azeglio (Gabaccia 2000: 10)—those mass migrants often knew little of the "nation" to which they were supposed to belong. Instead, the relevant homeland was local, toward which the attitude often took the form of *campanilismo,* the term used for the southern Italians "whose attachment did not extend beyond the earshot of the single belltowers *(campanile)* of their" hometowns (Luconi 2007: 466–467). While the mass migrants of the twenty-first century mainly originate from states where nation building is more advanced, the proliferation of hometown associations among contemporary immigrants testifies to the continuing weight of the *patria chica* ("the little homeland") and the strength of the loyalties it inspires.

Though pervasive, cross-border migrant localism competes with other, often broader cross-border social collectivities. In the last age of migration, as already noted, cross-border political solidarities also took the form of internationalism. At the time, internationalism competed with other long-distance particularistic solidarities linking migrants to existing, but more often putative, would-be nation-states. Internationalism, albeit under a somewhat different name, remains a force today, but it is mainly found among labor and human rights activists, *not* international migrants.

By contrast, what the literature calls migrant long-distance nationalism (Anderson 1998) is alive and well, though *long-distance patriotism* might be a better term because it can encompass the range of home country attachments in their benign as well as more malign or aggressive forms. Unlike the turn of the last century, today's migrants generally come from long-established nation-states, most of which impart their peoples with a sense of national identity, both through socialization and opportunities for political involvement in national life. Although the literature on Mexican migration, for example, has focused mainly on Mexican bilocalism, data from the World Values Survey show that Mexicans exhibit high and growing levels of national pride (80 percent saying "very proud" in 2000); the survey also shows that Mexicans report levels of local attachment that are comparable to those found in the United States and that are declining in importance. Though not incompatible with local attachments, national identity provides the better fit with the immigrant experience because social circles in the new country almost always expand beyond local ties. Local loyalties are also hard, almost impossible, to transmit to the next generation. As opposed to the relatively homogeneous hometown, the host country context is far more diverse, yielding exposure to persons of the same national background but originating in a myriad of hometowns, as well as a nationally heterogeneous population. Consequently, among the second generation, the first generation's hometown localism gives away to a broader homeland attachment; the result, as the historian Kevin Kenny has noted, is a "retrospective sense of premigration national identity that" becomes "part of their American identity" (2003: 24).

The key point, however, is that interest in and involvement with homeland matters fundamentally differ from the bilocalism that characterizes long-distance migrants, whether moving *within* or *across* states. In attending to the country left behind, the people thought of as "immigrants" are instead behaving as "emigrants," living in one territory but loyal to the people and polity of another. Cross-national allegiance of this sort can sometimes be accepted, but not always, which is why the effort to belong to both worlds—"here" and "there," "home" and "host"—involves a delicate, hard-to-maintain balance. While the activists may find a way to keep a foot in both worlds, the rank and file often ends up developing loyalties to the political community where they actually live.

## Conclusion

The continuing controversies over the meaning and utility of the concept of "transnationalism" obscure a more profound difficulty: identifying the phenomenon of interest and the intellectual puzzle it poses. International

migration inherently generates cross-border connections: migrants' remittances, letters, phone calls, visits, and investments in their home communities yield feedbacks spurring additional departures. By channeling
newcomers to established settlements, cross-border networks also reduce
the social, psychological, and sometimes economic costs of migration,
thus putting it in reach of a growing population. These ongoing feedbacks
also explain why migrations, once begun, are so difficult to stop.

The growing scholarly interest in matters transnational has had the
virtue of highlighting these connections and their ubiquity—linkages
ignored by traditional preoccupations with immigrant assimilation or
integration. In these approaches, everything of importance transpires
*within* the boundaries of the states on which the immigrants converge,
converting an inherently political phenomenon involving the encounter
between aliens and nationals into a matter of the relationship between
minorities and the majority. Focusing on the cross-border dimension also
demonstrates that population movements across borders inherently raise
issues related to rights, citizenship, political participation, and national
identity in both home *and* host societies—questions obscured by the traditional intellectual division of labor between research that is either home
society *or* host society focused (Waldinger 2003).

The scholarly challenge involves identifying the mechanisms generating
*and* attenuating cross-border connections. As noted earlier, international
migrations inherently yield ties and flows extending back from receiving
to sending states. These connections lead to greater connectedness, driving
down the costs of cross-border exchanges; migrants' movement to a rich
society provides them with the resources needed to keep up cross-border
ties even as they move ahead in their new country. Those resources combine with the new freedoms made possible by emigration to produce continuing engagement with homeland politics, often providing the migrants
with greater levels of influence than previously experienced. Seeking to
access those resources while controlling migrant behavior, sending states
develop policies aimed at engagement with their diasporas.

On the other hand, a variety of factors embed migrants in the receiving
country's national social field, tearing them away and differentiating them
from the people and places left behind. Initially, territory may have limited significance in structuring the social field linking host and home, but
time sharpens the social boundaries between "here" and "there." Though
migrants and stay-at-homes may stay connected, migration pulls them
apart, as each undergoes experiences that the other cannot completely
share. Despite distance-shrinking technologies, cross-border engagement
remains costly, reducing the population motivated or able to keep up home

country ties. As the migrants' social relations shift from home to host societies, on-location costs grow, raising the burden of cross-border exchanges, while the growing difference between migrants and stay-at-homes makes benefits decline. Because the political infrastructure connecting migrants and their descendants to the home state is often weak and incomplete, involvement with home country social collectivities entails significant effort and correspondingly high opportunity costs; by contrast, the host country offers lower-cost opportunities to participate on site, which in turn generates rewards with which home states cannot compete. While *some* migrants and immigrant offspring maintain involvements with home country collectivities, those engagements are shaped by interests and preferences born out of the migration experience; given the costs of cross-border political connections, those involvements are both episodic and asymmetric, allowing the migrants to intervene at home but impeding collaboration with stay-at-homes.

Moreover, national identity remains relevant on both sides of the territorial divide. While migration shows the social scientist that social relations are not inevitably contained within states, nationals in both sending *and* receiving states tend to *believe* that territory and identity *should* coincide. Thus, while migrants are often motivated to sustain a connection to the people, town, region, or nation left behind, members of the nation-state societies to which the migrants have moved frequently find these displays of concern and affection disconcerting. It is not simply that the migrants are failing to detach themselves from their old worlds—as social science wisdom and popular belief prescribe. In a world of mutually exclusive nation-states, rather, persons with foreign attachments are open to question, and all the more so when the relevant nation-states co-exist on less than friendly terms. Consequently, even while *some* migrants and their descendants may continue to identify with the home community, they do so as residents and sometimes members of a foreign country. As their lifestyles, preferences, and behaviors are no longer fully native but rather reflect the experience and patterns prevailing in the place where they actually live, their claims to belonging are met with skepticism, if not rejection, by the stay-at-homes. While not sufficient to prevent all migrants and migrants' descendants from maintaining multiple memberships in home and host societies, these cross-pressures make it increasingly difficult for many, as we shall now see.

# CHAPTER THREE

# The Dialectic of Emigration and Immigration

EVERY IMMIGRANT is an emigrant, every alien a citizen, every foreigner a national. Though this duality lies at the heart of the migration process, it is one that scholars all too often evade. For the proponents of assimilation, the people crossing borders are just *immigrants,* moving to settle, which is why they quickly adapt to the ways and respond to the expectations of the new society they have joined. By contrast, the proponents of transnationalism see the migrants as *emigrants,* keeping up contacts and involvements with the people and places left behind. The transnational perspective provides a useful corrective to the conventional viewpoint, which overlooks the inherently cross-border nature of migration itself and the ways in which population movements across states always build other, subsequent bridges across boundaries. While the transnational perspective rightfully emphasizes this cross-state dimension, it is nonetheless too pat, pretending that migrants can lead lives across borders, when in fact the dialectic between immigration and emigration is a source of constant tension.

The people crossing international borders are active makers of their own destinies, continually seeking to move ahead. Yet they do so under circumstances and conditions not of their own choosing, which is why the decision to move to the territory of another richer state simultaneously empowers the migrants, allowing them to triumph over adversity, but also forces them to confront a set of new, painful dilemmas from which there is no escape. In this chapter, I develop a new perspective on the tension between immigration and emigration, showing how the intersocietal relations produced by migration across borders are shaped by the influences of place, space, nation, and state. *Like* the scholars of transnationalism, I understand international migration as a regular, recurrent process extending social relations across states. *Unlike* those scholars, however, I explain how those cross-state networks collide with the forces that cut social ties at the water's edge.

INTERSOCIETAL CONVERGENCE   In opting for life in another country, the migrants pull one society onto the territory of another state, unintentionally and unconsciously producing a convergence between here and there. Intersocietal convergence—labeled the "transnational social field" by the scholars of transnationalism—results from the migrants' own survival strategy. The newcomers turn to one another for help in order to solve the everyday problems of migration: how to move from old home to new, how to find a job and settle down, how to pick up the skills needed to manage in their new world. In the process, the migrants extend and embed their networks, creating a new community where the density of familiar faces, tongues, and institutions reproduces the world left behind. As the home country society gets transplanted onto receiving states, *alien* territory gets turned into a *familiar* environment, putting in place the infrastructure needed to keep up here–there connections and providing the means by which migrants can sustain identities as home state *nationals,* even while living on *foreign* soil.

Moreover, for many, though not all migrants, cross-state connections often comprise part and parcel of the familial survival strategies that propel migration in the first place. That pattern holds best for labor migrants—exemplified by the Italians of yesterday's era of mass migration and the Mexicans of today's—among whom movement from poor to wealthy societies is a way to generate resources at the point of destination to be used at the point of origin (Massey et al. 1987; Gabaccia 2000). Migrations of this sort send one household member to a place where wages are high, who in turn transmits savings to be spent on consumption and/or investment in a place where the cost of living is low. Families with members abroad also secure an informal insurance system because the income from migrants working overseas can offset the losses that take place when things go wrong at home. Agrarians subject to unpredictable changes of all sorts—whether floods, drought, high seed prices, or low harvest prices—find particular benefit from the risk reduction that remittances provide, but as volatility is more likely to hit developing rather than developed countries, migration can yield insurance effects for city-dwellers as well as ruralites (Taylor and Martin 2001).

Hence, connectivity is part and parcel of the migration experience itself: what flows across borders—information, resources, and support—provides ample motivation for family members separated by space to maintain strong social ties. Of course, migration of low-skilled laborers, usually of peasant background, is only one variant on the many migration types. High-skilled labor is far more likely to be welcomed as well as wanted, yet these streams often involve a temporary, sometimes circular component, as exemplified by the foreign graduate students enrolled in American universities or the foreign engineers on short-term contracts in high-technology companies. By definition, refugees and asylum seekers cannot go back, at least not as long as the homeland conditions that expelled them persist. While for some the breach is definitive, for others the ties to the places and, more important, people left behind remain compelling.

Reinforcing the strength of those connections is the fact that family migration often involves a multistage process. Sometimes, entire nuclear families move in one fell swoop. But the risks and uncertainties involved in the move to a strange, often distant place make serial migrations a common pattern. At the turn of the last century, as Donna Gabaccia (2000) has explained, young Italian men headed off for the Americas, leaving behind their married "white widows" (as contrasted to the true widows, clad in black), with some of these married spouses later following their husbands across the Altantic. Historically, a similar pattern characterized Mexican migration, especially from the beginning of the *bracero* program in the early 1940s up until the legalization of undocumented workers in 1986. In other cases, however, such as the migrations leaving from the Philippines, wives are more likely to depart than husbands. Alternatively, a young, unmarried person moves abroad and then, whether formally or informally, later sponsors the movement of the person who will then become his or her spouse. As for minor children, they are less costly to take care of if left behind with spouse or grandparent; children may follow once the migrating parent develops the earnings capacity needed to allow families to move from the relatively low-cost place of origin to the high-cost place of destination, sometimes doing so in tandem, in other cases, serially, one by one. In yet another pattern, a spouse returns home, leaving migrant children in the care of the parent who has opted for long-term residence in the place of immigration. And it is rare that every significant other changes place of residence. Migration is generally for the young, not the old, which is why obligations to aging parents at home often keep remittances, letters, phone calls, and visits flowing well after roots in the host country have become deeply established.

While at the turn of the twenty-first century, as at the turn of the twentieth, social and economic considerations of these sorts stretch migrant kin networks internationally, an added pressure is at work today, namely, receiving states' ever-greater focus on migration control. Under these circumstances, the emigrants are often those most likely either to gain passage through legal means or to get around the obstacles meant to discourage residence or entry by those without authorization. In either case, the opportunity is too important to be foregone, leaving family members—a category especially likely to include children—lacking that option and thus having no choice but to stay behind. Though reunification may later occur, the process is often protracted and uncertain, proceeding at the whim of institutional and legal factors over which migrants have no control. As family reunification has become increasingly costly, hard, and time-consuming, so too have cross-border family ties become more common and persistent (Mazzucato and Schans 2011).

Thus, in myriad ways, migration pulls kinship networks across borders, entwining the survival strategies of migrants in the place of destination with those of the relatives still in the place of origin. Because the migrants rely on the stay-at-homes, those exchanges are bi-directional, going well beyond the receipt of funds furnished by those who have moved abroad. Parents leaving children behind rely on grandparents to provide care; migrants planning to return home after migration count on their kin and friends to look after houses built with the savings from remittances; alternatively, remittance houses can be used to subsidize the stay-at-home sibling responsible for everyday care of aging parents. Moreover, disaster isn't reserved for the stay-at-homes: migrants who have lost jobs may turn to the stay-at-homes for material assistance; likewise, the latter have a role to play in furnishing the home country documents—sometimes only available on-site—that the migrants need in order to consolidate their place in the society of residence (Mazzucato 2009).

These connections produce greater connectedness. The social ties between points of destination and origin keep the migrations flowing: information about the opportunities found elsewhere leaks out beyond the initial circle; veteran migrants help newcomers, who in turn tend to show up where the previous movers had settled; ongoing contacts— letters, phone calls, return visits—tell the stay-at-homes that they would do better moving elsewhere. As long as new arrivals keep coming, the connections are refreshed, with the newcomers' intense interest in keeping up ties to the stay-at-homes making it easier, more convenient, and cheaper for the old-timers to do the same. Though with time many migrants put down roots, large numbers maintain ongoing connections to the people from whom they are now separated by borders, sending back remittances, making the occasional trip back home, purchasing ethnic products made in the home country, and communicating with relatives and friends at home. The burgeoning of these cross-border connections, as well as their growing complexity, swells the size of the market, creating economies of scale and opportunities for specialists in the provision of here–there connections, lowering the cost and increasing the convenience of maintaining home society ties.

But keeping the connection often proves elusive: a variety of factors embed migrants in the nation-state society where they actually live, tearing them away and differentiating them from the people and places left behind (Waldinger and Fitzgerald 2004). Initially, territory has limited significance in structuring the social field linking host and home; with time, however, social boundaries are rearranged so that they increasingly align with the national borders of the states in which migrants and stay-at-homes reside. Consequently, although the scholars may insist that the migrants create transnational communities suspended between "here" and "there," the reality is otherwise: the migrants find that they are betwixt and between their new and old homes, *in* the country of immigration but *of* the country of emigration. Neither one nor the other, the migrants are *foreigners* (Mexicans, Italians, Senegalese, and so on) *in* the country where they reside, but *immigrants* (French, Germans, Americans, and so on) whenever they return back *home*.

PLACE  From the start, place matters, and far more than either scholars or migrants would like to think. Distance-shrinking technologies— ranging from the letter to the telegraph, to the telephone, to the worldwide web, to the mobile phone, to the no-cost phone conversation held over Skype—do bring "here" and "there" closer. However, the chronocentrism of contemporary social scientists—convinced that today has no parallel in what went before—leads them astray. A long-term perspective highlights the continuing synergistic effects of long-distance migration and long-distance communication. Thus, during the last era of mass migration, changes in literacy, technology, and public infrastructure made the transoceanic and transcontinental delivery of letters increasingly predictable and fast: rail tied interiors to ports and ships moved across the seas at increasing speeds (Moya 1998). What had taken a year in the late eighteenth century, fell to a few weeks by the mid-nineteenth and dropped to roughly a week a half century later, with lower postal rates and higher literacy on both sending and receiving sides sending volumes still higher (Sinke 2006). Hence, the exchange of letters was often more than adequate to keep migrants and home communities tightly connected, propelling a stream of "transatlantic gossip" and keeping migrants under the "social surveillance" of hometowners both "here" and "there" (Gabaccia 2000: 87).

When read aloud to the neighbors by the village's one literate resident, the letter also had a broader informational impact that today's email— sometimes deleted *before* it is read—is unlikely to possess. On the other hand, everything is *not* the same. The advent of the Internet allows migrants and stay-at-homes to communicate instantly and almost without cost, with a spontaneity approaching the conditions of face-to-face contact. With videoconferencing, bringing together "image, sound, and simultaneity" (Mattelart 2009: 12), long-distance communication moves yet closer to interaction on site.

But there is no death of distance, as it simply cannot be killed. The same global inequalities that propel migrations from poor to rich countries deprive the stay-at-homes of the technology most likely to facilitate long-distance contact. In contrast, the migrants gain from the surrounding, technologically advanced environment but often without fully benefiting from its potential. Held back by the inequalities experienced before and after migration, the advances in telecommunications technology often exceed both their skills and their ability to pay. As for those fully up-to-date on the technology front, there is no way to erase the effects of having changed longitudes: even if free and of the highest quality, no telephony will put Vancouver and Manila in the same time zone. Things are easier if relocation keeps one in the same time zone—as with Mexican immigrants in Texas communicating with relatives in Guadalajara, or Moroccans in Paris talking to relatives in Tangiers. However, even those best situated, whether in terms of geography, technology, or both, cannot fully escape the liabilities of contacts that take place via long distance.

Unlike face-to-face communication, communications separated by space have a discontinuous, erratic, removed character not found when people are interacting in place. Those discontinuities yield an across-the-board impact, but they particularly affect those displaced by long-distance movements since migration often loads the content of communication with hard-to-handle matters. Emails or texts can be sent at any time, but these media essentially function to communicate information, not the emotions required to maintain close, and especially intimate, relationships

(Giglia 2001). Moreover, communicating about the resources flowing plentifully from points of destination to points of origin—in particular, finances, whether funds to be sent or money that was spent—is inherently difficult, which is why conflict so often results. Unlike a face-to-face encounter, where meaning is conveyed by gesture not word and where messages can be received and sent at the very same time, the phone often proves inadequate for the task. In the requests for remittances, the migrant, unwilling to tell her family just how hard things are abroad, hears an endless set of demands; in the reluctance to send more money, the relatives at home hear a familiar voice grow foreign and cold. Absence of physical presence also strikes at the connection that migrants *and* stay-at-homes hold in common: separation means that the two no longer share the same experiences and, above all, the home that they once held in common. For the migrants, the place of origin is likely to be fixed, stuck in time; in contrast, those still on the ground know that it is changing, responding both to shifts in the immediate environment as well as signals from the migrants.

All the while longing for the place left behind, pragmatism, rather than nostalgia, rules the migrant's day, shifting key social relations—spouses, children, parents—from point of origin to place of destination. The strategy of sending workers to states where wages are high while leaving families in states where the cost of living is low works in the short run but proves hard to sustain over the long term. For a while, migrants can manage to subordinate personal needs to the imperatives of family members afar, but as the sojourn continues, postponing the dream of return to next year and then the year afterward, the capacity to maintain the necessary level of deprivation proves more than many migrants can bear. Spending more in the place of destination disrupts the migrants' ability to maintain the international family economy on which a trans-state way of life depends. The next logical step is to relocate family members so that they are all living in the place where wages are earned; however, that change further upsets the balance between spending and earning since it also reduces the capacity either to send resources home or to squirrel them away for investment at some later point in time (Piore 1979).

As the social center of gravity crosses the border, the cross-border ties weaken, if only because the costs are high and the rewards tend to diminish. Moreover, time and distance weigh heavily in the balance, inevitably imposing costs and creating barriers for those who want to maintain contacts with the stay-at-homes. Despite distance-shrinking technologies, cross-border engagement remains costly, reducing the population motivated or able to keep up home country ties. The most successful immigrants may have the resources needed to keep up a constant pattern of travel and satisfying long-distance communication, but the very same factors generating the capacity for cross-border engagement, namely, deeper, more effective engagement with the receiving society and its members, weaken the motivation to keep up the connection to the place earlier abandoned.

By contrast, resource constraints weigh heavily on the many who would like to sustain the connection: forced to pick and choose among the available options, they are apt to fix on a combination of lower-cost activities as opposed to those that are the most resource-taxing. Though vital, economic success does not guarantee access to the full array of cross-border connections: only those lucky enough to combine economic resources with the legal entitlements needed to move freely back and forth across borders can pursue the full range of cross-border connections. As for the rest, increasingly severe receiving-state efforts to impede entry and permanent settlement tend to yield territorial capture and immobility (Hernández-León 2008). In the meantime, contacts in the new environment cross ethnic boundaries, yielding ties to nationals whose social worlds are largely, if not entirely, encompassed by national borders and which, in turn, tend to absorb interest and time at the expense of long-distance, cross-border relationships.

SPACE   The capacity to maintain successful, satisfying, continuing connections is not simply a matter of resources, whether technological, economic, or political. No less important is the fact that the people on the two sides of the chain are no longer one and the same—an ironic result of the same global inequality that triggers migration.

Resource containment provides the motivation for boundary-crossing: migrants leave home, departing for richer states, because displacement lets them capture the wealth contained in the developed world, an option not available were they to stay in place. In that sense, migration provides a way to exploit the world's rich, gaining access to the wealth that remains within borders and thereby funneling some of those benefits back to the people confined to poorer states.

The duality at the heart of the migration experience means that the emigrant orientation proves sticky, continuing to exercise influence even as the movers turn into immigrants and put down roots that make return difficult. Yet even while facing the place of origin, the migrants are no longer the people they were when they departed from home. Over time, they are not simply *in* the rich countries to which they have moved but rather *of* those countries as well. Though the specifics of the migrants' new homes vary from one territorial unit to another—which is why nation and national identity also matter—the democratic countries of the developed world share much in common; consequently, the encounter with the behaviors, institutions, and resources contained within those spaces yields similar effects, regardless of the precise point on the globe.

Migration transforms the migrants. To some extent, that process conforms to what the literature calls "acculturation," absorbing the tastes, preferences, and behaviors of the specific national society in which the migrants have settled and acquiring the skills appropriate for that setting, most notably, the dominant language. Language is both a symbol and a tool of membership, functioning simultaneously as the means of communication and as a meaning-laden indicator of group membership since the capacity to speak a common tongue defines the boundaries between insiders and outsiders. For these reasons, language possesses powerful emotional connotations, well beyond its instrumental value. Home, as Alfred Schuetz noted decades ago, is where shared meanings and understandings can be taken for granted, which is why he understood " 'to feel at home' [as] an expression of the highest degree of familiarity and intimacy" (1945: 370). Precisely for that reason, as noted far more recently by Brubaker and colleagues, "the experience of speaking 'one's own' language is often associated with a feeling of phenomenological comfort, a sense of being at home in the world" (2006: 254).

The conventional literature focuses on the society of *immigration,* concerned with the linguistic boundaries between groups of foreign and native origin living in the *same* territory. Bringing in the *cross-territorial* dimension raises a different question: how does the acquisition of *host* society language competence affect functioning in the language of the *home* country? The answer is likely to depend on the degree of language shift. To the extent that the first generation retains the mother tongue for most purposes, using the dominant tongue only in those domains where its use is required, the capacity to communicate across borders, as if they had not left home, is likely to continue undiminished. But not every immigrant retains their same level of proficiency. In particular, those who migrate as children are more likely to resemble those foreign-origin children born in the country of *immigration:* exposed to the mother tongue at home, but using the dominant tongue in all other domains, relegating the mother tongue to kitchen-level proficiency. Hence, the shift from the immigrant to the dominant tongue might *reduce host society* social boundaries between foreign-origin minorities and native-born majorities while also *increasing* the *cross-border* social boundary between stay-at-homes in the country of *emigration* and immigrants and their foreign-born offspring residing in the country of *immigration*. If home is where the heart is, the emotional attachment to the place left behind is likely to be sundered if the capacity to speak as if one had never left home has also been lost.

But the conventional conceptualization of acculturation is too narrow and too rigid, assuming the separation of culture from social structure and equating the distinctive, cultural elements of the new environment with the particularities of any one place. Instead, migration entails a change in the interior of the person, one both entailing and resulting from practical adaptations to a different social structure, the nature of which is generic to the wealthy, technologically advanced, bureaucratized societies on which the migrants have converged. The initial problems are those of everyday competence: for example, learning how to make change in a new currency or relating prices to those encountered back home, discovering the ways in which higher earnings and higher cost of living have to be balanced in order to still have money left over to send home, or coming to master the time demands of work schedules more rigid than those known at home (Peñaloza 1994; Pribilsky 2007).[1] Those same imperatives lead the migrants to pick up the tools needed to comprehend and appropriately respond to the behavior and expectations of the people and institutions around them, whether when shopping, driving, or looking for a job. Just how the migrants stand in the eyes of the others around is among the lessons absorbed: insofar as they realize that they are not fully wanted or accepted, they have all the more reason to retain their attachment to the people and place left behind. On the other hand, as the migrants grow increasingly proficient in reading the national code, they also perceive that equal treatment, even if violated in practice, is the norm and one with sufficient appeal that it might be sent home. Likewise, interaction with institutions provides instruction in a different style of administration, one whose bureaucratic ways may induce a preference for rules and predictability that is unlikely to be satisfied by institutional practices in the place left behind.

But there are also imperceptible changes imposed by the new routines, though often later accepted: accommodating to a longer, more precise, more demanding work schedule, which in turn leaves less time to others but may also breed a preference for timeliness. Likewise, there are new behaviors prompted by opportunities or experiences not acquired before: the option to satisfy material needs previously repressed or those newly acquired, after which might come the financial pressures that accompany consumption, in turn reducing one's capacity to help others or infusing every form of help with explicit expectations of return.

Even migrants who start at the bottom quickly gain access to the good things that the rich societies have to offer, leading habits obtained before migration to erode. In the societies of *emigration,* scarcity induces scarcity consciousness: spending today proves too risky when tomorrow is uncertain; better to economize for the fallow period that is sure to come. The same factor leads to the bridling of individual wants: when survival depends on the support and involvement of others, gratifying the self at the expense of those around one means cutting oneself off from help at a time of inevitable need.

But self-sacrifice in the interest of the intimate collectivity is not the way of the *immigration* societies of the rich world. From the standpoint of the developing world, the wealth of the developed world does indeed trickle down to the rich countries' poorest residents, which is precisely why international migration is an upward mobility strategy par excellence. The immediate fruits of that upward mobility take the form of the everyday amenities that the people of the developed countries take for granted: indoor plumbing, hot and cold drinkable water, heated (and sometimes even air-conditioned) residences, gas cooking, and electric lighting (Dreby 2010: 30). Shortly thereafter comes consumption: once the newest arrivals learn how to manage money, they then discover that they can both save money to send home *and* buy more than they ever purchased before. Hence, the newcomers quickly "adapt to abundance," to borrow the description coined by the historian Andrew Heinze (1990). As Heinze pointed out, patterns and norms of consumption are the most readily detectable and easily learned of the new society's ways, especially since better settled relatives and friends, having already assimilated these lessons, are there to pass them on. Satisfying in and of itself, consumption also sends signals: to the others around one in the society of immigration, the clothes, the car, and the jewelry convey the message that one is just like them and not a bit less; to those still at the point of origin, possessions are a way to telegraph that one has made it and in ways that the stay-at-homes have not been able to attain. Consumption produces further consumption, in part because it allows for the expression of an individual identity that had been suppressed in an economically more constrained environment. And it also yields further individuation, providing a means to satisfy the self apart from the collective unit and often in defiance of its preferences and expectations.

Hence, the migrants' continuing engagement in the contacts between "here" and "there" demonstrates *both* the enduring power of the home country connections *and* the factors that weaken those ties from within. Thus, rather than jettisoning the place left behind, the migrants often want to engage with it. However, they do so with a combination of assets and liabilities: assets resulting from the resources and experiences acquired in the years abroad, and liabilities resulting from the gap in expectations, preferences, knowledge, and contacts produced by the years of absence.

Moreover, the migrants typically engage in ways that involve exporting aspects of the foreign reality that they have encountered and internalized, an activity labeled as "social remittances" by the sociologist Peggy Levitt (1998). For a minority, engagement takes the form of concerted efforts at producing change, optimistically, via democratization (Shain 1999), a goal that does not necessarily coincide with the preferences of home country elites. Alternatively, the migrants may pursue involvement through collective investments in hometown projects, designed to furnish the stay-at-homes with some of the benefits that the migrants identify as their gains from movement abroad, albeit goals that may be tenuously related to the priorities of the communities from which the migrants come.

But the most powerful demonstration of the migrants' transformation can be seen in the individual but parallel actions that they undertake on their own. As an example, consider the houses that the migrants construct in their hometowns and what those homes signal about the people who build them (or have them built) and the messages these investments send. On the one hand, the remittance house, to borrow the phrase coined by the architectural historian Sarah Lopez (2010), testifies to the continuing pull of the place of origin—an attraction difficult to explain from the rational choice point of view adopted by the scholars emphasizing assimilation in the reception society because so many of these houses turn out to be wasteful palaces in which their owners never live. But on the other hand, the remittance house demonstrates how deeply the immigrant has been transformed by the experience of living in a different, much richer country with distinctive consumption patterns and very different expectations regarding the relationship between the individual and the community, not to speak of the new, more privatized needs that the destination society breeds. Moreover, it is via this paradoxical relationship to the home society that the emigration message springs: what better way to demonstrate the benefits gained by migration than by bringing them home and in a form that no one can ignore?

NATION   The duality between *emigration* and *immigration* belongs to the social aspect of population movements across borders. But precisely because these flows take people across states, they entail an inherently political dimension, creating yet another source of tension.

In traversing frontiers, migrants produce intersocietal convergence. However, the states the migrants leave *as well as* those they enter are linked to meaningful social identities understood in territorial terms. Since national identity is relational, defined in contrast to alien states *and* people, the migrants' quest to belong both "here" *and* "there" is contested by nationals on both sending *and* receiving sides. Whether in place of origin or in place of destination, the prevailing view is that "we" are "here," while "they" are "there," in alien states located on the other side of the border and where the aliens are contained. Thus, while migration shows the social scientist that social relations are not inevitably contained within states, nationals in both sending *and* receiving states are disinclined to accept the message, *believing*, instead, that territory and identity *should* coincide (Waldinger, 2007c).

Emotionally tied to the people, town, region, or nation left behind, migrants often seek to sustain these connections. However, members of the nation-state societies to which the migrants have moved frequently find these displays of concern and affection disconcerting. In the societies of the developed world, monistic political cultures have weakened under the impact of globalization, tending instead toward pluralism. Hence, holding on to premigration identities is increasingly acceptable as long as these are accompanied by an attachment to the place where the migrants reside and people among whom they live. Thus, while multiculturalism flourishes in one form or another, it is profoundly asymmetric: the newcomers can retain ties to the old country and aspects of its ways, but they need to master the native code. Moreover, no one expects nationals to take on the foreign ways of their new foreign-origin neighbors. Language remains a potent symbol of national unity, which is why the nationals throughout the developed world not only expect the newcomers to learn the native tongue but want it to remain dominant. Indeed, the United States exemplifies this tendency: a somewhat greater acceptance of cultural diversity is accompanied by an emphasis on learning English, with public opinion not ready to insist on "English only" but strongly endorsing "English first" (Citrin and Sides 2008: 39). Similarly, ethnic political organizations are tolerated but are also viewed as possibly undermining national cohesion; the political loyalties of the foreign-born are open to suspicion, and there is widespread support for the views that there are too many immigrants and that national borders should be better controlled— evidence that the residents of the developed world can be more accepting of foreigners who wish to become nationals without ever becoming one-worlders.

In general, the immigrants and their descendants respond positively to this message, concluding that one does better if one can present oneself to be just like everyone else. Engaging in the necessary adjustments is often acceptable to the people earlier willing to abandon home in search of the good life; the everyday demands of fitting in, as well as the attenuation of home country loyalties and ties, make the foreigners and their descendants increasingly similar to the nationals whose community they have joined. Some groups do effectively retain certain ethnic attachments and old-country ways while adding on a national tool-kit; nonetheless, there does not seem to be any case in which the foreigners and their children wish to appear as if they are "fresh off the boat." Indeed, all the evidence points to the contrary: remaining a greenhorn entails far too many disadvantages. In contrast, picking up the linguistic, cognitive, and interpersonal tools needed to get by and then get ahead in the new society proves far more rewarding. Though native-born residents of global cities, hearing strange tongues, worry that a Tower of Babel will be soon among them, in reality, foreign languages quickly lose ground to the dominant tongue. Some groups, especially Spanish speakers in the United States, add English to continued mother tongue facility. But the views of such alarmists as Samuel Huntington (2004) notwithstanding, the old pattern remains in place: the immigrants' children reserve the mother tongue for private places; in public, it is a dominant-language-only (or at worst, mainly) world.

Of course, *some* migrants and their descendants may continue to identify with the home community. They tend to articulate a new, deterritorialized view, redefining the nation as a community encompassing its nationals, wherever they might live. That perspective often resonates with the concerns of sending states and their officials because the greater resources secured by movement to a richer country invariably yield consequences for home communities and populations. For the most part, the emigrants' cross-border involvements are strictly social and highly particularistic, directed at the migrants' kin and no one else. However, private actions undertaken *abroad* have profoundly public consequences *at home*, as demonstrated by the huge flow of migrant remittances traveling from rich to poor countries. Hence, the migrants' cross-state engagement invariably yields home country responses, one component of which involves retaining the loyalties of the people who voted with their feet for life in another state.

Living on *foreign* ground, the emigrants' claim to *membership* in the national community in the place where they no longer live is contested. As Nancy Green felicitously noted, the expatriate can easily slip into the *ex*-patriot (Green 2012: 7), in which case exit may be seen not as departure but rather as desertion and hence disloyalty. Sentiments of this sort are widely shared, as evidenced by the historically negative portrayal of emigrants in Mexican popular or political culture or by the terms applied to Israeli emigrants, who, unlike the immigrants to Israel, went down, not up. And then there is the characterization of the Cuban exiles as *gusanos* ("worms") offered by the Castro regime. Further vulnerability lies in the *immigrants'* presence on the *foreign* grounds where they actually reside. The claim to identity with the stay-at-homes may ring true to some but definitely not all because those with in-person contact can readily detect the ways in which the *immigrants* (variously described as "gringoized Mexicans;" "gold-chainers," which criticizes the conspicuous amount of jewelry worn by Dominicans returning to the island from the United States; "riches Marocains de l'Europe" instead of "residents Marocains a l'étranger," conspicuously dotting their hometowns with US- or European-styled "dream houses") have become *unlike* those who have stayed behind. Hence, political actors have tangible reasons for contending that nationals *there* have become increasingly like *them,* no longer fully belonging to the national *us* that still live *here.*

STATE    The very same population movements that knit societies together also transplant the migrants into a distinct, separate political environment. While controls around that territory may impede the back-and-forth movement needed to sustain homeland *interpersonal* ties, separation at the territorial line is the source of the political feedbacks that immigrations recurrently produce. The receiving state's borders yield two effects, keeping *in* wealth while keeping *out* the tentacles of the sending state, thus providing the migrants with both resources *and* the political protection against home state interests that might seek to control them. Consequently, life *abroad* gives the immigrants *home* country political influence never previously experienced, while their new political environment recurrently gives rise to social movements built in the place where the migrants *live* but designed to effect change in the place that they have *left.*

The irony is that exercising influence at home results from entry into an alien state where arrival *never* yields instant citizenship, and acceptance into the policy often follows only after long years of residence. Exclusion from receiving-state citizenship entails vulnerability: most important is the threat of losing any right to residence. Nonetheless, once present on the soil of a democratic society, migrants enjoy at least some rights, which is why conflicts suppressed at home often burst into the open when migration entails movement to a less coercive environment. As social boundaries are relatively diffuse, migrants develop close ties to citizens, generating allies with unquestioned political entitlements. Because the immigrants' cause can be framed in terms that resonate broadly—whether appealing to beliefs in human rights or self-determination—they find additional ways to bridge the internal boundary of citizenship. Depending on the circumstances, the *immigrants* can gain receiving-society membership by proxy, connecting to organized receiving-state interests whose unquestioned rights of intervention help secure the space for autonomous, migrant social action. Hence, moving to *foreign* soil gives the *emigrants* a powerful *home* soil punch.

Emigrant politics take a variety of forms. In some cases, as with the Irish, Tamils, or Croats, migrants engage in state-seeking nationalism, seeking to build a new state out of an existing, multiethnic polity. In other cases, they pursue regime-changing nationalism, trying to replace the old regime, whether from left to right, as with the anticommunist Cuban exiles in Miami, or from right to left, as with Salvadorans who flocked to the United States in the 1970s and 1980s. Other emigrant political actors and movements have more pacific goals, most notably regaining home country membership, as evidenced by the many campaigns for expatriate voting rights. With the vote in hand, many expatriates then engage in campaigning, encouraging visits by homeland leaders and contributing funds to homeland parties.

Accompanying emigrants are more widespread private actions with homeland consequences of an inherently political nature, the most prominent being the large-scale transmission of resources. For these reasons, emigrants' decision to vote with their feet almost invariably yields sending-state efforts at diaspora engagement, seeking to sustain national loyalties beyond national borders. The portfolio of relevant policies is vast, ranging from monitoring the emigrants to activating their national solidarity, to protecting them and furnishing them with services, to providing them with incentives to continue transmitting resources across borders, to extending the ballot to persons who live and vote from abroad.

While the actions of sending states *and* of emigrants extend politics across borders, the capacity to maintain a viable political connection runs up against the constraint of extraterritoriality, limiting sending states' capacity to connect to nationals living *abroad* while constraining emigrants' capacity to connect to the *foreign* polity outside the boundaries of the country where they actually reside. Thus, for sending states, the practice of diaspora engagement proves difficult, as opposed to the rhetoric, which is cheap. Symbolic measures are available to any state, no matter how weak or incapable of servicing its citizens at home. The stratagem is not a bad one because it tugs on the membership sentiments of the emigrants, who are not only ready to help less fortunate fellow nationals living at home and deprived of a functioning state but are willing to do so for free. Going beyond symbolism, however, means expenditures of a nontrivial sort. As noted by a Mexican diplomat, attending to the needs of a population that "has decided to leave the country and settle permanently in the United States" adds to the obligations of states "with so few resources and so many domestic problems" (González Gutierrez 1993: 225). Not surprisingly, opposition from voters, lobbyists, or demonstrators who have opted to stay behind gets in the way of efforts to "implement promised policies of [emigrant] inclusion" (Ostergaard-Nielsen 2003a: 5). Moreover, even when resources are available, sending states can engage the emigrants with only a limited number of tools. Because the migrants have crossed territorial lines, using coercion to achieve the usual goals of extracting resources or ensuring political compliance is no longer an option. For the most part, sending states can only exercise influence, doing what they can to mobilize resources that might engage, mobilize, and protect those citizens who have opted to build lives on the territory of another state.

Likewise, displacement to the territory of a different state, representing a new people, can be a source of homeland leverage for those still interested in the place left behind, but typically it yields impacts that work in the opposite direction. Home states can do relatively little for the migrants in the territory where they actually live (Fitzgerald 2009), reducing motivations to purely symbolic or intrinsic rewards, which are unlikely to be compelling for most. Options for participation are also limited, with obstacles high. Although home country political parties maintain foreign branches, and candidates travel abroad to garner expatriate support and material assistance, campaigning on foreign soil costs considerably more than on native grounds, especially if the former is a developed and the latter a developing society. Where they exist, expatriate electoral systems might attract greater migrant attention, but none can reproduce the national voting infrastructure on the territory of another country (Nohlen and Grotz 2007).

Absent mobilization, the pressures to detach from home country politics intensify. Political life is fundamentally social: participation responds to the level and intensity of political involvement in one's own social circles, which in turn generates political information (Rosenstone and Hanson 1993). However, the circumstances of settlement are likely to lead to spiraling disengagement. Even areas of high ethnic density rarely possess the ethnic institutional completeness and political infrastructure that would stimulate engagement with home country matters. The migrants' status as immigrants orients them toward receiving-state institutions, and media practices—even if conveyed via a mother tongue—provide at best modest coverage of home country developments. Absent powerful inducements, clear signals, and the examples of significant others, the costs of participation may easily outweigh its benefits. Since, by contrast, immigrants often realize that they will settle in the places where they live and where political participation is also easier, so all pressures lead to disconnection from home country politics.

## Conclusion

Though failing to deliver on its promise, the transnational perspective has nonetheless performed a useful scholarly function. By attending to the many cross-state connections, which international migrations *invariably* produce, it has moved migration studies beyond the largely unconscious, implicit nationalism of established approaches, highlighting important aspects of the migrant phenomenon that prior research had largely ignored. The incidence of immigrants' cross-border activities is therefore beyond debate. The challenge is how to understand the processes that put them in place and maintain them, even as these very cross-border connections come under pressure, weakened by the impact of place, space, nation, and state.

In departing from their *home* state and opting to live on foreign soil, migrants displace social relations to the territory of another state, producing a convergence of societies. How to understand this displacement depends on one's point of view. From the standpoint of receiving states and their people, migration produces the arrival "here" of foreign persons who should have stayed "there," in foreign lands. The perspective at the other end of the chain is not all that different: the national "we" can longer fully be found "here," with "us," but rather "there," with "them" in their foreign lands.

The migrants, in contrast, find themselves between here and there. Over the short to medium term, they often succeed in maintaining a bridge, keeping in touch with and trying to remain true to the people and places that they have left behind. The motivation to do so is also potent: inertia keeps at least some of the migrants' significant others rooted in home territory, thus prolonging the migrants' home country orientations.

The long term, however, looks different, as *intersocietal convergence* recedes in the face of *intersocietal divergence*. Distance yields effects that few can escape, changes in communication technology notwithstanding. In the end, the absent cannot be present, no matter how strongly they insist otherwise: migrants and stay-at-homes inevitably undergo different experiences, producing differences that accent the impact of geographical distance, and core social networks shift from old to new homes. Moreover, both foreign-born and especially their offspring take on the traits of those around them, willy-nilly picking up the everyday habits and tools that make it easier to fit into the new environment and adapting to the greater abundance and individuation of the socioeconomic context in which they live. While the move into a new political jurisdiction, combined with the economic resources resulting from life in a richer country, generates political influence for homeland-oriented activists, political boundaries yield different effects for most. By voting with their feet for residence in a different state, the migrants create new obstacles for long-distance engagement. On the one hand, home states have limited scope for solving the *immigrants'* problems in the place where they actually live; for the *emigrants,* on the other hand, cross-border involvement in the place from which they departed entails high costs and few benefits.

Even though the *emigrants* insist that they still belong to the "we" of the society of origin, those who remain behind are rarely of the same opinion; in their view, rather, at heart these are *immigrants who* are no longer like "us" but are rather like the foreign people among whom they live. In fact, the stay-at-homes are not entirely mistaken since the longer the *emigrants* stay abroad and the more deeply they implant their roots in new soil, the more different they become from those who never left home, which lends a foreign character to the demands directed toward the community of origin. The nationals of the society of reception are willing to tolerate the immigrants' foreign attachments, but only up to a point; the more insistently and visibly the immigrants engage abroad, the more they threaten their acceptance among nationals, who tend to see the immigrants as "them" from "there," and not as part of the "us" that belongs "here."

In the end, scholarship needs to understand the factors that promote *and* supplant cross-border involvements. That goal requires a departure, from both the views of the globalists who see immigrants living in two worlds as well as those of un self conscious nationalists standing with their backs at the borders. A better perspective emphasizes the collision between the processes that recurrently produce international migrations, extending social and political ties across states, and those that cut those linkages at the water's edge, transforming immigrants into nationals and shifting their preoccupations and social connections from home to host states. Applying that optic in the chapters to come, I will show why the immigrants are so often between here and there, keeping touch with and trying to remain true to the people and places that they have left behind while simultaneously shifting loyalties and allegiances to the place where they actually live.

# CHAPTER FOUR

# Cross-Border Ties

## *Keeping and Losing the Connection*

MIGRATION INVOLVES the crossing of a territorial but not necessarily a social boundary. Once described as the "uprooted," migrants are now often described as "the transnationals." That label almost surely goes too far, but it is certainly true that many, perhaps most, of the migrants maintain some tie to kin, friends, and community in the country where they were born.

Ties so often stretch across borders because the displacement from the core social network at the point of origin is almost always partial. To varying degrees, parents, spouses, children, siblings, and more distant relatives may remain at the point of origin or may return there after a sojourn in the destination country; either way, the migrant's inner circle is likely to extend across territorial boundaries. And the connections are not simply a matter of people, but of things. Migrants depart without necessarily abandoning the properties they own at home: while those things are often the objects of the migrants' investment plans, they also comprise commitments that can reinforce the dependency on relatives or friends at home looking after the migrants' assets.

Consequently, international migrations inherently pull one society to the territory of another, producing *intersocietal convergence*. That convergence can be seen from both ends of the chain: origin as well as destination. As migration within the Americas is so focused on the United States, the view from the sending countries, as found in a 2010 survey, dramatically shows how many people have gained a US-based connection as migrant numbers have grown. The density of connections varies tremendously from one place to another: in giant Brazil, a tiny fraction of the population reports that a close relative, previously living in their household, now resides in the United States; in Haiti, by contrast, 37 percent answered yes to the very same query.[1] When the question gets broadened—asking respondents whether they have *any* relative, not just close kin, living abroad—the proportion gets even higher, hitting the 50 percent mark in a recent Mexican survey. Overall, among the countries in close proximity to the United States, the pattern is unmistakable: these states no longer include all their nationals, with very large proportions—in the case of Jamaica, over a third of the population—living in the territory of some other state.

Unfortunately, no source of information provides the corresponding receiving-state data: we simply do not know what proportion of *immigrants* in a country of destination still has close relatives living in the country of origin. But a variety of sources suggest that, for a large fraction of the immigrant population, the familial circle is found in both country of emigration and country of immigration. For example, 20 percent of interviewees queried in a nationally representative 2006 survey of Latin American immigrants in the United States had a child still living in the country of origin; among respondents with children, that fraction rose to just over one-quarter. Almost 70 percent of all respondents were also sending remittances to support relatives still at home. While those with children abroad were the most likely to do so, they only accounted for a fifth of remittance senders. Parents were actually more likely to be remittance receivers than children, with 40 percent of the sample sending help to their fathers or mothers; another 7 percent was transmitting funds to siblings. Piecing together the information on children's location and remittance recipients tells us that almost 60 percent of these respondents still had a close relative living outside the United States. The data on Asian immigrants in the United States does not allow for the same degree of detail; nonetheless, a large-scale 2012 nationally representative survey of Asian Americans found that over two-thirds of the foreign-born respondents report having immediate family members (spouse, parents, or siblings) still living in their home countries.

People left behind can later join their migrant relatives in the country of destination. But migrants also leave behind material investments that are often completely immobile—as in the case of property—and whose value, whether for reasons having to do with sentiment or some projected future use, may be such that the migrant wants to keep the asset in place. Again, the information needed to paint a complete picture of migrants' home country *material* interests is lacking, but the available data give us a glimpse of the nature and extent of these connections. For example, a 2002 survey of Asian immigrants in the greater San Jose, California, area found that fully one-sixth owned property in the home country and that 8 percent still had a business there. In turn, those investments provided reason for continued contact: 10 percent of all respondents who traveled did so for business, as did a full quarter of those who returned home once a year or more. Looking at the nationally representative 2006 survey of Latin American immigrants discussed above reveals some striking similarities. In this case, one-third of the respondents owned some asset at home, most commonly a house. However, unlike the Asian immigrants queried in San Jose, very few (3 percent) possessed a home country business and the home country property owners were no more likely to travel home than those with no assets in the country of origin.

Thus, to put it colloquially, being out of sight does *not* mean being out of mind. The migrants most certainly do move, but many of their most important social relations as well as significant material assets stay put. Yet something else is involved: namely, the interdependencies between migrants "here" and their connections "there," which emerge clearly from detailed analysis of the survey of Latin American immigrants. Holding home country property and having left children behind *each* has a powerful impact on the likelihood of remitting and frequent communication.

## The Technology of Cross-Border Connectedness

Thus, international migration *inherently* produces cross-border connections. In turn, those connections produce greater connectedess, swelling the size of the market, creating economies of scale and opportunities for specialists in the provision of here–there connections, and lowering the cost and increasing the convenience of maintaining home society ties. Today, however, scholars tell us that there is something entirely new under the sun: ongoing declines in transport and communication costs and the advent of entirely new means of communication between migrants abroad and communities at home are transforming those connections altogether. Many analysts insist that the technological changes of the current age of mass migration have had a transformative effect, providing "the basis for the emergence of transnationalism on a mass scale" (Portes et al. 1999:

223), making the migrant "the representative of a new culture of mobility, which entails international geographic mobility and also digital mobility" (Diminescu 2008). New forms of information communications technology (ICT), in particular "permit easier and more intimate connections" (Levitt 2001b: 22) among migrants and stay-at-homes, allowing "them to be actively involved in everyday life there" (22), whether making familial decisions or planning weddings across long distances. Robert Smith's ethnography of a sending community in the Mexican state of Puebla provides an emblematic description of these changes: This is a region

> both marginalized and transnationalized . . . the roads are in worse repair, vegetation is sparser, and the mountains are covered with sere shrubs; yet numerous travel agencies list prices for flights to New York, signs advertise videos and cell phones, and parabolic television antennas . . . sprout from the roofs of the houses. Internet cafes have popped up, linking migrants and stay-at-homes by email. As the Mixteca drives people north, technology moves in to keep them in touch with their relatives who stay behind. (2006: 39)

And for the most fortunate of migrants, "technical inventions" have allowed "ordinary people . . . to implement their own brand of long-distance enterprises," as with the immigrant businessman breathlessly described as "on his way to the airport to pick up a consignment of foreign goods shipped the previous day while talking on his mobile telephone to a home country partner and sending a fax to another" (Portes et al. 1999: 223–234).

The ways in which technological change has reinforced connections to people, assets, and communities left behind can be seen in the exponential growth in the volume of international telecommunications, with more rapid growth in US-bound traffic from developing as opposed to the Organization for Economic Cooperation and Development (OECD) countries (Kapur and McHale 2005: 124–125). Just as the declining cost of postage hastened the flow of letters back and forth across the Altantic a century ago, "cheap calls" have been described as "the social glue of migrant transnationalism" (Vertovec 2004). International telecommunication may not be free, but it is not terribly expensive because competition within the telecommunications industry constantly drives prices down and mobile telephony has significantly expanded access at the other end of the chain, where migrants' friends and relatives live. Moreover, migration can provide the synergy needed for an infrastructure that can knit here and there together. Cross-border population movements have helped drive the growth in international telephone traffic: an analysis of 160 countries between 2001 and 2006 shows that a 10 percent increase in the size of bilateral migrant stocks was associated with a three-person increase in bilateral telephone traffic, a more robust effect than that produced by short-term visitors, bilateral trade, and bilateral foreign direct investment stocks (Perkins and Neumayer 2010).

The diminishing costs of telecommunication; the extension of service to rural areas in the developing world; and, most important, the advent of the cell phone has put communication by voice in reach for migrants and stay-at-homes in many corners of the developing world, with voice conveying a direct emotionality that the letter cannot always convey. For migrant kin living in rural areas, the change has been dramatic, as discovered by anthropologist Peri Fletcher, who observed migration's impact in rural Jalisco, Mexico, during the 1980s and 1990s:

> The extension of a phone line to Napízaro in 1989 made daily involvement much more of a reality. The phone, located in a small *tienda* at the top of the town, serves as a conduit of information about jobs in the United States. People now know that they will be informed quickly in case of illness or other family crises. . . . They are no longer out of touch for weeks and months at a time. Grandparents warn children that their parents will be told of misbehavior the next time they call from *allá*. (1999: 134)

While the advent of the phone reduced isolation, access in rural areas often remained difficult, as documented by Sarah Mahler, who found that, in the late 1980s, migrant kin in a high-emigration region of El Salvador struggled to gain access to the phone:

> Only six phones serve the two towns and no phones are protected by booths so there is absolutely no privacy for callers. Moreover, the national telephone company controls the services and a local operator in each office places calls. (Mahler 2001: 604)

By the early 1990s, things had improved on the migrant side because calling cards dropped costs for those unable to afford a phone, though access was still problematic and communication was a struggle. Research in the Senegalese River basin in Africa tells a similar story, though one entailing even greater change: in the 1960s and 1970s, communication was slow and difficult, often relying on personal emissaries, the trustworthiness of whom was often in doubt. By the early 1990s, a few telephones were found in the villages, limiting the options and frequency of communication for most. As of the mid-2000s, the expansion of the mobile network combined with increased competition "permitted a more individual and widespread use of the mobile telephone, even in the most distant villages" (Sargent, Yatera, and Larchanché-Kim 2005). The capacity to connect via the phone significantly altered relationships between migrants and their kin, allowing for an instantaneity, rapidity, confidentiality, and capacity to hear the voices of close kin that was widely appreciated. A particularly innovative Australian study examining communication patterns on *both* the sending *and* the receiving side found that, prior to 1990, contact mainly involved the exchange of letters, often sent weekly or every other week, with the telephone, less widespread and often considered unreliable, used only rarely. The early 1990s saw phone usage pick up smartly (Wilding 2006).

The advent of the Internet occurred by the end of that decade, allowing migrants and stay-at-homes to communicate instantly and almost cost-free, possibly yielding a spontaneity approaching the conditions of face-to-face contact. Members of the migrant network based in the Antipodes, described in the Australian study mentioned above, quickly adopted the Internet as a supplement to the phone, leading to a sharp uptick in the frequency of communications. Of course, home access was often lacking on both sides of the migrant chain. But the absence of a link at home may simply be an impediment to be skirted via the use of cybercafés, which have proliferated on both sending and receiving sides, often emerging in the latter amid thriving ethnic commercial enclaves where a clientele of common origins transforms the cybercafé into a form of immigrant sociability. The experience of Ecuadorian immigrants to Spain and their relatives at home in Ecuador provides a window onto these changes. As of the mid-2000s, "the acquisition of personal computers and related technology [was] still a luxury that only a few Ecuadorians c[ould] afford" (Mejia-Estévez 2009: 396), but the number of Ecuadorian cybercafés quadrupled over the first four years of the new millennium. Across the Atlantic, in Spain, immigrant entrepreneurs rushed to open up cybercafés catering to their co-nationals, whose patronage grew as the cybercafés offered an ever larger panoply of services targeted at the immigrants' needs:

> The owners of the cybercafés *(locutorios)* have made communication the point of entrance in order to offer multiple services. In effect, practically all the cybercafés offer the service of sending remittances . . . parallel to access to telephone, internet and sending of remittances they offer other types of services such as the sale of prepaid phonecards, sending of savings, conversion of American system videos to the European or visa versa . . . food or other Latin American products. (G. Ramirez 2007: 18–20)

Beyond email are the potentialities unlocked by videoconferencing, which lets immigrants and kin at home communicate face-to-face regardless of distance. The effects can be dramatic, as found by Graciela de la Fuente in her ethnography of Bolivian immigrants in Spain:

Many of them make recourse of the web camera in order to see how their sons and daughters are physically, as much as to know if they are sick or if they have had piercings, as to be able to follow their growth, the changes that they experience with age, or, simply, to attend to daily experience: see the little children play or to see whether their homes are in order. This tool permits them to see them in real time, to observe their gestures and physical features. Thanks to this technology, they feel that they have control over what their children do and can feel that they comply with the decisions taken from a distance. This technology introduces nonverbal communication as a key element. For them it implies an indispensable additional value to exercise motherhood. The corporal movements and gestures permit them to know the emotional situation of their children: if they are sad, happy, preoccupied, or if they tell them the truth or lie. (2011: 24)

Taken together, these many changes in telecommunications technology provide reason to think that migrants, though separated by long distance, can maintain the daily relationships characteristic of proximity. As Diminescu writes, "Today, the virtual bond—via telephone or email—makes it easier than before to stay close to one's family, to others, to what is happening to them, at home or elsewhere" (2008: 567).

While the letter, the phone call, the email all let migrants transcend distance to stay in touch with their kin at home, nothing fully replaces in-person contact. The ethnic tourism of immigrants and those of their relatives lucky enough to get the visa needed for a short stay is a growth business. It attracts investors eager to serve this market and help it grow while also triggering the interest of sending states attentive to the rewards to be reaped from temporarily returning migrants. Always on the lookout for new customers, airlines have concluded that ethnic tourists and foreign workers comprise a growth market, with the result that they make efforts to attract "visiting friends and relatives" traffic (Michaels 2007). A case in point is Morocco, where ethnic tourism has been a remarkable success. The number of migrants visiting Morocco almost tripled after the turn of the millennium, a flow that entailed roughly three million visits by migrants and their descendants during 2006 (de Haas 2007: 32). Moroccans traveling from Europe have the option of driving home; while geography is such that many migrants cannot avail themselves of this cost-saving possibility, air travel between source and destination countries has boomed, as exemplified by the 350 percent gain in air travel between the United States and Colombia recorded between 1975 and 2006,[2] or the still more impressive tenfold increase in United States–El Salvador air traffic between 1990 and 2004, or the spread of daily air travel to Central America from a growing number of cities in the United

States (Orozco 2005). The emergence of this traffic corridor, almost entirely dominated by migration-related travel, has in turn triggered new commercial strategies, further making connectedness easier and cheaper (Programa de las Naciones Unidas para el Desarollo 2005).

## Why and How Place Still Matters

In the view of many scholars, these cross-border activities comprise a "transnational social field," encompassing migrants and stay-at-homes. However, while ties may extend from "here" to "there," cross-border linkages neither come together in a single package nor persist in stable form. First, the intensely connected themselves engage in cross-border activities of a varied sort: sometimes cultural, sometimes economic, and sometimes political (Levitt 2001). Second, few migrants engage in "transnationalism." For the most part, they maintain cross-border connections on a selective basis: some send remittances; others may travel; others stay in touch by phone. Furthermore, a sizable minority of them abandon the cross-border connection altogether. In some cases, the migrants *want* to cut ties, having left home precisely because they found the home country social or cultural environment to be stifling or their kin to be dominating, difficult, or unkind. Cross-border engagement is also costly, reducing the population motivated or able to keep up the home country tie. Likewise, resource constraints compel those more strongly attached to friends and family at home to pick among the available options. Only migrants equipped with the material resources *and* the legal entitlements needed to move back and forth across borders at will enjoy the full array of cross-border connections. At the other end of the chain, the costs of travel and, more decisively, border controls keep the stay-at-homes in place (Arias 2009). Unlike the circulation of information—flowing from one receiver to one sender and back—the circulation of people has spillover effects beyond the immediate circle, especially where the small size of sending communities makes for frequent contact between returning migrants and their stay-at-home neighbors. Hence, as the circulation of people stops or slows down, simultaneous awareness of events in place of destination and place of origin inevitably declines.

Moreover, proclamations of a technology-driven "death of distance" warrant a skeptical second look. To begin with, the effort to keep up cross-border contacts runs up against the hard, physical constraint of space: some forms of time and space can be compressed, but not all. In particular, migrants moving across an east-west axis inevitably move into time zones at some remove from those of their kin and friends back home, a factor impeding communication, regardless of its speed or quality. Physical distance also generates coordination problems not encountered when contact is face-to-face and part of the routine, everyday reality. Instead, migrants abroad and their significant others at home have to make appointments, which are always vulnerable to disruption if some unexpected event or even a distraction puts someone at either end out of touch. Consistency and frequency also matter since information gets quickly out-of-date. Thus, when contacts lapse, communication may reveal that neither migrant nor stay-at-home is fully aware of the other's reality, thus heightening the impact of absence.

But the capacity to keep up connections goes beyond matters of distance and geography. Equally important is the paradox of international migration itself: movement is inherent to migration, which is at once the effect and the cause of movement. On the one hand, the impetus to migration stems from the territorial containment of resources, which are unequally distributed across the world. Those resources do not leak out across the boundaries of the resource-rich states, so they can be accessed only by crossing borders. On the other hand, those very same inequalities separating receiving from sending states also diminish the capacity to keep up ties since the technological infrastructure needed to maintain cross-border contact is most developed in the countries of *immigration* but lags far behind in the countries of *emigration*. Those disparities also affect the immigrants, who are often handicapped by the legacy of the resource constraints impinging on the places from which they departed: arriving with lower levels of education (in some cases, limited literacy) and little prior technical exposure, they find it difficult to take full advantage of the technological potential available in the place where they actually live.

Last, because migration is at once a difficult and a transformative experience, maintaining effective, satisfying contacts across borders proves problematic, even when the technical capacity to interact—whether remotely or in person—is available. In large measure, those impediments also derive from territorial containment, in this case, not just of resources but of the behavioral patterns and expectations generated by life in a different social, economic, and technological environment. Hence, while migration extends identities and social relations across states, those cross-border connections are persistently eroded by the many forces that lead social relations to converge with territorial boundaries.

## A New World of Communication and Contact?

As noted by Raelene Wilding, technologies that now seem ordinary have recurrently been accompanied by radical and utopian visions of impact, which is why the grand visions common in the migration scholarship "rarely stand up to empirical scrutiny" (2006: 127). Today's world undoubtedly furnishes new forms of communication, but it is neither clear that the pattern of innovation at the millennium involves a radical rupture from the past nor that current forms of communication yield results more profound than those experienced in the past.

Thus the literature is largely preoccupied by the speed of communication, at the expense of communication's social context. Oral communication, proceeding via intermediaries, has long been an alternative, remaining common among Italian immigrants to North America in the immediate postwar decades and among sub-Saharan and North African immigrants in France throughout the 1980s. Though the messenger may have pledged confidentiality to the sender and the receiver, the very fact of relying on an intermediary gave oral communications a social character, lost when contact shifted to the more individualistic exchange via the written word (Sayad 1991). Serving as a stand-in for the migrant ("It was like seeing you here," wrote a mother in Italy to her son in Montreal after a visit from one of his migrant friends [quoted in Cancian 2010: 52]), the courier was then—and is still now—also an instrument for transmitting gifts, not just words. Precisely because of their materiality, gifts have a lasting quality and the capacity to symbolize the presence of the person far away; as oral communication is inherently ethereal, it can't fully substitute for the loss entailed in distance.

Letters and literacy go hand in hand; indeed, during the last era of migration, the migrants' need to communicate when there was no other tool but the written word provided powerful motivation to gain at least the basic reading and orthographic skills needed to stay in touch with those still at home (Sierra Blas 2004). Moreover, the information conveyed by a letter arriving in a peasant village often traveled well beyond the recipient, especially if the latter had difficulty reading, in which case a literate member of the community read its contents to all the assembled villagers. As historian David Gerber explained, "the classic 'America Letter' . . . was produced as much or more for the community as for the more intimate confidences of a private relationship and served more as a form of social intelligence than as a means for sustaining emotional ties" (Gerber 2000). Consequently, the information and gossip it channeled sufficed for the closure needed to keep migrants in line and connected to the stay-at-homes.

Although the transoceanic letter during the last age of mass migration was probably not as common a phenomenon as today's email or phone call, its effect may have been greater for precisely that reason; its materiality also meant that the communication had a less transient impact. The accounts left by turn-of-the-twentieth-century migrants themselves demonstrate how closely they attended to the letters arriving from overseas, with photographs—a regular component of the transatlantic letter from the late nineteenth century on (P. Fitzgerald 2008)—conveying an image of the new world that any recipient could understand:

> I was receiving letters from my sister, my uncle, and aunts from America; they also sent their pictures. They were dressed so nicely that I could not understand how simple workers could afford such things. For a long time, I was deliberating about America—what a strange country it is. A photograph shows that they are well fed, and in addition they send money to their relatives . . . After prolonged deliberation I decided to risk my savings for a ticket, if only to see it with my own eyes and try my luck there. (quoted in Morawska 1985: 78)

The continuing synergistic effects of long-distance migration and long-distance communication enhanced letters' effects, tightening bonds across the Atlantic. In and of itself, the need to communicate with distant relatives spurred the spread of literacy and the diffusion of the practice of writing (Caffarena 2012). Long-term changes in literacy, technology, and public infrastructure prior to the last age of migration hastened the delivery of letters across continents and oceans, even as the number of correspondents burgeoned. Though yesteryear's speeds pale in comparison to today's, the mail nonetheless provided the means by which European migrants sent home "a rain of gold" (Esteves and Khoudour-Castéras 2009).

## The Fragility of Cross-State Connections

Thus the literature has overdrawn the contrast between the supposedly "closed" world of the past and the more "open" present; it has also raised an empirical red herring since the question of the impact of differences in the speed and volume of communications "then" and "now" is simply unanswerable. Most important, the case studies that have so heavily influenced contemporary scholarship convey an unrealistically high estimate of the type, durability, and frequency of connections criss-crossing today's immigrant networks. An exemplary description comes from Peggy Levitt's portrayal of Dominican migrants in Boston and their home community whose many frequent interchanges were seen as creating this transnational village and making it likely to endure . . . Migrants and non-migrants . . . remained in close touch. More than half of the villagers spoke by phone to their relatives in Boston at least once, if not twice a month. . . . Nearly three quarters of those who migrated returned home to visit; more than half had been back to Miraflores between two and four times. (2001b: 53)

Undoubtedly, contacts between sending communities and migrants abroad *sometimes* take so regular and recurrent a form. But one needs to remember that the cross-border infrastructure generated along the Caribbean-US axis may not provide the right model for the rest of the world. Though living in the first world, refugees from war-torn parts of the world are unlikely to be able to communicate with their kin with comparable ease. The same often holds true for much poorer, less developed places than the Caribbean islands, where even regular postal service is not yet a reality. Migrants of this sort, as noted in an Australian study, are apt "to rely on networks for friends and kin travelling in and out of the region to deliver letters, photographs, and videos," evidence that the communication "methods of hundreds of years ago remain the most reliable in this context" (Baldassar et al. 2007: 132).

Moreover, communication depends on both means *and* motivation; the latter is not always in place. As the historical and ethnographic literature so amply documents, some migrants depart precisely *in order to* cut the connection. For others, contact lapses out of inconvenience, forgetfulness, the press of daily events, or unexpected and unwanted difficulties: factors of inevitable influence when friends and family are far away. In the early twentieth century, the *Forward,* a New York Yiddish daily with a mass circulation, "received letters from distant places, from abandoned wives in Russia and Galicia, asking that their husbands be located in America" (Howe 1976: 179). At the other end of the hemisphere, in Buenos Aires, "many newspapers, such as the *Laurac Bat,* of the Association of Basque Emigrants, published long lists of unclaimed letters and requests for information about relatives who had disappeared" (Sierra Blas 2004: 124).

Any number of circumstances can lead to disconnection; among the most important are the migrant's own failure or the creation of a new family, leaving the spouse and children left behind to fend for themselves. Jason Pribilsky's ethnography of both Ecuadorian immigrants in New York City and their kin back home found that many wives "waited in anguish when remittances failed to arrive; weeks passed without phone calls from husbands abroad," gaps that were sometimes unintentional, other times intentional, caused by husbands, "intimidat[ing] their wives with deliberate silence" (2007: 265). Writing about Mexican transnational families, Joanna Dreby similarly noted that "when fathers perceive failure and feel they cannot fulfill their role as family provider in terms of sending money home, communications with their children ceases" (2010: 81). Although communicating with family at home may be relatively cheap, it nonetheless entails some costs, making the resources to calling and staying in touch a matter of conflict within immigrant families.

Quantitative sources confirm these qualitative accounts: while pervasive, linkages are far more fragile, more fragmented, and more infrequently recurring than the literature suggests. At the emigration end of the chain, data from the 2007 Pew World Survey for thirty-five developing countries show how widely social networks have stretched across national lines: 32 percent of respondents regularly write to, telephone, or visit friends or relatives in other countries; 16 percent connect with people living in the United States. Moreover, these connections are circuits for the flow of scarce resources: 8 percent of the respondents with foreign contacts receive money regularly, with another 23 percent receiving money once in a while.[3] That so many receive financial transfers underlines the significance of these ties across borders; on the other hand, one has to note that words get passed from place to place a good deal more frequently than does money.

By the end of the twenty-first century's first decade, a quarter of Latin Americans reported that a former member of the household was living abroad, a pattern still more prevalent in Central America and the Caribbean, where more than half of Haitians indicated that a relative resided outside the country. But these migrant kin bear little resemblance to the image of the plugged-in hometowner avidly communicating with friends and relatives abroad. While technology may create the *potential* for daily contact, data from the Latin American Public Opinion Project— a hemisphere-wide set of nationally representative surveys—indicate that 7 percent of Latin Americans related to migrants living in the United States avail themselves of this possibility, with still lower proportions in El Salvador (5.2 percent), Guatemala (4.6 percent), and Mexico (2.4 percent). Moreover, contact is as likely to be frequent as occasional or nonexistent: hemisphere-wide, the proportion reporting that contact occurs twice a week or more (37 percent) is just marginally higher than the proportion reporting that contact rarely or never takes place (34 percent). Only in Jamaica and the Dominican Republic does a majority of migrant kin report weekly contact with migrants in the United States, a strong contrast with Mexico, where the proportion losing contact with kin in the United States exceeds the fraction engaged in twice-weekly communication. Although analysis of the survey shows that communication is more common when the parent at a home is a mother and less common when the migrant's relative lives in a rural area, controlling for background factors does little to alter the basic pattern.[4]

Receiving-side reports do not quite align with the patterns generated by sending-side information; however, they nonetheless show that national borders do cut frequently the tie linking immigrants to kin at home, as can be seen from data drawn from a broad range of large-scale, representative surveys of Asian and Latin American immigrants, of which some were conducted on a national basis, others on a regional basis. Across the surveys, the very great majority of respondents maintain contact with relatives or friends at home. Nonetheless, the surveys suggest that one or two out of ten migrants sever the connection altogether, a proportion that appears to be higher among Asians than among Latin Americans. Across all groups, moreover, only a minority appears to engage in weekly contact. In some cases, as among immigrants from the Dominican Republic—who consistently maintain a more intense pattern of cross-border engagement—a majority is in touch with relatives at least once a day. But among Mexicans— the very largest group—only half are in weekly contact with kin or friends in Mexico, a proportion a good deal lower among Asians as well as among immigrants nationwide. At the end of the continuum, almost all Cubans have fallen out of frequent contact with relatives on the island.

Further insights come from the 2003 Detroit Arab American Survey. While this study is of an unusual, relatively advantaged immigrant population and thus yields conclusions that may not fully extend to other groups, it nonetheless provides information on communication patterns and usage so far unparalleled by any other source. While the majority (roughly 60 percent) had arrived in the United States within the past twenty years, the great bulk (75 percent) reported having family *as well as* friends in Michigan. By contrast, more than 90 percent reported having family abroad, but only 60 percent claimed to still have friends living outside the United States. Moreover, monthly communication had a strongly local tilt, with respondents displaying a modest propensity for Michigan-based family over foreign kin but a very strong tendency toward regular communication with local rather than international friends. Cross-border ties also decayed with the length of respondents' settlement in the United States: after a quarter century or more of residence in the United States, one-third of the respondents were no longer in regular contact with family as well as friends living abroad.[5]

Returning to a more panoramic view, most migrants report that they have traveled home at least once since moving to the United States. Yet almost all the surveys show that a large minority—in the neighborhood of 30 percent—report that they have never returned home since arrival in the

United States. Indeed, a closer look at the data on the ethnic tourism of immigrants reveals a much less dynamic market than the overly enthusiastic literature suggests. The number of international visitors arriving in Mexico for the purpose of seeing relatives—a population likely to consist mainly of Mexican-born persons residing in the United States—has been largely stagnant since the late 1990s. While travel to the Dominican Republic by Dominicans living abroad doubled between 1993 and 2003, and rose by another 35 percent by 2010, the total market share accounted by ethnic tourism of this sort actually declined over the same period. Likewise, the surveys indicate that the typical immigrant is likely to send some money home at least once a year or more. Across all surveys, a still more substantial minority reports that remittances are rarely or very infrequently sent, a proportion that rises to 60 percent among Asian immigrants in a nationally representative sample who were queried in 2008.

While for many immigrants home connections attenuate or get cut altogether, the typical arrangement nonetheless involves the retention of *some* home country connection. Rarest, however, is the pattern so emphasized in the literature, where the "transmigrants" appear as the emblematic figure, suspended between two communities, living "lives across borders, participating simultaneously in social relations that embed them in more than one nation-state" (Glick Schiller 2003: 105–106). For evidence, we return to the 2006 nationally representative survey of Latin American immigrants discussed at the beginning of this chapter. Focusing on cross-border remittances, travel, and communication, analysis of the survey shows that most respondents fall into the category that I have called "the connected," maintaining one or two activities, but not all three. A smaller group consists of the bordered, those whose cross-border activities have tailed off altogether. However, the so-called transmigrants—those engaged in remittance sending, frequent communication, and regular travel—comprise the smallest group, roughly one of out of every ten respondents. Moreover, multivariate analysis shows that among the survey's typical respondents (married, employed, middle-age Mexican women living in the United States for fifteen years), even fewer—about five out of every one hundred—are likely to maintain cross-border connections of the strongest, most consistent sort. Colombians were a bit more likely to fall into the transmigrant category, as were respondents with children abroad or retaining property ownership in the home country. Regardless of which variable was assessed, however, the probability of falling into the transmigrant category never rose to the one-in-ten level.[6]

A variety of factors, to be discussed at greater length below, helps explain how and why these home country ties weaken, sometimes entirely falling away. Distance is not dead but rather alive and well. Though not the only influence, long-distance dislocation contributes strongly to the fraying of migrant–home community connections. To begin with, technology can compress some aspects of migrants' relocation but not all of them. While it now takes only a few hours to cross the Atlantic, as opposed to ten days during the last era of mass migration, the time entailed in long-distance air travel has barely declined since the advent of the jet decades ago.

While telecommunications costs have dropped significantly and are continuing to decline, the material is far from the only consideration affecting the pattern of talk. When interactions regularly take a face-to-face form, the telephone complements the communications that occur on-site. By contrast, with dislocation, phone talk has to substitute for face-to-face communication, with the result that calls are made less frequently but last longer. The working day structures the time available for telephone talk of this sort. Long calls, in particular, are more likely to take place in the evening, when most people have returned home and the key domestic chores have been done (Licoppe 2004). Given, the rigid, hectic, work-oriented schedules of the immigrants, weekday evenings may not afford the time or peace of mind needed to call relatives at home. Not surprisingly, a study of telephone calls in two heavily immigrant New York City neighborhoods found that domestic calls peaked weekday evenings, whereas international calls prevailed during the weekends (Rojas 2010).

Moreover, it matters greatly whether migration proceeds along a north-south or east-west axis, as the first keeps time zone differences down and the second expands them. Mexican or Maghrebian migrations, for example, rarely extend beyond a one- or two-hour time difference from the migrants' home. But the more global the migration, the more likely that time zone differences impede convenient communication. As noted in an Australian study, migrants moving internationally but within the same time zone from Singapore to western Australia called constantly; by contrast, those migrants from more far-flung destinations proved far more constrained, typically making a weekly call on Sunday, "the largest window of opportunity for catching both migrant and parent home at an appropriate time" (Baldassar et al. 2007: 113).

Thus, distance inevitably changes the rhythm of communication, giving it an intermittent cadence, punctuated by silences that prove difficult to avoid, even with the best intentions. The silences are meaningful, though hard for either side to interpret definitively; moreover, they add to the burden that each conversation has to carry, making the contact planned in advance increasingly different from the everyday face-to-face contact. The more important the role of premeditation and planning, the more distant the interaction gets from the routine, taken-for-granted, everyday nature of face-to-face contacts. To be sure, migrants with the full array of communications technology at hand manage the inherent problems of long-distance communication among intimates with greater ease. But these are resources on which less-skilled, more hard-pressed migrants cannot always count. And regardless of technological conditions in the place of immigration, the capacity to shrink distance depends on the options available in the place of emigration, precisely where resource shortages triggered the emigrants' own decision to leave for somewhere else.

## Contacts across Distance

Regardless of the geography of communication, we still know surprisingly little about the long-distance interactions between migrants and their kin. Despite all the hype about the Internet, questions related to migrants' digital literacy; their attitudes, skills, and knowledge of informatics; their use of the Internet; their access to broadband; their degree of confidence in the Internet; and their view of its value added are among the many matters that researchers have yet to explore fully (Borkert, Cingolani, and Premazzi 2009). Nonetheless, we can turn to a variety of sources to fill in the blanks. Close inspection of these data indicate that the image of the wired and footloose immigrant, communicating across borders in real time or traveling to home and back with little bother bears a tenuous relationship to reality: "the experience of the connected migrants, neglecting those without a connection, yield[s] a particularly truncated image of the realities of migration" (Mattelart 2009: 30).

Access to distance-shrinking technologies varies on receiving *and* sending sides. Migrant densities boost international calling rates, though impacts and incomes are positively correlated in both receiving and sending states (Perkins and Neumayer 2010). Access to the Internet and mobile phones peaks among the high-income countries on which migrants from the developing world converge (Hamel 2009). Nonetheless, the capacity to call far-removed friends and relatives is far from universal. As Joanna Dreby found when studying Mexican immigrants in the United States and their children left behind,

> Not all parents have easy access to a phone in the United States. Many do not have land lines and either use cell phones or public pay phones. Nearly all use calling cards, which offer the best rates to Mexico, but numbers often ring busy during peak calling times. (Dreby 2010: 62)

Indeed, data from surveys back up Dreby's ethnographic account, showing that immigrants fall behind natives on many indicators of telecommunications use. Cell phones may be thought of as universal, but as of 2011, a nationally representative sample of Latino immigrants in the United States showed otherwise: 45 percent still lacked a cell phone. And, as found in a similar survey conducted the prior year, a third of the cell phone owners never texted and a slightly smaller fraction used no voice application at all.[7]

The Internet may indeed eventually overhaul cross-border interactions, but conditions on the receiving side provide any number of reasons to suspect that transformation lies on the distant horizon. To begin with, digital divides frequently reproduce preexisting inequalities; characteristics that depress Internet use in the general population—lower incomes, lower levels of education, and lower levels of wealth—are often more pronounced among the foreign-born. Moreover, the role of networks in diffusing digital access may yield yet another impediment: as access to social support helps users learn how to use information technology (IT) and users with larger digital networks find Internet use more rewarding and profitable, low average rates of Internet use among immigrants may increase the costs of learning and delay diffusion. A French study of cybercafés in a heavily immigrant Parisian neighborhood suggests just how these factors might keep immigrants off the Web:

> The practice of the internet is still not well known in ethnic neighborhoods and is constrained by equipment that is still insufficient or poorly distributed in the migrants' country of origins. The absence of adapted technology (Arab keyboards, for example) and facilitators can be invoked, because the managers of these boutiques usually keep to their strict commercial role. The obligatory passage via writing and mastery of the keyboard comprises a constraint that videoconference does not succeed to lift: this technique necessitates a prearranged appointment, taking into account time zone differences, and unlike the phone call, the communication is taken in charge symmetrically by both parties, regardless of the resources, which makes this practice all the more difficult to put into action. (Scopsi 2004)

Research conducted in the United States shows that Internet usage rates among immigrants fall well below the national level (Fairlie et al. 2006). The best available trend data from the first half of the millennium indicated that the immigrant–native gap had widened at a time when most other digital divides had narrowed (Ono and Zavodny 2008). More recent data point to some amount of catch-up: as of 2012 (Lopez, González-Barrera, and Patten 2013), Latino immigrants lagged behind whites in the rate of going online (69 percent versus 87 percent) and owning a computer

(69 percent versus 87 percent), with data from 2010 showing even greater disparities in home Internet connection (45 percent versus 75 percent), and broadband connections (35 percent versus 69 percent) (Livingston 2011). However, a closer look using data from four waves of the National Latino Survey (2006, 2009, 2010, 2012) and the 2007 Pew Hispanic Center Health Survey suggests that the digital divide is closing slowly, if at all, and that the sources of Latino disadvantage keep digital access low. Thus, among the foreign-born, multivariate analysis found no statistically significant change between 2006 and 2010, with only the latest survey year, 2012, showing a significant upward bump. For the entire six-year (2006–2012) period, the typical respondent—a forty-two-year-old, married, Spanish-dominant Mexican man, with a primary school education and nineteen years of residence in the United States—had a one in five chance of using the Internet. Though younger immigrants were good deal more likely to use the Internet than their older counterparts, even among the twenty-five-year-olds, usage rates didn't reach the 30 percent level. By contrast, among respondents sharing all the same characteristics but reporting bilingualism rather than Spanish dominance, usage rates were just above 45 percent, while among those with a high school education but otherwise similar to the typical respondent, usage rates were just a few percentage points above the halfway mark. Unfortunately, data limitations make it impossible to track how the most recent changes in the use of technology matter for cross-border communications. Nonetheless, as the digital divide remains wide, results from a nationally representative survey conducted in 2006 are still likely to be illuminating. At the time, only 28 percent of Latin American immigrants sent email, of whom barely one-half used email to communicate with friends or family in the home country. Email use was far lower among Mexican immigrants, with only 11 percent sending email and not quite 6 percent using email to keep in touch with friends or family at home.[8]

Data drawn from the Detroit Arab American Survey provide a more detailed though entirely consistent portrait. Most of the 732 foreign-born respondents queried by the survey possessed either a mobile device, used a computer, or made some use of the Internet (whether for reading the newspaper, email, or some other activity). However, 32 percent were not connected in any of these ways. Although 61 percent had a cell phone, no other usage pattern crossed the 50 percent mark. Just over one-quarter of respondents reported reading the newspaper over the Internet. Only one-fifth could be considered fully wired, using each telecommunication modality. These discrepancies in usage fully reflected the inequalities within the group: the least educated respondents were unlikely to report any form of connection whatsoever compared to three connection modalities among the most educated. Income differences yielded similar though slightly smaller effects.

Thus, the digital divide hampers access to the means of long-distance communication on the receiving side; it matters even more at the other end of the chain, where poverty as well as infrastructure capacity ensure that physical distance still matters, that the "immobile" can't fully keep up with the mobile. As late as the early 1990s, Sarah Mahler found that migrant kin in rural areas of eastern El Salvador still struggled to find an available working phone, as noted earlier; however, things quickly changed soon after, with cell phone access soaring. In 2000, El Salvador had a mobile phone-to-user ratio equal to 35 percent of that in the United States. Over the next nine years, cell phone penetration quadrupled, pushing El Salvador, like Guatemala and Jamaica, well beyond the United States.[9] Still, phone access in today's sending societies remains far from universal, with the Latin American average still below that of the United States, and the poorest Western Hemisphere societies, like Haiti or Nicaragua, lagging far behind. And in rural Latin American areas, mobile telephony is far from taken for granted (Peres and Hilbert 2009: 56).

Thus, for most, though clearly not all, stay-at-homes, a telephone is likely to be in reach. But there are often resource asymmetries because the cost of calling can be systematically lower for the migrants than for their more resource-deprived relatives in the sending country. As Miller and Madianou found, even the introduction of international calling cards based on prepaid credit did not manage to push costs down to a level that home country callers could afford, which is why only one of their Philippines-based subjects had purchased such a card, which, at the time of the interview, remained unused (2011: 462). Consequently, in these families, children could generally not afford to call their mothers, with the result that inbound outdistanced outbound calls by a ratio of 7:1 (467).

Internet access shows even greater asymmetries because the world is far from being equally wired. In general, the digital divide across countries grows as gross domestic product (GDP) per capita declines; in Latin America, the declining gap in mobile telephone access coexists with a widening gap in computer, Internet, and broadband access compared to the OECD countries (Peres and Hilbert 2009). Though the contrast to the United States is not quite so unfavorable, it still demonstrates how little progress has been made. Whereas rates of Internet use in the Dominican Republic, El Salvador, Guatemala, Haiti, Mexico, and Nicaragua moved closer to the US pattern during the 2000s, the gap in computer access and bandwidth size remained virtually unchanged.

Hence, while migrants in the cities of the developing world may find that obstacles to online access, though significant, are gradually falling, their relatives in isolated villages in Mexico or Haiti (as of 2007, among the world's worst ranked on the International Telegraph Union's information communications technology (ICT) Development Index [Balboni et al. 2011]) are far more likely to be off the grid. In Latin America, the greatest socioeconomic digital divide is found in countries with the lowest overall ICT penetration rates, which, like El Salvador or Honduras, also happen to be significant exporters of people. Throughout the hemisphere, the very rural areas from which so many migrants come also report the lowest rates of Internet penetration (Grazzi and Vergara 2011). As of 2007, rural areas in Mexico, Honduras, and El Salvador registered ICT penetration rates of 6 percent, .1 percent, and .1 percent, respectively (Grazzi and Vergara 2011: 17). Moreover, as demands for carrying capacity increase, the divide between migrants in technologically advanced countries and their relatives at home is likely to increase. In Latin America, broadband access remains mainly concentrated in cities; more generally in the developing world, multiple platform communication technology is still available "primarily to those in urban areas and affluent enough to afford the related costs" (Miller and Madianou 2011: 461).

Furthermore, the deficiencies afflicting the general population affect the stay-at-homes as well because a significant proportion of them simply lack the capacity to keep up regular contact. Data from the Latin American Public Opinion Project show that, of the migrant kin living in Mexico, one-fifth possesses neither a cell phone nor a land line; just over one-third has both a cell and a land line. Not surprisingly, Joanna Dreby (2010) found that many of the Mexican immigrants she interviewed in the United States had to make arrangements to call their children in a neighbor's home or in a local business providing phone service. Access to the newer technology of the Web is still more limited: of the migrant kin living in Mexico, barely one-sixth uses the Internet as frequently as once a week, and two-thirds never use the Internet; not surprisingly, Internet use is lowest in the small towns and especially the rural areas, where most migrant kin are found. Communication increases when the means of communication are at hand, with particularly strong effects in rural areas, where migrant kin possessing both cell phones *and* land lines are three times less likely to lose contact with relatives abroad than those with no phone at all.[10]

That immigrants and stay-at-homes communicate with difficulty, sometimes falling entirely out of touch, should not bring us back to the rightly discredited view that migration involves a complete uprooting. Instead, the lesson to learn is that migrants and stay-at-homes have to work hard to stay connected and that, despite all the technological advances of the Internet age, there is no transcending distance.

## Losing the Connection

Still, continuing migration means continuing connectedness: given the rates of international migration, the global cities of the developed world are hubs of contact, linking migrants with far-off kin and communities. But the view gleaned from examination at the aggregate level may be misleading because it includes the recent arrivals—whose connections are almost always more robust—with those who are putting down roots and may consider the receiving country to be the country of adoption. The crucial question concerns change over the long term: do connections wither as the migrants change, adapting to their new set of circumstances in ways that make them increasingly different from the people left behind?

Analysis of the 2006 survey of Latin American immigrants in the United States, discussed throughout this chapter, sheds light on the mechanisms by which immigrants retain attachments to the transnational social field or instead pull back to the society where they actually reside.[11] While the scholarly enthusiasts of transnationalism insist that cross-border activity persists even as immigrants put down roots in the country of destination, the survey, containing information on remitting, phone calling, and travel home, points in a different direction. First, migrants seem to be picking and choosing among possible cross-border activities; greater host country commitments affect the capacity to maintain ongoing home country ties, *selectively* drawing migrants out of the home country connection altogether. As indicated by the data on travel, migrants find regular face-to-face contact— the type of cross-border activity most likely to reinforce ties between migrants and stay-at-homes experiencing very different realities—difficult to sustain; the probability that a respondent would have taken a recent trip was barely one out of three. Though the survey's respondents engaged in a lot of cross-border communicating, the analysis shows that everyday contacts falter even though telephone communication occurs at low cost and legal status has no bearing on one's ability to pick up the phone. Thus, the typical migrant—a Spanish-dominant person residing in the United States for under twenty years—has a one in three chance of rarely or never calling home. For English-dominant migrants and child migrants, the probability of never or rarely calling home is over one in two.

Second, the frequency of phone calls home and the probability of remitting decline with length of stay, with phone calls falling steeply in the early years and bottoming out with extended US residence. Patterns of recent travel change in a different manner: they first increase during the first fifteen to twenty years of residence, only then to diminish. An otherwise typical migrant with only five years (instead of fifteen) of residence in the United States has a slightly *higher* probability of remitting than her more settled counterpart and is also a good deal more likely to call home weekly. However, she is *less* likely, by 5 percentage points, to have traveled back to Mexico at some point in the prior two years—a pattern probably related to the prevalence of unauthorized status among the more recent immigrants, for whom border crossing is therefore most difficult. Age at migration also matters: child migrants often leave at too early an age to have developed the strong ties that can be sustained despite distance and time. Indeed, migrants that came as children to the United States are much less likely to call weekly and much more likely never to call at all. In fact, the typical child migrant is more likely *never* to call than to call at least once during the prior year.

The survey also sheds light on the mechanisms by which immigrants maintain an active connection to the home country or instead cut those ties. The language use variables provide striking results: shifts away from the foreign tongue consistently yield reduced home country attachment. Language, of course, is the essence of communication: it is difficult to feel at home or believe that the stay-at-home other is just like oneself if the meanings of speech can no longer be taken for granted. Migrants who have adapted to the new national society in which they reside by adopting its language are likely to experience exactly these effects.

The effects of settlement variables highlight the factors that keep home country ties alive and well. As noted earlier, those connections are often part and parcel of the familial survival strategies that initially trigger migration. As the survey shows, migrants with continuing home country personal or material commitments are the most likely to maintain ongoing linkages to the place left behind. Migrants who have instead shifted commitments from home to host society are likely to lack either the motivation or the resources to maintain home country connections of the same intensity.

By contrast, policies and politics appear to both connect migrants to the transnational social field and detach them from it. Country-of-origin differences underscore the mechanisms yielding detachment. Among Salvadorans, the probability of remitting is exceptionally high, which comes as no surprise because these immigrants come from a country where remittances account for over 10 percent of GDP. On the other hand, the probability of recent travel is less than half the rate predicted for the typical migrant. While the greater distance between the United States and El Salvador may be one factor, the much lower prevalence of legal status among the Salvadorans is likely to be highly influential. While Cubans remit like the Mexicans, they show a far lower propensity to travel. Here, the issue is not lack of legal status but rather US restrictions on travel to Cuba that were then in force. Either way, political constraints on international travel make it particularly hard to "live lives across borders." These impediments are likely to have long-term effects: the longer one is bordered and the more time elapses before face-to-face contact is renewed, the greater the difficulty in reviving or maintaining the cross-border connection.

On the other hand, migrants who acquired US citizenship are more likely to remit than otherwise comparable respondents who have retained a foreign nationality; they are no less likely to have engaged in recent travel or to have called weekly. However, acquiring US citizenship increases the probability of being both "bordered" and "transnational," at the expense of falling into the connected category. This paradoxical pattern is likely to reflect the dual effects of citizenship, which gives migrants the same freedoms as nationals, allowing those so inclined to cross borders as they please (and as their resources allow). But becoming a US citizen also detaches some of these new Americans from their home country connections, reflecting citizenship's role as one of the means by which states "embrace" their peoples.

## Conclusion

International migrations inevitably pull "here" and "there" together. For some migrants, producing that convergence was the goal that initially impelled them to leave home. Displacement to a richer country allowed them to establish a bridge that they could then use to send resources home to their significant others still residing in a poorer place. For other migrants, intersocietal convergence was an unintended result of moves designed to accomplish long-term goals best pursued in the country of destination. But few of the long-term settlers leave everyone behind; if the core social network shifts from "there" to "here," the process is usually protracted, with the result that information, ideas, emotions, gifts, loans, and people keep flowing between destination and origin, and back. As so many migrants are seeking to keep up connections, these countless individual but parallel and completely uncoordinated efforts to maintain ties improve the options for everyone else because the demand for connected-ness generates an infrastructure designed to make it happen.

While at the mass level, connectedness persists, its regularity is hard to maintain. The very same factor that motivates the migrations—namely, international inequalities—yields inequalities in the capacity to stay in contact. While physical distance may not be as constraining as in the migrations of years gone by, its impact is inescapable. The brute fact of location keeps long-distance rhythms off balance: when it is noon in Los Angeles and 3:00 a.m. the next day in Guangzhou, it is consistently hard to find the right time to talk, with the effort required making it a conver-sation of a completely different type. Even when time zone matters less, life gets in the way. The long day in the factory, the commute home, and the struggle with children leave little time for conversation with faraway relatives, whose everyday experiences are of a very different kind. When contact grows intermittent—the prevailing pattern, as we have seen—communication can divide rather than connect, reminding migrants and stay-at-homes that neither knows the other's reality and making them realize that physical separation has produced estrangement. Maintaining flows through the migration circuit requires inherently scarce resources and unevenly distributed capacities—most notably, money and the freedom to move between "here" and "there." And while *some* significant other is likely to remain "there," over time, the key members of the social network tend to relocate to the place of destination, reducing motivations to keep up the tie while increasing the demands for resources spent in the place where the migrants actually live.

In the end, the limits to cross-border connectedness stem from the very nature of international migration itself. Migrants build those connections precisely because resources are tied to location: the better life is found away, *not* at home. Migration is generally good for the migrants because they too benefit from the rewards of residence in a richer place. But in seeking a better future elsewhere, the migrants also enter a cage, where their home country ties inexorably wither.

# CHAPTER FIVE

# Engaging at Home from Abroad

## The Paradox of Homeland Politics

THOUGH INTERNATIONAL migration is an inherently political phenomenon, the study of migrants' political behavior is only now
moving from the field's periphery to its center. This scholarship mainly
focuses on receiving societies and hence *immigrant* politics, whether
involving political participation by persons who may or may not be citizens; learning the rules of a new and foreign political system; and last,
gaining political influence and office. Echoing the long-standing interest
in the retention of cultural beliefs or practices imported from the society
of origin, students of *immigrant* politics have sought to understand the
impact of political experiences and conditions in the society of origin *on*
political behavior in the society of destination.

However, as I have argued throughout this book, this preoccupation
ignores the duality at the heart of the migrant phenomenon. The people
opting for life in another state are not just *immigrants*, but also *emigrants*,
retaining ties to the people and places left behind. Using connections
to make their way to the new country, the migrants find themselves
among their fellow foreigners. As we have seen, that co-presence produces
a familiar rather than alien environment and also facilitates the maintenance of cross-border activities. While for many, cross-border involvements are strictly social and highly particularistic, all migrations also
include at least some migrants who keep up political as well as social
connections.

This chapter zeroes in on those home country political engagements as they unfold in the United States, a process heavily influenced by the United States' distinctive political structure and political culture. As with the long-distance social ties (which were examined in the previous chapter), long-distance emigrant politics reflects the paradox of population movements across borders. While inherently entailing mobility, migration is impelled by the unequal, territorial containment of resources, a feature of social life that both gives the migrants newfound leverage over states and peoples left behind *and* constrains their capacity to maintain cross-border connections. Cross-border migrations moving populations into developed, democratic states give the migrants capacities never previously possessed. Once in the receiving state, migrants obtain newfound leverage, benefiting from both the wealth of the economic environment and from the freedom of a polity no longer controlled by the home government. While home country politics is rarely salient among the migrant rank and file—who often had little premigration political experience and whose lives in the country of destination unfold independent of political matters at home—things take a different turn among the politically oriented. The new political environment provides the space for autonomous migrant social action, unfolding in the place of *destination* but oriented toward the place of *origin*.

Hence, population movements across borders inevitably produce migrant homeland political activism. But because the relevant political interactions extend beyond the migrants and their homelands to encompass host states and national peoples, the international dimension also proves constraining. Migrants' foreign entanglements run the risk of reminding nationals of the foreign, often unwanted, often suspected alien presence in their midst. While host states may tolerate and even support migrant engagement with homelands abroad, acceptance is contingent on the degree of stability and tranquility of the broader international order. When international troubles arise—as they invariably do—host states are apt to act in ways that restrain and possibly punish migrants insisting on maintaining a cross-border political connection.

*External* influences can thus limit homeland engagement; by contrast, *internal* influences, most notably the receiving state's political opportunity structure, work in the opposite direction. Pursuing emigrant politics, homeland activists frequently take the path of immigrant politics because mobilizing resources in the destination country is best done with the political skills required by that environment. Moreover, as all migrants begin without citizenship, influence is exercised only via contacts and interaction with mainstream political figures; since entry into the receiving-state polity is the key to greater influence, activists initially motivated by home-land concerns often move deeper into host state politics, whose rewards are also hard to ignore. In the United States, immigrant politics is all the more attractive because the political culture validates the pursuit of home-land politics and the political system makes it possible. Though certain limits cannot be crossed, emigrant politics yields a predominantly integrative impact, making homeland politics an apprenticeship in Americanization.

## Migrants and Politics across Borders

In opting for life in a new country and leaping over the borders separating home and host societies, international migrants paradoxically knit those societies together. The connections established by migration could explain why all politics need not necessarily be local, but can, under the circum-stances generated by migration, extend across borders. After all, the types of dislocations envisaged by the scholars who earlier thought of the migrants as the "uprooted" would leave no place, in the cross-border sphere, for the social interdependencies on which political behavior so frequently depends. By contrast, the continuing contacts between movers and stay-at-homes—whether involving long-distance communication or the in-person encounters entailed in the visits made by migrants returning home or by relatives traveling to see the migrants in their new homes—provide the context in which political information can be transmitted or simply gleaned.

Homeland political interest is likely to be at its lowest ebb among those who fall out of the cross-border circuit entirely, but as we have already seen, only a minority cuts the tie altogether. As for those who remain con-nected, some cross-border exchanges do not involve communication—remittance sending, for example, can be done electronically—which means that some of the interactions across borders may be entirely devoid of political content. Likewise, contacts that take place long distance may not yield political information of the same quality or with the same con-tent as exchanges occurring in person. Politics might well filter into the course of weekly communications typically focusing on other matters. In-person visits, however, will yield opportunities for the transmission of indirect information that can be gleaned only *in situ*, as when a visit coin-ciding with a homeland political campaign brings the migrant face to face with the politics that she had left behind.

Moreover, migration itself may trigger homeland responses that *directly* transmit political signals, as will be discussed at length later in this book.

Thus, since long-term, large-scale migrations frequently yield return visits that are recurrent and patterned, as in the annual pilgrimages made by countless Mexican migrants for a one-week celebration of their hometown's patron saint (Massey et al. 1987: 143–145), they can also lay the basis for institutionalized contact with homeland political leaders, who make their presence known to the otherwise absent sons and daughters (Fitzgerald 2009). And while politics may generate little interest among the rank and file, the resources actually or potentially mobilized by the minority of migrant activists are likely to gain the attention of homeland political leaders—giving them all the more reason to connect with migrants whenever they have the chance. Last, the migratory circuit itself may yield a strong sense of home community membership, as exemplified by the growing number of hometown associations. As we will see in Chapter 8, however, these organizations are locally focused, oriented toward philanthropy, and sometimes abjure partisan politics altogether. However, they necessarily connect migrants with politics, sometimes transforming engagements that are meant to be purely civic into involvements of a more distinctively political sort (Fox 2005).

Ironically, the *political* boundaries separating "here" from "there" increase the resources available to migrant activists and diminish the constraints they confront. Passing from one political jurisdiction to the next, the migrants escape the long arm of the home state because its coercive capacity stops at the border. Moreover, residence in a democratic society entails at least some rights, even if those rights are contested and variable. Immigrants to the United States have consistently enjoyed a bedrock core of rights, as evidenced by Chinese immigrants at the turn of the last century, who effectively used the courts to protect their standing. Even in the late nineteenth century, these much despised immigrants were able to find allies whose membership went without question and who saw good reason to support immigrant rights, whether for reasons of ideology or self-interest (Salyer 1995). And as liberal democracies are relatively open societies in which persons with an unauthorized presence can nonetheless connect to citizens as coworker, neighbor, classmate, friend, or even lover, migrants develop close social ties to persons with political entitlements that are taken for granted.

Over the long term, the material and the political combine. The same logic that propels a transnational family economy supports trans-state political projects: because migrant activists collect funds in countries where wages are high in order to support political mobilization in countries where costs are low, small contributions from low-wage migrant workers give exile activists the resources needed to make a difference back home. Even among the most disadvantaged migrants, not all stay at the bottom; many experience upward movement, with some of the more successful putting their means, as well as their contacts, at the disposal of the trans-state activists. That the migrants mobilize in a more powerful country, with a capacity for acting in ways that could help or harm home country regimes, also adds to their impact. While opponents in exile may be blocked from exercising direct influence at home, their host society location—as well as host society allies—gives them the option of connecting to host society policy makers whose views home society actors are less likely to ignore.

Moreover, with the acquisition of formal citizenship—available to many foreign-born residents, though not those in an unauthorized status—migrants formally enter the polity, obtaining both the full package of rights and the legitimacy that comes with being a passport holder of the state in which one actually lives. In the past, both the public and scholars assumed that new citizens would abandon home country affiliations, but many now contend the opposite. Once acquired, citizenship cannot be withdrawn, which is why naturalized citizens may be prepared to express homeland loyalties more forthrightly than their noncitizen counterparts. Indeed, some research indicates that naturalized citizens are more, *not* less, involved in cross-border engagements (Guarnizo et al. 2003). Receiving-society citizenship may actually enhance opportunities for engagement since ethnic lobbying provides both a socially approved means of maintaining dual home and host connections as well as motivation for sending states to keep up the connection with nationals who also enjoy host country citizenship. As we will see, some "new Americans" have persistently followed this route.

Passing over the line from alien to receiving-state citizen doesn't necessarily lead to the reciprocal: some immigrants *can* gain receiving-state citizenship while *retaining* home country citizenship. While naturalized citizens can no longer turn to their home governments when trouble arises on receiving-state soil, those immigrants who remain aliens do have that option; indeed, home states retain obligations to their emigrant citizens, duties that, according to international law, receiving states must allow to be fulfilled. Consequently, embassies and consulates function as outposts of sending-state sovereignty, providing a platform where emigrants can continue to interact with sending-state officials as if they were still at home. The broad range of services provided abroad—whether entailing document provision, cultural and educational programs, or interventions with a range of receiving-state authorities and agencies—allows sending states to keep up contact with migrants and demonstrate their relevance and political capacity—even to citizens who have chosen to live abroad.

## Knowledge and the Social Logic of Politics

Migration is an *implicitly* political act, as the migrants vote with their feet, *against* the state of origin and *for* the state of destination and the institutional structure that supports its economy, the public goods it provides, and the personal security it ensures. While economically induced migrations are *explicitly* apolitical, representing exit, *not* voice, an *implicitly* political conclusion may lay behind that apolitical act. As argued by Mexican sociologist Arturo Santamaría Gómez in words that could easily apply to countless other migrations, "The deepest experience, the most strongly felt discomfort of the migrants toward the Mexican government was the conviction that with a 'good government' they would not have had to leave their country" (1994: 165). The migrants' behavior often reflects widespread cynicism toward political action, institutions, and leaders, and it is also often the product of childhood socialization, the lessons of which may last for a lifetime. Moreover, not everyone leaves, but rather only those who decide to take matters into their own hands, so the migrants may also be less disposed from the outset to look to government or politics to provide a solution for their needs. If moving to a richer country usually turns out better for the migrants, it can reinforce the same cynical political worldview that motivated the very decision to leave. And from that perspective, as noted by the French sociologist Albano Cordeiro, the migrants' "lives owe nothing to the intervention of some political context, have no relationship with anything that the 'politicians' can say or do. Politics appears like something completely external to their lived experience." To the extent that the migrants are convinced that "I don't owe anything to anyone" or that "politicians never put food on my table," that view may be very difficult to change, absent some powerful experience to the contrary (Cordeiro 2005: 49).

Moreover, politics is unlikely to have been of salient importance *before* migration, as a variety of sources suggest. Three-quarters of the Mexican immigrants queried by the Latino National Survey in 2004, for example, had no prior political experience before leaving Mexico. Political experience was even less common among Asian immigrants: queried in 2008, not quite 5 percent reported some involvement in a political organization or party before leaving home for the United States.[1]

Migrants detached from home country politics before leaving home are unlikely to reconnect once abroad. To begin with, younger, not older, people are more likely to depart for a foreign land. As most electoral systems bar minors from voting, many migrants are likely to leave with little, if any, experience in formal politics and limited prior exposure. Political conditions at home are also an influential factor: undemocratic, partially democratic, or even democratizing nations may provide limited opportunities for engagement with electoral politics, even for those eligible to vote prior to migration. Data from the Latino National Survey, for example, indicate that only 47 percent of the nearly four thousand Mexican-born respondents voted before emigrating. Hence, any subsequent formal engagement with the homeland polity—as in the expatriate elections sought by many politically oriented emigrant activists—would mean that the typical expatriate voter would also be casting a ballot for the first time. Hence, they would also belong to precisely that population whose political participation is heavily affected by the high transactional costs associated with an initial vote (Plutzer 2002) as first-time voters everywhere have to clear hurdles—registering, finding the polling station, learning how to cast a vote, differentiating between political parties—that experienced voters have already negotiated.

Moreover, even for migrants with experience in and exposure to homeland politics, the mechanisms facilitating engagement when "in country" lack force in the expatriate context. As noted, some migrants fall out of contact with kin and friends back home, but most keep up the connection. However, because those ties often connect to particularized sets of significant others but not to political communities, they may *not* provide the vehicle by which relevant home country political stimuli cross borders. Furthermore, by providing migrants' associates with remittances that effectively substitute private for public resources, cross-border linkages might foster political *disengagement* among the *stay-at-homes* (Goodman and Hiskey 2008), which in turn might lead the flow of political information and stimuli moving from home country to host country to shrink.

No less important is the local social environment in the receiving country. Political and social life are deeply intertwined: the individual paying no attention to politics picks up her ears when her neighbors begin to talk about the next election. Otherwise too busy to go out and vote, she may make the effort when she sees her friends standing on line at the polling place. Those social triggers are all the more important for migrants who arrive detached from homeland politics; social networks linking less politically attentive migrants to those more politically engaged *could* transmit the needed signals, but apart from migrations where the presence of political exiles looms large, the group attuned to homeland political developments is typically small. Moreover, political organizations are needed to provide the spark, drawing attention to political matters and providing the motivations needed to engage in a political activity that typically yields no direct benefit. Grabbing the voter's attention is the job of political parties, which they do reasonably well as long as politics remains domestic. The expatriate situation, however, greatly complicates party efforts at mobilization: campaigning on foreign soil consumes scarce resources, all the more so because the costs of doing business are far higher in the rich country where the migrants reside than in the poorer place from which they came and where most voters live. Having departed the territory, migrants have also taken themselves out of the electoral registers used to identify and activate likely voters, which further complicates the job of any organization that would want to activate homeland loyalties. Emigration states also hesitate to promote cross-border campaigning since visible manifestations of *emigrants' home country* loyalties might impede *host society* acceptance (Ostergaard-Nielsen 2003b).

In the absence of parties and social networks tying politically aware emigrants to their less attentive compatriots, disengagement is likely to be self-reinforcing, with the circumstances of settlement possibly producing spiraling effects. Though geographic convergence is the modal pattern, areas of high ethnic density may not *all* possess the ethnic institutional completeness needed to stimulate engagement with home country matters; political messages are likely still weaker in areas of lower ethnic density. Absent powerful inducements, clear signals, and the examples of significant others, remaining motivations to attend to home country political developments, let alone participate, may not suffice. Of course, immigrants may still find that their hearts beat strongly for home, as demonstrated by the intensity with which so many immigrants follow homeland sports. But it is one thing to know all the members of the national soccer team and recall the great games of the recent past, and it is another to focus on the far less enjoyable, far less edifying game of homeland politics, which also gets little attention from anyone else (Cordeiro 2005: 47).

While immigrant incorporation in the destination country might yield politicizing impacts that could later be conveyed to core network members at home, many migrants long remain in a state of nonincorporation. Until they become citizens, migrants stand outside the polity, which keeps them distant from the efforts at mobilization that so often trigger political interest and knowledge. For example, the 2006 Mexican Expatriate Survey found that three-quarters of the immigrant respondents could neither correctly report the month of US congressional elections nor the party then controlling the US House of Representatives. Similarly, nearly one-third of the nationally representative cross-section of Mexican immigrants in the United States, polled by the Latino National Survey in 2004, could not correctly answer *one* of the three questions about political knowledge asked in the survey, had *never* contacted an elected official in the United States, and did *not* identify with a US political party. Only a small fraction of these same interviewees described themselves as "very interested" in politics, so it seems likely that many immigrants find themselves in an environment where politics is of low, if any, salience.

Moreover, the long interval between arrival and naturalization provides an extended opportunity for reorienting political interests from homeland to host country—opportunities all the easier to fulfill when interests in homeland politics are modest or minimal from the start. Though immigrants begin as foreigners, undergoing an extended period of exclusion from the polity, noncitizens, including those lacking in legal status, are exposed to political messages broadcast to the wider audience to which they often belong (e.g., the viewers of foreign-language television). Like citizens, noncitizens are affected by government policies, motivating them both to attend to receiving-society politics and to participate (Verba et al. 1995; Leal 2002), whether by communicating with political officials, going to meetings, or engaging in protests (like the spring 2006 immigrant rights demonstrations in the United States), even if electoral participation is barred. Thus, even before entering the receiving-country polity, immigrants receive political signals and encounter opportunities for political participation, which might focus their attention on host society political matters. Subsequent acquisition of citizenship might open the gateway to deeper, more extensive engagements, which, in turn, may generate a deeper sense of receiving-society membership. If, as Zolberg and Woon have argued, immigrants "change themselves" under conditions in which the nationals "hold the upper hand" (1999: 9), and the latter continue to view persons with foreign loyalties as suspect, new citizens may be motivated to discard home country for host country political identity. In that case, a twofold capture could ensue, with receiving states "caging" the populations residing on their territory and constraining ties beyond the territorial divide (Mann 1993), while also "embracing" the newcomers, creating incentives and opportunities for civic and political participation in host country institutions, as a result of which still deeper attachments to the new national people are likely to be made (Torpey 1999).

In addition to these distinctively *political* factors, changes in the social structures linking migrants to their home communities might further curb involvement in expatriate voting and interest in home country matters. As noted, international migrations inherently yield ties and flows extending back from receiving to sending states. Over time, however, for all but a minority those ties decline. Living in two different societies, migrants and stay-at-homes undergo experiences that the other cannot completely share, which in turn may pull them apart. Despite distance-shrinking technologies, cross-border engagement remains costly, reducing the population motivated to keep up home country ties. Since settlement often leads social relations to shift from home to host societies, on-location costs also grow, in turn raising the burden of cross-border exchanges. As connections attenuate and migrants realize that they have moved for good, exposure to and interest in home society matters may also dwindle.

## Homeland Disengagement

The extensive body of research on Mexican immigrants in the United States—who comprise one-quarter of the United States' foreign-born population—highlights the limits of rank-and-file home country involvement. In voting with their feet, Mexican immigrants have acted in a way that reflects widespread distrust of Mexico's political system and its leaders. As noted by one highly influential US student of Mexican politics, surveys of the Mexican population show "very low levels of respect for political institutions of any sort and the persons associated with them," indicating "a general lack of trust in government" (Camp 2007: 73). Indeed, when interviewed by a team of Mexican sociologists, Mexican immigrants in Los Angeles repeatedly sounded this point of view:

> The perception that the interviewees have of Mexican politics is in general negative, repeatedly associated with corruption, violence, poverty, and incapacity to govern, independent of the political party. A very significant indicator consists of the fact that, of the 90 interviewees, there was not one positive opinion about politics in Mexico. (Alarcon et al. 2012: 298)

As imported attitudes take so negative a turn, only some offsetting factor could trigger engagement from abroad. However, that hurdle looms high because premigration political engagement is relatively scant. Thus, the National Latino Survey shows that a majority of immigrants (62 percent) did *not* vote in Mexico prior to emigrating to the United States. As noted above, an even larger proportion had no premigration involvement in a social or political organization. Inattention to US politics, noted earlier, parallels lack of interest in Mexican politics: 72 percent of the US-based respondents polled by the 2006 Mexican Expatriate Survey reported that they paid no or little attention to that year's US congressional election, as did 74 percent of those respondents when asked about the presidential campaign in Mexico. The same survey found that, compared to Mexicans in Mexico, Mexican immigrants were far less likely to talk about or pay attention to Mexican politics (McCann et al. 2009). Almost two-thirds of the Mexican immigrants queried that same year by a nationally representative survey undertaken by the Pew Hispanic Center agreed with the statement, "I am insufficiently informed about Mexican politics to vote." Indeed, when asked by the 2006 Mexican Expatriate Survey to identify the slogans adopted by two of the Mexican presidential candidates, 79 percent answered incorrectly and only 3 percent could provide both right answers (McCann et al. 2007).

Though no other single national origin group compares in size to the Mexican immigrant population, overall levels of homeland political engagement seem quite similar. Of the roughly nine hundred respondents born in East, Southeast, and South Asia who were queried by the 2000–2001 Pilot National Asian American Political Survey, only 8 percent reported involvement in politics or political party membership *prior* to arrival in the United States, and still fewer—only 6 percent—claimed to have participated in any activity related to their home country *after* migration. Similarly, only 4 percent of the 4,582 foreign-born persons queried by the 2008 National Asian American Survey reported involvement in activities dealing with their country of origin (Wong et al. 2011: 77). Barely 5 percent reported having had premigration political experience. Ninety-four percent of Colombian, Dominican, and Salvadoran migrants surveyed randomly by the Comparative Immigrant Entrepreneurship Project said that they *never* participated in campaigns to support home country political candidates; 96 percent also reported that they *never* contributed to home country electoral campaigns. Similarly, only 1 percent of Dominican migrants voted in the 2004 election for president of the Dominican Republic, even though the newly implemented system of expatriate voting made it easy to cast a ballot from abroad.

Thus, even as many migrants maintain ongoing connections to contacts at home, involvements in home country political matters are rarely intense and get attenuated in relatively short order.[2] For example, analysis of the National Latino Survey shows that relatively few migrants completely fall out of contact with relatives in Mexico; not surprisingly, these migrants showed markedly lower levels of interest in Mexican politics than did their typical counterparts who were tightly connected to friends and family in Mexico (those calling or contacting weekly and sending remittances). However, these same migrants took little interest in home country politics. Moreover, migrants who were especially connected were not especially concerned with homeland matters, as illustrated by the finding that respondents who visited Mexico every year paid no more attention to homeland politics than did those who were yet to return after migrating. Settlement also mattered: interest in Mexican politics diminished with mounting years of residence in the United States. In addition, those planning to return to Mexico and those still owning property there were likely to be more interested in Mexican politics than the typical respondent, who neither owned property in Mexico nor planned to return. Though most respondents reported little engagement in politics before migration, those who had voted or had been involved in some non-electoral political activity or a social movement were likely to retain a higher interest in Mexican politics. Yet even these engagements failed to inoculate migrants against the disconnecting impact of the new environment. Even among the members of this group, interest in Mexican political matters waned as residence and commitments in the United States deepened.

Immigrants' capacity to engage in home country politics falls off for much the same reason, as indicated by the responses of Mexican immigrants surveyed in 2006 in order to gauge likely levels of participation in the 2006 Mexican presidential election—the very first in which emigrants were allowed to vote.[3] As with the respondents to the Latino National Survey, these immigrants remained closely connected to relatives at home, yet they had limited knowledge of basic aspects of the Mexican electoral system, let alone the specifics of expatriate voting rights. For example, presidential elections take place every six years, a fact known by almost 90 percent of Mexicans *in Mexico,* but barely half of this sample of Mexicans *in the United States* knew that 2006 was an election year. Those elections are *consistently* held in July, as are the legislative elections that take place every three years. Yet when asked in January 2006, more than four-fifths of the respondents did not know that elections would be held in July of that year.

Moreover, differences in the intensity of home country ties had little impact on levels of knowledge, with the exception of the small minority maintaining especially intense cross-border activities. The few (8 percent of this sample) who traveled to Mexico three or more times in the prior year knew more about electoral procedures than those who did not travel back home at all; however, the latter—comprising most of the sample— knew as much about election procedures as those who had traveled back once or twice (25 percent of the sample). Similarly, those calling home regularly seemed to know more about basic electoral procedures but were no more likely than others to have the detailed knowledge about the specific registration procedures required to cast a vote abroad. Remitting was also associated with inconsistent results: respondents remitting several times yearly had more knowledge than those remitting occasionally or not at all; however, the latter were no less knowledgeable than those remitting with the greatest frequency. Lack of information does not imply complete disengagement. Most respondents followed Mexican news; these respondents knew more about voting procedures, especially regarding details, than did less attentive respondents. On the other hand, those claiming to follow news closely were relatively unfamiliar with the basics of *when* the election would take place: only 57 percent of respondents who said they followed Mexican news closely knew that 2006 was a presidential election year; still fewer—27 percent—also knew that the election would be held in July and that expatriates had the right to vote.

Consequently, the bounded nature of the new environment yields two contradictory effects. On the one hand, it generates resources and provides protection, furnishing homeland-oriented activists with significant leverage. On the other hand, it deactivates the migrant rank and file, though the extent of that effect varies with the circumstances of migration and the degree to which a politicized identity was imparted prior to or during migration. The typical labor migration, involving displaced peasants with strong local but weak national identities and little involvement in national political structures, tends toward disengagement. By contrast, if refugee movements are impelled by politics, they tend to breed a more lasting political disposition, especially when the émigrés are of elite origin. The migrants arrive with political skills and other forms of cultural and social capital that can be put to political ends. The size of "a supportive constituency available for mobilization" (Wald 2008: 275) therefore varies depending on migration type; so too do the resources that can be gathered through mobilization. However, almost all migrations include at least some persons who remained involved in homeland matters; because there is often a large constituency that resonates to the homeland call at least occasionally, the hard core is rarely alone. The denominator also matters: where the numbers are huge, as with Mexican immigrants in the United States, any cause that engages the energies of 1, 2, or 3 percent of all migrants can impel significant numbers into action. Likewise, migrations involving numbers that are absolutely small but loom large relative to home country populations—as in the case of Caribbean islands—can yield influence that home state leaders ignore at their peril.

THE VARIETIES OF EMIGRANT POLITICS    Migrant political activism comes in various forms, ranging from the ideologically motivated undertakings of exile elites to the ad hoc, uncoordinated efforts of rank-and-file migrants seeking to help, and therefore also to change, their hometowns. If *emigration* is an *implicitly* political act, in which migrants register their distaste with the home government through exit, *immigration* provides the opportunity and resources for voice, allowing the migrants to *explicitly* express those grievances and seek means of resolving them. The international nature of these activities ensures that international events and tensions yield spillover effects on migrants' capacity to mobilize and organize in the destination country in order to affect the place of origin. The more those efforts are principally affective and symbolic, the greater the migrants' ability to ward off the negative boomerang from events abroad. By contrast, action that is explicitly political and concerted is less buffered, both from receiving-state conflicts that diaspora politics might trigger or exacerbate as well as from the potential repercussions occurring when homeland politics is perceived as running counter to host country interests.

Moving to a foreign country often yields a change in identity, teaching immigrants that they are not simply members of the hometown "little country" but also members of the larger "national" community. Prior socialization and the experience of being treated as a strange foreigner triggers long-distance patriotism, which provides the means and the vocabulary for activating solidarity with either compatriots or a state from which one is geographically removed. The most popular form of long-distance national solidarity is one that doesn't cost anything, namely, "symbolic ethnicity" (Gans 1979). Illustrating this phenomenon is the long history of recurring ethnic parades and festivals found in America's immigrant cities—providing a public space open to all, whether the occasion is St. Patrick's Day or Cinco de Mayo, celebrated by Mexican immigrants since the late nineteenth century. Here migrants and their descendants gain a one-day opportunity to express concern for the place left behind, in a context of good feeling, where the home country flag can be happily waved without the risk that anyone will take offense. Migrant philanthropy (as when American Jews raised funds for distressed co-ethnics living in eastern Europe in the aftermath of World War I or Salvadorans came together in order to send money and supplies to relieve compatriots traumatized by natural disasters) also exemplifies this more benign form of migrant long-distance nationalism, albeit in a slightly more demanding, committed form. Home country loyalty can also turn migrants and their descendants into ethnic lobbyists, an outcome facilitated by precedent because mobilized homeland loyalties have been an enduring aspect of the American ethnic scene (Smith 2000). Converting immigrants into lobbyists greatly interests the leaders of today's economically struggling sending states, who value gaining access to the resources of the United States even more than the donations produced by migrant philanthropists.

However, because the migrants have moved into a distinctive political environment and have gained degrees of freedom never previously possessed, entry into a foreign political environment can trigger more aggressive forms of long-distance nationalism. A common outcome is the *exo-polity* (Dufoix 2003), in which emigrants challenge the home state. In some cases, this involves *state-seeking* nationalism targeted at an existing multiethnic state, with the goal of creating a state for a "people" that doesn't yet have one. Other cases entail *regime-changing* mobilization, which is undertaken with no thought of changing the territorial order but is directed at changing the government of an existing state.

The long-distance state-seeking and regime-changing mobilizations of migrants differ in their goals but less so in means. They both demand clear-cut opposition to the sending-country regime, and they both yield polarization among the migrants whom they seek to mobilize. Consequently, politicization "tends to invade all community space, forcing everyone to take sides" (Dufoix 2002: 68). Since both require heightened in-group solidarity, they tend to sharpen conflict and competition with the various out-groups with whom the migrants interact. Hence, internally focused and externally focused aggressiveness may go hand in hand, as exemplified by the experience of Cuban Americans, who simultaneously experience intense internal strife over the future of a post-Castro Cuba and highly fractious relations with their Haitian, African American, and white American neighbors (Eckstein 2009). Moreover, the migratory and ethnic connections that cross state borders also provide the vehicle for diffusing conflicts from home country to host country or adding international tensions to social antagonisms of mainly domestic origin. Thus, disputes based on home country polarities yield internecine conflicts that belie claims of a transnational "community"—as in "the war of the little Italies" earlier in the century (Diggins 1972) or clashes between nationalists and Communists in contemporary Chinatowns (Liang 2001). Alternatively, opposing home country loyalties can create adoptive country cleavages, as illustrated by contemporary disputes between Arab Americans and Jewish Americans (Shain 1999); the earlier frictions between African Americans and Italian Americans, which were spurred by Italy's invasion of Ethiopia during the 1930s; or the discord between Japanese Americans and Chinese Americans, which was provoked by Japan's invasion of China (Stack 1979; Chen 2000).

DUAL LOYALTY   Moving across borders into the territory of a rich democratic state, migrants gain economic and political resources, which in turn give them newfound opportunities to affect change back home. But the capacity to build and maintain here–there connections is not a matter for the migrants to decide on their own. The immigrants are also foreigners, whose lives involve ongoing connections to foreign people and foreign places. Even though popular cultures have become more cosmopolitan, and intellectuals often tend toward xenophilia, foreign ways and affiliations to foreign places leave immigrants open to question. As the scholarly transnationalists correctly note, some of the immigrants want membership in two social collectivities, not just one. But while the American public often tolerates, and indeed sometimes accepts, homeland loyalties, it expects that the claims of the immigrants' new social collectivity will come first. Not surprisingly, those who think of the nation as a version of the family writ large take umbrage at demonstrations in which immigrants wave the flags of the states of *emigration* (Huntington 2004).

Consequently, how to manage the competing claims of new and old lands has been a persistent immigrant dilemma. In her essay "Loyalties: Dual and Divided," which appeared in the landmark *Harvard Encyclopedia of American Ethnic Groups,* published in 1980, Mona Harrington argued that the United States' political culture facilitated the pursuit of home country ties: individual liberty was valued over loyalty to any collectivity, the nation included. Furthermore, the belief in American exceptionalism encouraged the idea that American ideals could be appropriately exported by immigrants still concerned with the country they left behind. On the other hand,

> The open expression of dual loyalties inevitably raises problems of conflicting loyalties with the potential for causing trouble both within the United States and between the United States and other countries. . . . The problem for Americans since World War I and since has been to try to define the point at which loyalty to the United States makes it unacceptable for ethnic groups to maintain attachments to the homeland or to promote its causes as one of the many types of privately formed interest that Americans are supposedly free to express and support. (Harrington 1980: 104)

That issue remains far from resolved. In the early 1990s, well before the tensions generated by September 11 cast new suspicion on immigrants' homeland loyalties, nationally representative public opinion polls showed that the public saw African American and Asian, Hispanic, and Jewish Americans were "open to divided loyalties and therefore less patriotic than 'unhyphenated' Americans" (Smith 1994: 9).

If there is a latent predisposition to view cross-state social action as disloyal, the relationship *among* states further affects the conditions under which international migrants and their descendants can pursue "homeland" interests. A peaceful world encourages states to relax the security/ solidarity nexus, whereas international tension leads states to tighten it. The specifics of the relationship between particular sending and receiving states matter even more. Homeland loyalties extending to allies, neutrals, or weak states can be tolerated easily; those connecting to less friendly, possibly hostile states and powerful states are more likely to be suspect.

While states have *often* wrongly suspected international migrants of "dual loyalty," they have not *always* erred, as the more astute students of transnational phenomena knew from the start. Thus, in their foundational writings on transnationalism, Nye and Keohane noted that "governments have often attempted to manipulate transnational interactions to achieve results that are explicitly political: the use of tourists as spies or the cultivation of sympathetic ethnic or religious groups in other states are examples of such 'informal penetration'" (1971: 340). That migrant cross-border social actors are more likely to be opponents than servants of the home state does not necessarily please receiving states concerned with international stability, the undermining of which is precisely what migrant long-distance nationalism can sometimes entail.

The last century of political cross-border activity provides ample demonstration of the ways in which international conflicts affect emigrant political engagement. In the United States, war first provided the occasion for destroying German America and later for interning the Japanese. The same set of considerations led the United States and all the other western democracies to intern "enemy aliens" in both world wars (Panayi 1993). But the contemporary era of mass migration belongs to a different world, or so it appeared until just recently. With the winding down of the Cold War, the factors facilitating trans-state ties have been embedded in a more pacific world order, in which national allegiances have been allowed to overlap, as opposed to the mutual exclusivity expected for most of the twentieth century. Not all groups are equally lucky in this respect. Immigrants who come from countries with unfriendly relationships with the United States run the risk of falling into the "enemy alien" trap, which is why long-distance nationalism in all of its forms (including that of the time-honored ethnic lobby) proves so hard for Arab Americans to pursue.

Yet when foreign attachments and entanglements are subject to suspicion, even long-standing forms of home country involvement undertaken by the most established of American ethnic groups encounter problems. Case in point, the Irish American lobby, whose relationship to Irish Republicans in Northern Ireland turned around after September 11, 2001. Whereas Irish American politicians had long turned a blind eye to the violent tactics pursued by at least some Republican factions in Northern Ireland, that tolerance vanished along with the twin towers. The most ardent Irish Republicans found an increasingly chilly welcome, whether in the White House, the Congress, or among corporate chieftains of Irish descent. Nor were rank-and-file Irish immigrants exempt from the security-driven changes in migration control policies: noncitizen Irish immigrants—especially, but not only the undocumented—worried about their ability to remain in the United States; Irish American organizations viewed the Patriot Act as "potentially harmful to the interests of the Irish community across the United States" (Cochrane 2007: 227). On the other hand, assimilation blocked cross-border spillovers from the opposite side: although Protestant loyalists in Northern Ireland seized the opportunity provided by 9/11 to cast the Republicans as enemies akin to Al Qaeda, the homeland no longer captivated the attention of the millions of Protestant Americans with roots in Northern Ireland, for whom genealogy remained the sole remaining Irish connection (Ó Dochartaigh 2009).

## An Apprenticeship in Americanization

Thus, while movement to a new polity typically leads the immigrant rank and file to disengage, it simultaneously provides politically active and oriented emigrants with the opportunity to exercise homeland influence far greater than any experience prior to migration. The quest to exercise influence on "homeland" issues yields unintended effects. Doing so effectively compels an orientation to the host country political game, thereby fostering entry into that polity. In the United States, moreover, the political structure and political culture make the pursuit of homeland loyalties one of the means by which the immigrants become Americans.

The country's pluralistic political structure facilitates the *legitimate* mobilization of immigrant and ethnic trans-state social action. Since politics at the different levels of government—federal, state, and local—is loosely connected, immigrants can link up with readily accessible political actors, namely, local or state officials, who see practical benefits in endorsing homeland causes and little reason to worry about how their positions might be perceived in Washington. New York's political figures, for example, long attended to the importance of the "three I's" of Italy, Israel, and Ireland; conditioned by that background, they did not require prompts from social scientists to extend their political antenna to Santo Domingo or Port-au-Prince once the city's demographics changed. While local leaders react to constituent preferences, federalism facilitates that response: with no responsibility for issues of war and peace, local politicians can engage in the symbolic politics of ethnicity. Not only are local politicians largely immune from pressure to conform to expectations for national unity, the politics of national disunity can produce its own benefits. In championing the cause of Cubans eager for a more hard-line approach than that adopted by the Clinton administration during the 1990s, or the very different cause of Salvadorans opposed to US military aid to El Salvador during the 1980s, local political leaders rallied their electoral base—whether directly, as in the case of Miami, or indirectly, as in Los Angeles, where the deeds done in the name of the undocumented and vote-less Salvadorans nonetheless galvanized other Latino voters.

Motivating all forms of interest group politics, fragmentation also encourages ethnic lobbying. Politicians accustomed to accommodating the needs of special interests find nothing strange in similar-sounding requests from immigrant or ethnic activists as long as the frame is appropriate, as with appeals to furthering democracy, self-determination, or human rights. The same political structure that creates opportunities for the most narrow of economic interest groups also generates a political space that favors the pursuit of homeland causes. Because the US Congress is "a decentralized entity, with many points at which legislation can be either initiated or blocked" (Smith 2000: 88), groups with a small, even insignificant electoral base can gain influence and effect alliances that produce tangible results.

Although American Jews represent the classic case, Armenians provide the better example. The group is small, with just over four hundred thousand people of Armenian ancestry living in the United States as of 2012. Not only is Armenia poor and lacking in resources, but also it is in conflict with both a more powerful neighbor (namely Turkey) and a resource-rich neighbor (Azerbaijan), alliances that seem to be in the interest of the United States. The diaspora is more impelled by ideological than material considerations than is the Armenian government, and it is made up mainly of persons originating in Turkey and the Middle East, but not the *current* Republic of Armenia. Thus, it is also less inclined toward accommodation with the country's neighbors than is Armenia itself.

Nonetheless, US policy has proved remarkably responsive to the highly organized, though fractured Armenian lobby (Paul 2000; Gregg 2002;

King and Pomper 2004). A special addendum to the 1992 Freedom Support Act, designed to give aid to the former Soviet republics, specifically prohibited Azerbaijan from receiving US assistance as long as Azeri hostilities toward Armenians continued. Despite opposition from oil companies and pro-Israel lobbies, this policy remained in place until the events of September 11 made national security concerns the foremost foreign policy influence. While the US government now provides aid to Azerbaijan, the continuing material and military support it furnishes to Armenia is far more generous.

The explanation for this surprising and paradoxical history stems from the factors already mentioned. Though few, the Armenians are concentrated in places that, by accident, turned out to be linked to politicians of primordial importance. One such concentration is located in the Massachusetts congressional district from which John F. Kennedy began his political career more than sixty-five years ago, only to be succeeded by Tip O'Neill, later Speaker of the House. Furthermore, the same institutional structures that facilitate the mobilization of all sorts of interests within Congress serve to advance the agenda of the Armenian diaspora activists as well. Following the good example of the automobile industry, diaspora activists have convinced congressional representatives to form an Armenian caucus, which currently includes roughly 25 percent of the House.

While US political structure facilitates the mobilization of homeland loyalties, American political culture encourages and legitimates it—even though pursuing that strategy runs the risks noted above. Identification with the place left behind has a strong reactive component: for immigrants who have experienced rejection, or sometimes just incomplete acceptance, rallying to the cause of the homeland or simply commemorating the accomplishments of its culture and people can compensate for the hurts endured in one's new land. Moreover, connecting with the homeland generates pride and thereby helps gain membership in the club. For that reason, as Ezra Mendelsohn has pointed out, throughout American history "support for nationalism abroad and integration at home was not contradictory, but in fact, perceived to be complementary" (Mendelsohn 1993: 133).

Indeed, homeland ties have such extraordinary appeal that they have been created when none previously existed. One example is the "black Zionism" of the nationalist, back-to-Africa movement spearheaded by Jamaican immigrant Marcus Garvey in the 1920s, who praised Zionism as well as Irish nationalism, upholding both as models for African Americans to follow (Lewis 1984). Though Garveyism is long dead, the idea of a connection to a homeland, no matter how far removed, continues to resonate among African Americans, as demonstrated by the efflorescence of Afrocentrism and the lobbying efforts on behalf of a variety of African issues by African American organizations (Shain 1999). Similarly, long-dormant homeland connections can be reactivated by homeland events and crises, even among long-settled populations. Thus, in the late 1960s, when Northern Ireland's "troubles" began, Irish Americans of many stripes—whether militant nationalists, prominent mainstream politicians like the late Senator Edward Kennedy, or corporate leaders of Irish descent—turned their antenna back to the Emerald Isle, seeking to support the Irish Republicans, even though the result was to generate friction between the United States and its "special ally," the United Kingdom.

Not only are homeland loyalties repeatedly triggered, but recurrence provides legitimacy for each successive group of homeland-oriented immigrants. In the early 1900s, Zionists and Polish nationalists pointed out that they were acting no differently than other, much longer established American ethnic groups (Mendelsohn 1993). Similar claims are heard today. In particular, today's homeland-oriented migrant activists—as well as their homeland supporters—are eager to learn from and imitate that most successful of diasporas, namely, American Jews. Writing about Dominicans, Levitt reports, "Several leaders mentioned the example of the Jewish American community as the model they wished to emulate. Just as the Jewish American lobby favorably influenced US policies toward Israel, so the Dominican migrant community could generate support for favorable sugar quotas, terms of trade, and development assistance" (2001: 134). Hindu nationalists trying to build a social movement in the United States had the same idea: indeed, the publisher of the newspaper *India Abroad* hired the director of a Jewish American organization to head the India Abroad Center for Political Awareness in 1993 (Mathew and Prasad 2000: 520). According to Prema Kurian, community leaders consistently maintain that

> Hindu Americans should emulate the model of Jewish Americans. As a highly successful group that is integrated into mainstream American society ... while maintaining its religious and cultural distinctness, close community ties, and connections with the home country, American Jews are viewed as a group that has been able to "fit in" *while remaining different*. This is the route to success that Hindu Americans also want to adopt in their quest to stake a position in American society. (Kurien 2004: 372; emphasis added)

One could cite countless other examples—for instance, Jean-Baptiste Aristide, who led a popular revolt against Haiti's dictatorship in the early 1990s, "called on Haitians in the North American diaspora to emulate

American Jews," by supporting the homeland through pilgrimages and donations (Richman 1992: 196). Still, one wonders whether every group can exercise the same influence enjoyed by the Jews. For the moment, however, that is the path that many take, in which case it makes sense to get lessons from the experts, as did Mexico's Institute for Mexicans Abroad when it engaged the American Jewish Committee and the Jewish Anti-Defamation League to train key members of the Mexican diaspora (Bayes and González 2012).

## Conclusion

The risk of the game is that of losing equilibrium, of pushing homeland mobilization so far that it awakens the suspicions of the Americans who are normally ready to accept long-distance loyalties as long as the American flag is not abandoned. But experience, both historical and contemporary, indicates that the Americans shouldn't be worried. Over the long term, those mobilizations produce effects that the emigrants couldn't have imagined at the beginning: agitation in favor of home country interests serves as an apprenticeship in US politics, attaching the cross-state activists to the American political system and giving them the contacts and competencies needed for successful engagement.

The history of the left-wing activists from El Salvador, who began arriving in the United States in the late 1970s as part of the refugee exodus from that country, provides an ideal case in point. From their arrival, these activists began reviving their movement, simultaneously following two paths. One led them to their compatriots, an easy connection to establish as immigrant social networks funneled the refugees into the same neighborhoods where prior migrants—whose emigration had been impelled by economic reasons—had installed themselves. Here, the activists mounted demonstrations in front of the Salvadoran consulate and marches in the nearby streets and parks while also concentrating on collecting monies for comrades fighting in El Salvador. Simultaneously, the activists tried to develop alliances with sympathetic Americans, some of whom shared the activists' specific political convictions, many more of whom simply opposed US aid to El Salvador (Gosse 1996; Hamilton and Chinchilla 2001; Perla 2008). At the time, the activists had no thought of settling permanently in the United States; rather, residence on US soil was temporary, to end once the left had won the war. After a decade of bloody fighting, the civil war stopped in 1992, when both sides realized that neither could gain victory. A few activists returned to El Salvador, but most realized that they had actually put down roots in a new home, an awareness fully shared by their less politicized compatriots.

Thus, although the activists retained linkages to relatives, friends, and comrades still at home, priorities quickly changed: from then on, the needs of the *immigrants* dominated the agenda. Instead of mobilizing compatriots in order to transform the country of *emigration,* the organizations that had been established for that very goal now decided to provide services that would allow *immigrants* to settle down securely in the United States and move ahead in their new home. Although sudden, this reorientation was the inevitable consequence of everything that the activists had previously done. As Arpi Miller argues (2011), in attaching themselves to Americans ready to act in solidarity with the Salvadoran left and the Salvadoran refugees, the activists developed connections with leaders who could help them pursue the strategy involved in this second phase: namely, integration. In much the same fashion, their earlier efforts, undertaken with the goal of influencing American politics toward the country of *emigration,* turned out to serve other goals—namely, that of providing an apprenticeship in the politics of the country of *immigration.* Without the contacts and skills acquired in the efforts to change El Salvador, the activists could never have pursued their new strategy of changing the conditions affecting Salvadorans in the United States since that pursuit required help from government and from foundations. Each step along that road reinforced the orientation toward *immigrant* politics, deepening the skills needed to maneuver in the US political world and strengthening and multiplying contacts with US political figures.

Of course, the pursuit of *immigrant* integration doesn't imply abandonment of the country of *emigration.* Activists heading Salvadoran immigrant organizations retained close ties to kin and friends at home; to some extent, they remained engaged in home country politics. Both activists and rank-and-file immigrants also devoted time, energy, and resources to associations oriented toward the place of origin. But these continuing connections notwithstanding, the course had been set, as illustrated by this concluding, personal anecdote.

In spring 2006, vast immigrant rights demonstrations swept the United States. Wanting to participate in one of these rallies, I went to the headquarters of a Salvadoran immigrant organization, at the invitation of one of my students, who had long been an important activist in the group. Arriving in front of their building, I saw several dozen people congregating on the sidewalk, all wearing the organization's T-shirts and each one equipped with an American flag. Knowing that the American flag was more likely to be flown by those who find themselves on the right, not the left, I asked myself whether I hadn't somehow gotten the address wrong. But after checking, I realized that the address was indeed right. Rather, what had changed in this organization located in the heart of Salvadoran Los Angeles were its goals and demands: although proud of their origins, these immigrants wanted to become Americans. The demand is completely reasonable; more difficult to understand is the reaction of the Americans, who hesitate to accept a population that has put down very deep roots and will never go home. It is here that we find the heart of the phenomenon of interest: the recurrence, indeed, the inevitability, of international migration and its collision with states and people who insist on cutting themselves off from the foreign world around them, as well as the foreigners who are no longer willing to stay behind borders.

# CHAPTER SIX

# Emigrants and Emigration States

THE PEOPLE crossing borders actively shape their own destinies, doing what neither home nor host state wants, getting ahead by making effective use of the resource that they almost all possess—one another. A move to the territory of another richer state can fulfill the migrants' objectives, improving their own lives while helping the kin and communities left behind. But in relocating not just to a different country but to an entirely different type of place, the migrants find themselves transformed in ways that they rarely expect, often producing distance from the people, places, cultures, and loyalties left behind.

With this chapter I shift to an examination of the internal tensions and contradictions arising among people who are simultaneously immigrants *and* emigrants. In doing so, I put the cross-border dimension front and center, an endeavor that helps define international migration as a distinctive field of study, one encompassing but going beyond *immigration* and *assimilation,* as those words are conventionally defined.

This chapter develops an overarching framework for understanding the interaction between emigrants and the states and societies they have left behind, with a particular emphasis on what I will call the political sociology of emigration. The perspective elaborated here is broad, encompassing a wide range of migrations and stretching historically over a century and a half and more. The following two chapters take the arguments developed in the immediate pages to follow and focus more narrowly. Whereas this chapter identifies the dynamics entailed in the interactions between emigrants and emigration states, the next chapter shows them in action, comparing two different, recent episodes in the relationship between Mexico and Mexican migrants in the United States. I then further tighten the focus in Chapter 8, looking at what happens when migrants living in the United States try to do good for the communities left behind. Throughout all three chapters, I attend to both receiving and sending contexts, showing how cross-state population movements recurrently generate ties linking places of origin and destination even as the migrants' insertion into a different society and distinctive political unit weakens those very same connections.

## The Political Sociology of Emigration

This chapter develops a political sociology framework for analyzing the interaction between emigrants and emigration states. The chapter emphasizes the dualities at the heart of the migration phenomenon: immigrants are also emigrants, aliens are also citizens, foreigners are also nationals, nonmembers are also members, the politically excluded are also political participants. At once *of* the sending state but not *in* it, *emigrants* are members whose everyday connections with kin and communities left behind yield both persistent cross-border involvements and reciprocal obligations; residing abroad, however, their claims to *home* society belonging are undermined by their presence on *foreign* soil and the changes induced by exposure to a *foreign* way of life and standard of living. At once *in* the receiving state but not *of* it, the *immigrants* can access the economic and political resources available in their new location *abroad,* gaining leverage for use in the *home* left behind. As *aliens,* the migrants' rights are circumscribed and as outsiders of *foreign* origin, their acceptance is uncertain; these two vulnerabilities can be aggravated if migrants' continuing *homeland* involvement triggers the suspicion of *host* state nationals.

The migrants' combination of resources and vulnerabilities activate interventions by *home* states seeking to influence and protect nationals abroad. While extension to the territory of another state keeps options inherently limited, in crossing boundaries to connect with *emigrants,* sending states are providing services to their own *citizens* and, for that reason, have enhanced access rights. In engaging abroad, sending states can also draw on a variety of tools to simultaneously reinforce *emigrant* loyalty weakened by distance, monitor opposition facilitated by the emigrants' extraterritorial location, and also resolve problems of *immigrant* integration. Those efforts, however, are checked by challenges of two types, one related to the greater resources and autonomy enjoyed by *immigrants* by virtue of their residence on *foreign* grounds, the second emanating from receiving-state *nationals* anxious about the *foreigners* in their midst and the *foreign states* to which they still have allegiance. Hence, the politics across borders provoked by cross-state migrations yields a series of unpredictable conflicts, sweeping up migrants, nationals "at home" and "abroad," as well as receiving- and sending-state officials in a complex, unstable relational nexus.

The framework developed in this chapter is designed to apply to only a subset of international migrations, namely, those that are *truly* international *and* take migrants from poorer, developing states to richer democracies. As such, the framework remains encompassing, both temporally and spatially; it extends from the transatlantic migrations of the mid-nineteenth century to the contemporary south-to-north migrations converging on the Americas; Europe; the Antipodes; and, increasingly, East Asia (South Korea, Japan, and Taiwan). By contrast, other migrations—whether those within the European Union, for example, or those leading to the Persian Gulf—fall outside the chapter's purview. While some variables may apply to migrations of these sorts as well, the interactions linking immigrants/emigrants, states, and publics in both sending and receiving contexts fundamentally derive from the conditions that arise from migration from poorer to richer democratic states. Likewise, migrations from colonies to the metropole, while sharing many of the traits of interstate migration, remain *internal* to the empire and hence lack the international dimension that is crucial to the process of interest here. However, once colonial migrations become postcolonial—as with Indians in the United Kingdom or Surinamese in the Netherlands—the relevant conditions apply. By contrast migrations that remain within a colonial framework—as in the case of Puerto Ricans to the United States or Martiniquais to France—fall outside the boundaries of the phenomena to which the framework developed here is meant to apply.

### The Duality of Emigration and Immigration

The political sociology of emigration is distinctive in departing from both scholarly *and* popular understandings of states, societies, and the world to which they are connected. Figure 6.1 displays a model of the world as conventionally depicted and understood: territorial boundaries separate

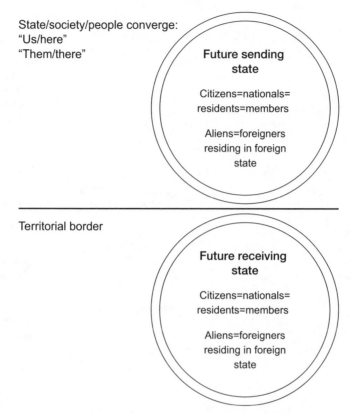

State/society/people converge:
"Us/here"
"Them/there"

**Future sending state**

Citizens=nationals=
residents=members

Aliens=foreigners
residing in foreign
state

Territorial border

**Future receiving state**

Citizens=nationals=
residents=members

Aliens=foreigners
residing in foreign
state

FIGURE 6.1.   World without migration: State/society/people converge: "us/here," "them/there"

states and societies. In this world, each state contains its people and no other; their social relations do not spill out geographically but are rather confined to the territory of their state. Since the citizenry virtually fills up the territory, the solid lines denoting the citizenry almost converge with those denoting the territorial borders.

The image shown in Figure 6.1 presents the worlds of methodological nationalism and of classical and conventional contemporary sociology, all framed by the assumption that society = nation = state. In this world, each state resembles the other: whether a future receiving or future sending state, each is the state of its citizens. In each, the citizenry comprises the people; in each, the people and the population residing in the state are one and the same. Likewise, the persons lacking citizenship are foreigners, all residing in alien states located beyond the territorial boundary. Hence, whether in one state or another, space, citizenship, and identity are all

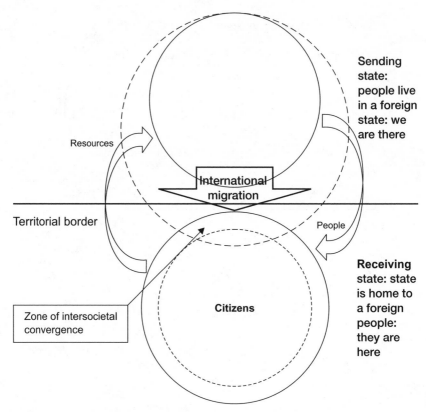

FIGURE 6.2.    World with migration

bound up in a similar way: "we" are "here," "they" are "there" (Painter and Philo, 1995).

Figure 6.2 presents a different picture. Here, in contrast to Figure 6.1, sending- and receiving-state societies are not separate but overlap. In opting for life in another country, the migrants pull one society on to the territory of another state, unintentionally and unconsciously bringing the isomorphism between state and society to an end. As seen from the receiving side, "they" from "there" have come "here"; as seen from the sending side, "we" from "here" have gone "there."

Convergence occurs because the people moving across borders are both immigrants *and* emigrants, retaining ties to the people and places left behind even while putting down roots in the place where they live. As we have already seen, the emigrants' own survival strategies link them to kin and communities still at home, creating an infrastructure that facilitates and reinforces those contacts. Thus, "here" and "there" come to overlap in a zone of intersocietal convergence.

This emphasis on the social processes of migration, and the cross-border links that it forges, leaves out the political dimension. The inherently political character of population movements across boundaries (Zolberg 1999) yields sending-state impacts that paradoxically stem from the very boundedness of the new environment. In a world characterized by *inter*-state economic inequalities, simply moving from a poor(er) to a rich(er) political unit gives migrants access to the wealth contained within that new state (Pritchett 2006). As those resources normally do *not* spill over to the country of origin, migrants quickly outdistance their compatriots still at home.

In opting for exit rather than voice, the *emigrants* retain home country citizenship but typically lose the options for home country political participation because territorial presence is the default condition for citizens' formal membership in the polity. By contrast, *immigrants* enter a new political jurisdiction as *aliens, inside* the territory of the receiving state but *outside* the boundary of its polity. Hence, the zone of intersocietal convergence is also a liminal political space in which presence on the territory of a democratic state yields protections, but far fewer than those enjoyed by citizens. While migrants to democratic societies "have a right to have rights," the basic fundament of citizenship, as famously described by Arendt (1951), to be meaningful, the right to have rights needs to be exercised. That activity is particularly difficult for aliens at the outer reaches of the liminal space between citizenship and the territorial boundary. As rights-claiming entails exposure when staying in the shadows may be the safer strategy, aliens may lack the full capacity to protect themselves from coercive behavior by receiving-state citizens (Bosniak 2006).

Nonetheless, by moving *abroad,* the immigrants gain *home* country political influence never previously experienced. The receiving state's borders do more than keep *in* wealth; they also keep *out* the tentacles of the sending state, providing the migrants with political protection against home state interests that might seek to control them (Adamson 2004). Moreover, the very same aliens standing outside the polity are also immigrants who are very much part of the society where they reside. Ties to citizens naturally develop out of proximity in neighborhoods, workplaces, and schools. The opportunities for political participation outside the electoral arena, inherent in any liberal democracy, provide the means for finding allies with unquestioned political entitlements. As *immigrants,* the migrants can frame their cause in terms that resonate broadly—whether appealing to beliefs in human rights or self-determination—finding additional ways to bridge the internal boundary of citizenship. Receiving-society membership can be obtained by proxy, when aliens connect to receiving-state interests, whose unquestioned rights of intervention help secure space for autonomous, migrant social action. For some, formal membership can eventually be obtained, with additional political entitlements occurring as the internal boundary of receiving-state citizenship is traversed. Hence, moving to *foreign* soil gives the *emigrants* a powerful *home* soil punch.

Thus, international migrations take nationals abroad where, as aliens, they encounter problems but as immigrants they gain resources, consequences that in turn yield home country *political* impacts and responses. While that pattern was visible during the last era of mass migration, it is especially notable now, when there is virtually no "emigration state" without a so-called diaspora that it is trying to engage. That effort to reconnect from afar takes any number of forms, whether entailing efforts to cultivate loyalty, keep cultural traditions alive, promote instruction in the homeland tongue, provide services, facilitate investment, or expand opportunities for political participation from abroad. However, as the emigrants have relocated to a new political jurisdiction, coercion no longer serves to gain access to resources or gain compliance; hence, sending states have no choice but to approach their nationals abroad with a totally different set of tools.

## Sending States and Emigrants

EMIGRANT CITIZENSHIP AND HOME COUNTRY ENGAGEMENT
Though migrants get treated as *aliens* the minute they step onto *foreign soil,* they remain *home country citizens* no matter where they go. Since citizenship inherently ties persons to states, international migration simultaneously weakens sending states' hold on their citizens *and* extends those states' reach beyond their frontiers (Green 2005).

That extension takes institutional form via embassies and consulates, which have long been recognized as outposts of extraterritorial sovereignty in which states can interact with nationals abroad as if they had never left home. As almost all states have citizens living in foreign states, whether as tourists, students, emigrants, or business owners, they also share a common interest in maintaining access, which in turn reinforces the rights accorded to consular activities. Long informally recognized, those rights are now protected by international law: signed by approximately 165 nations, the

1963 Vienna Convention on Consular Relations codified practices governed by custom and bilateral agreement between states, explicitly safeguarding activities related to protecting, assisting, and helping nationals (United Nations 2005).

Consulates and embassies provide a platform for a range of other activities. One component entails provision of documents, extending from passports and birth or death certificates to consular identity documents. Though no longer exercising a monopoly of force over emigrants living on the territory of another state, sending states retain their monopoly on the provision of official documents, leaving the emigrants, in their status as *aliens,* with no choice but to turn to the state of origin. The need for documents such as passports, identification cards, birth and death certificates, property titles—as well as help in other important matters, such as the repatriation of the dead for burial at home—produce regular visits to the consulate. Hard data on the frequency of consular contacts are difficult to find, but the best available source—a survey of return migrants to Algeria, Tunisia, and Morocco—indicates that two-thirds of all respondents had contacts with consular officials while living abroad, almost universally for reasons related to documentary needs.[1] Moreover, qualitative evidence from government reports, policy institutes, and the very rare academic study indicates that demand for consular services of this type is rising worldwide (Melissen and Fernandez 2011; White 2007).

Hence, though no longer able to cage their populations, sending states can use these outposts of extraterritoriality to embrace citizens abroad (Torpey 1999), as suggested by a survey of Mexican emigrants that found that more than half of those who cast a mail ballot in the first presidential election in which expatriates were allowed to participate had visited a consulate at least once in the prior year (Instituto Federal Electoral 2006). Thus, despite their extraterritorial location, consulates serve as a source of infrastructural power, permitting closer involvements. In some cases, sending states mandate that emigrants register with consular offices (Babiano and Fernandez Asperilla 2009); in reality not a demand but a request, that request does not always go unheeded, enabling sending-state officials to track, monitor, and manipulate their citizens abroad. Sometimes, the receiving state creates the clientele for consular services. As will be described in Chapter 7, post-9/11 demands for identification led millions of Mexican immigrants in the United States to obtain Mexican consular identification cards. In visiting the consulates, the emigrants provided Mexico with both the capacity to track a population that would otherwise have disappeared from its statistical records and the opportunity to foster connections with the state's broader diaspora engagement activities. A less benign case of the consular infrastructure put in place to keep track of Spanish guest workers in postwar Europe shows that the consular service can make emigrant surveillance and control its highest priorities. In general, the broader the consular network, the greater is its ability to connect with nationals abroad. At the turn of the last century, Italy's development of a full-fledged emigration policy entailed a substantial expansion of its consular corps (Choate 2009). During the interwar period, when the then-fascist state sought closer engagement with the only Italians it could not fully control, that infrastructure underwent further deepening, with fourteen consulates in France alone (for a population of roughly 500,000) given new mandates for overseeing emigrant welfare, mutual aid, and cultural and sports associations (Guillen 1982: 201–211). At the same time, but on the other side of the Atlantic, Mexico developed an expanded consular corps as growing numbers of Mexicans moved to the United States; arriving on the immigrants' heels, "consulates fostered *mexicanismo*, organized unions, developed community leadership, offered legal protections, spied upon the *colonia*, facilitated emigration, and, when required, participated in the massive removal of [Mexican] citizens from US territory" (González 1999: 9). Slightly later, post–World War II Spain, wanting remittances and a safety valve for its unemployed in the postwar years, encouraged emigrants to seek labor abroad, where they were followed by a network of sixty-eight labor attachés in western Europe who were charged with assisting and surveilling the expatriates (Babiano and Fernandez Asperilla 2009). A contemporary counterpart can be found in the consular infrastructure established by Mexico, which, as of 2013, includes fifty-one consulates in the United States, which in turn maintain traveling consulates to service emigrants living outside major metropolitan areas (Laglagaron 2010).

Of course, a sending state's ability to extend its sovereignty legally beyond its border is a matter of receiving-state discretion. A receiving state may sometimes assent to a greater extraterritorial presence, at other times not, especially when relationships with the sending state are unfriendly or hostile. Sending and receiving states that negotiate bilateral agreements, such as the *bracero* program (which imported Mexicans for work in the United States between 1943 and 1964), or the postwar European guest worker programs often want labor control and temporary migration without settlement. Hence, both sides collude to stifle independent migrant action, which is why sending states can extend surveillance and policing to the territory of the receiving state with the latter's assent. Thus, during the guest worker era, receiving-state police agencies worked hand in hand with consular officials from Spain, Morocco, Tunisia, and Algeria to keep immigrant troublemakers under close watch (Miller 1981). Similarly, receiving-state preferences that the guest workers return rather than settle provided a good match with sending-state efforts at retaining emigrant loyalty, which is why France, Germany, and the Netherlands were all willing to permit and even subsidize efforts by Turkey, Morocco, Spain, and Portugal to instruct emigrant children in home country languages (Iskander 2010; Koopmans et al. 2005). Nonetheless, as sending- and receiving-state interests are not symmetric, collusion goes only so far. As early as the 1920s and continuing thereafter, guest worker agreements in Europe guaranteed immigrant workers access to health and unemployment benefits, but frequent failure to fulfill treaty obligations led to unappreciated sending-state interventions (Rosenberg 2006; Rosental et al. 2011). On the other hand, by encouraging or at least tacitly accepting unauthorized migration, as France did with Spanish, Portuguese, and Italian immigrants during the post–World War II period (Weil 1991), and the United States did with Mexicans during the *bracero* era (Calavita 1992), receiving states undermined sending-state control potential.

Regardless of the circumstances of migration, sending states have privileged access to emigrant *citizens* abroad. But if retention of *home country citizenship* means continued vulnerability on the basis of *receiving-state alien status,* the immigrants lack all the protections needed to enjoy the full fruits of their place of residence. Hence, sending states often encourage immigrants to obtain receiving-state citizenship, which, if combined with persistent *homeland national loyalties,* converts the emigrants into lobbyists who can effectively mobilize on behalf of the place and people left behind.

Ironically, the *national* component of emigrant *citizenship* frequently gets in the way. Though home country citizenship status often does little for the emigrants, it retains deep value in its quality as a symbol of belonging. Hence, exclusive *sending-state* citizenship laws that forbid dual citizenship can reinforce migrants' tendencies to see the acquisition of receiving-state citizenship as a repudiation of the country in which they were born and the *national* family to which they still feel tied. Far better for sending states is accepting dual citizenship, thereby loosening membership expectations and freeing migrants to gain a secure place in the country where they reside. This is the very policy pioneered by Italy during the last era of mass migration (Cook-Martin 2013). Sending-state enactment of dual citizenship laws can yield just the effects intended, increasing rates of receiving-state naturalization and boosting the earnings of the newly naturalized, which in turn might increase their ability to send money home (Mazzolari 2009).

Motivations of this sort help explain the growth of dual citizenship, but they tell only part of the story. Ironically, dual citizenship is a policy in which sending- and receiving-state interests can converge. Because receiving states engaged in policies of *immigrant* integration also often see the ways in which their own exclusive citizenship policies stand in the way of *immigrant* belonging, they sometimes come to perceive that dual citizenship could serve as a transitional tool that fosters immigrant belonging. Empirical research shows symmetrical effects: enactment of *receiving-society* dual citizenship laws seems to yield rates of naturalization exceeding those found in receiving countries where citizenship is an exclusive status (Bloemraad 2007). Yet advocates of a more cosmopolitan approach have thus far had limited success in convincing receiving-state nationals. Instead, the national identity concerns triggered by the influx of foreigners surfaces in the form of anxiety over the dual loyalty of *immigrant* citizens, a factor often sufficiently powerful and broad to keep *receiving-state* citizenship an exclusive status (Hansen and Kohler 2005).

Those allergic reactions have made *citizenship status* increasingly hard to obtain. Toleration of immigrant dual citizenship is the general trend in western Europe, with most states currently far more accepting of dual citizenship than was the case in the early 1980s (Howard 2009; Goodman 2010). But naturalization requirements have followed a different path, involving more stringent residency requirements and more demanding procedures. To their misfortune, sending states can do little about these trends, an important source of their limited ability to engage with citizens abroad. Hence, the potential reach of *dual* citizenship is first and foremost limited by *host country citizenship policy.*

EMIGRANT MEMBERSHIP   As status, *citizenship* entails a relationship between the individual and the state whereby rights are institutionally guaranteed. Citizenship also has an identity component, related to membership in the political community (Joppke 2010). Unproblematic when polity, people, and population converge, membership questions become complicated when international migration relocates status citizens into an alien polity (Baubock 2003) because rights to political participation are often conditioned on territorial presence. Because so many *emigrants* keep cross-state social ties, some want to retain membership in the self-governing "we" of origin, even as they live "there." Consequently, emigration and the creation of a zone of intersocietal convergence breed demands for cross-border polity extension, allowing emigrants to participate as if they were still residing at home.

Migration is an *implicitly* political act: migrants depart in response to the state's betrayal of its people. That perception of injustice challenges *emigration* states seeking to retain emigrants' loyalty and their resources. Consequently, *membership retention* comprises a recurrent *sending-state* goal, as demonstrated ever since the late nineteenth century, when the emigration states of Germany, Italy, and even Greece provided "support to schools, libraries, and students" in an effort to "preserve the language and cultural identity" of emigrants and emigrant offspring living abroad (Paschalidis 2009: 278). Programs oriented toward cultural maintenance are now a standard component of emigration policy, testifying to the widespread concern over the lure of the *foreign* environment toward which the *immigrants* are ever more oriented. Another technique consists of transforming an act once seen as a symbol of misery into a sign of accomplishment. Many scholars have noted how Mexico's turn to diaspora engagement turned the emigrants from traitors to heroes, but examples can be found around the globe yielding similar efforts at expressing recognition, whether through statues; postal stamps; or special, commemorative days all designed to honor the emigrants (Poinard 1988).

While sending states seek to ensure that emigrants living "there" nonetheless retain their sense of belonging to the home country national "we," that goal resonates with at least some of the emigrants. Hence, both parties are likely to articulate a new, deterritorialized view, redefining the nation as a community encompassing its nationals, wherever they might live. In this new understanding, the national community goes beyond the limits of any single home state, including nationals abroad and at home, whether conceptualized as *italiani nel mundo; salvadoreños del mundo;* or as a member of a new extraterritorial unit, as illustrated by the late nineteenth-century designation of American Polonia, defined as "the fourth district of Poland" (Gabaccia et al. in Green and Weil 2003: 77); or the contemporary contention that Peruvians abroad comprise *El Quinto Suyo*, or "fifth department" (Berg and Tamagno 2006).

This deterritorialized perspective implies that the *emigrants* are one and the same as the people left behind, so emigrant membership also provides the rationale for claims on the people and place left behind. Typically, the migrants seek institutional recognition of their status as physically absent yet fully legitimate, engaged, protected members. As noted by Ostergaard-Nielsen (2003c: 762), "they ask for favorable investment schemes, tax and toll exemptions . . . , regulation of pension schemes and child benefits, and . . . extended channels of influence on politics at home, such as advisory councils, absentee voting rights, and the right to be candidates in elections." Ironically, these claims are often informed by the *immigrant* experience, reflecting a quest to export aspects of their exposure to *foreign* institutions—whether a more democratic polity or a more rationalized, more efficient state bureaucracy—back to the place where they were born. However, the emigrants are also apt to emphasize their economic contributions, thus exploiting their location in a richer, *foreign state* to reproduce clientelistic or paternalistic patterns, whether in the public arena or via the family members who depend on remittances abroad.

Living *there,* however, the emigrants are subject to dissimilation, the process, as explained by Fitzgerald (2012), whereby a political boundary creates *difference* between populations of common national background. Consequently, the emigrants' claim to *membership* in the national community in the place where they no longer live is contested. For those left behind, the periodic or annual return of the "absent sons" typically provides ample evidence of the degree to which the emigrants are not just *in* the country of destination but *of* it as well. By contrast, modernizing elites, who looked down at the emigrants right from the very start, are apt to see the migrants as representing some prior, shameful version of the country, now "frozen in time" (Fullilove 2008: 65).

Because *emigrants'* influence stems from the fact that they are beyond home state control, some home country nationals are also apt to view them as an *alien* force, and possibly even a Trojan horse acting in the interests of the *foreign* state on whose territory they reside. Last, because membership claims, when translated into policy, can have real effects, whether shifting influence to a hard-to-control group or requiring expenditures for nationals living not just on foreign but on high-cost grounds, political actors have tangible reasons for contending that nationals *there* don't fully belong to self-governing "we" still living *here.*

Conflicts over *emigrant* voting provide a window into the ambiguous, fundamentally contested nature of emigrant membership claims. Expatriate voting is usually the converse of the political challenge faced in democratic receiving states: immigration yields a gap between the state's demography, including aliens, and its democracy, limited to citizens, with the result that the people *in* the state and the people *of* the state are no longer the same. Emigration has like effects because the people *in* the state comprise only part of the people *of* the state, some of whom live elsewhere. In countries of *immigration, non*citizen *resident* voting provides a means of making the boundaries of the polity converge with the boundaries of the territory, furnishing immigrants as well as citizens the opportunity to influence the conditions under which they live. In countries of *emigration,* voting by *non*resident *citizens* extends the boundaries of the polity *beyond* the territory to include all the people, thereby allowing emigrants to affect decisions whose consequences have little effect on the expatriates but almost surely matter for the stay-at-homes.

Emigrant access to the ballot abroad pulls the polity beyond borders, signaling membership in a political community expanded beyond the original territorial base and corresponding to the intersocietal convergence produced by migration. Migrants' claims to be *emigrants* notwithstanding, *immigrant* status generates a distributional—"who gets what?"—consequence to the migrants' identity—"who is what?"—claims. The electoral machinery needed to service a dispersed migrant population is expensive, with the result that logistical arrangements abroad "often cost more per voter than elections organized in the home country" (Ellis and Wall 2007: 262). Furthermore, anything done in the rich *foreign* country where the emigrants live far exceeds the comparable costs at *home,* entailing expenditures from taxes paid for by the stay-at-homes and from which the emigrants usually abstain. The expenses can mount up, sometimes translating to no more than a very expensive exercise in symbolism. Spending those funds also entails doing more for people who, by virtue of residence in a more prosperous state, already have greater access to all the things that government can provide, not to speak of superior chances for individual advancement.

PROTECTING VULNERABLE NATIONALS IN FOREIGN PLACES     Since for many immigrants, receiving-state citizenship is out of reach, emigration policy is also affected by the liminal status and vulnerable position resulting from yet another duality: the fact that emigrants reside abroad as both *aliens* and as *foreigners.* As *aliens,* the emigrants lack the full set of rights, a deficiency that cannot always be compensated for by knowing the ropes, leaving them potentially defenseless. As *foreigners,* the emigrants are people who do not know the ropes: lacking the full set of tools for navigating their new environment, they are subject to harm, even if receiving-state citizenship has been acquired.

These vulnerabilities intensify the pressures toward engagement with the *nation* beyond borders, adding moral and political force to the obligations involved in serving citizens abroad. Though relocation abroad may move emigrants outside the formal political community, they are often seen as part of the imagined community, meriting the state's concern. The inability to hold on to their own undermines sending-state legitimacy; it also "highlights the source country's weakness vis-à-vis the destination country" (Fitzgerald 2009: 23), a matter of particular embarrassment when the flow leads from a former colony to the former metropole.

Though lacking authority over nationals who have moved to foreign territories, sending states may still be perceived as fully responsible for the fate of citizens, no matter where they live. In the contemporary world, "the death sentence of a citizen detained abroad, a case of international child abduction, a large-scale natural disaster can . . . become directly related to the image and prestige of individual politicians, the foreign ministry, and even the government at large" (Okano-Heijmans 2011: 25). Expectations for protection abroad impinge not only on poorer emigration states but on rich states that have long sent tourists and managers abroad and now find themselves engaging with an ever-larger expat population responding to globalization. The combination of rising expectations and growing need produces resource issues that strain the budgets of even developed states (National Audit Office 2005); the implications for emigration states are far more severe. As movement abroad leaves migrants exposed to the arbitrary exercise of receiving-state power and to depredation from the profit-seeking migration industry (Hernández-León 2008), emigration repeatedly puts the sending state at risk of highly emotive, often media-tized scandals signaling not just its limited capacity but its utter incompetence.

Examples from the last era of mass migration demonstrate the ways in which emigrants' vulnerability as *foreigners* led sending states to engage (Green 2005). Children numbered prominently among Italian emigrants of the mid-nineteenth century; treated as "little slaves," their experience provoked such controversy that the nascent Italian state intervened, stopping the practice by the 1890s (Gabaccia 2000). The development of mass emigration by the 1880s provided a booming market for shipping companies and shipping agents, whose cutthroat competition repeatedly led to disastrous consequences on the transatlantic voyage. The ensuing scandals produced yet another instance of state engagement: Italy imposed rules regulating the shippers eligible to depart as well as onboard conditions (Douki 2011). Emigration similarly created a remittance market, furnishing an opportunity for unscrupulous immigrant swindlers eager to cheat the immigrants of their savings. Again, Italy responded, contracting with the Banco di Napoli, a charitable credit institution, to transfer remittances from the Americas to Italy at reduced rates (Choate 2009).

Violence directed at migrants is another persistent source of threat. At the turn of the twentieth century, antagonism against Italian immigrants in France repeatedly led to anti-Italian rioting, in turn producing anti-French rampages in Italy as well as demands for a home state response, an action then surpassing Italy's capacity (Milza 1993). Singapore's 1985 execution of Flor Contemplacion, a Filipino maid, provides a contemporary parallel, an act that provoked uproar and controversy in the Philippines and subsequently a transformation of the Philippines' emigration policy, putting greater priority on foreign worker protection (Guevarra 2010). While this case arose in a context associated with minimal migrant rights, it differed only in degree from similar cases in more liberal societies in which police or border patrol brutality against immigrants generates moral pressures pushing sending states toward stepped-up emigrant protection. In 1996, for example, the beating of Mexican undocumented immigrants by California police officers triggered outrage in Mexico, with the major television station leading its newscasts with the story for an entire week and all major politicians railing against US violations of human rights, though not enough to satisfy the public (*Migration News* 1996). In the late 1990s, racist attacks against Moroccans in Spain and elsewhere in Europe triggered outbursts of *emigrant* indignation against *home* state leaders unable to provide protection, in turn leading Morocco to revamp its policies of emigrant engagement (Iskander 2010). As suggested by these contemporary examples, democratization at home aggravates the problems encountered by emigration states because newly empowered citizens concerned about the fate of co-nationals abroad can now bring pressure to bear (Fullilove 2008).

At the turn of the twenty-first century, the problems of *emigrant* protection have been further aggravated by receiving state *immigration* policies. Because *immigration* control inherently creates the category of the unauthorized migrant, *alienage* has an importance not previously possessed, rendering migrants vulnerable in new ways. No less vexing is the fact that *receiving-state rights* are unstable and uncertain. Though impressive by historical standards, the package of rights that democratic receiving states provide *all* persons is limited. Some analysts have hailed the advent of "postnational citizenship," claiming that foreign residents share the core rights of citizens (Soysal 1994; Jacobson 1996). Even these scholars concede that "postnational citizenship" extends to legal residents only, leaving unauthorized migrants at the mercy of the host state.

Trends toward the restriction of *immigrant* rights provide further impetus for added emigrant engagement. Toleration was long the de facto policy in the rich, receiving-state democracies; since the 1990s, greater efforts at border control have increasingly been linked to intensified efforts at internal control, leaving unauthorized migrants with fewer rights and at increased risk of deportation (Fassin 2011). Legal residents are better protected; however, even their rights can be rolled back. Lacking the franchise, legal residents cannot control their destinies as do citizens, one reason why many analysts have concluded that "postnational citizenship" amounts to much less than its early proponents claimed (Hansen 2009). As for *receiving-state citizens,* many favor diminished immigration *and* restricted immigrant rights. Whereas *emigrants* emphasize *national* belonging in order to gain membership in a state where they no longer reside, *host-society nationals* emphasize the *foreign* origin and character of the *immigrants* in order to restrict the rights of *aliens* in the place where they actually live (Chavez and Provine 2009).

Attacks on *immigrants* spur intensified home country efforts to protect *citizens abroad,* in which sending states often try to exploit the peculiar politics of *immigration* and the *domestic* fractures it yields. Since *immigrants* are often wanted even when they are not welcomed, sending states can connect with mainstream host society allies on both left *and* right for whom defense of *immigrant* rights is a matter of either principled commitment or, perhaps more powerfully, material interest. The more "porous" the receiving state, the easier it is penetrated by societal interests, making it open to *foreign* actors as well, who are probably most effective when partnering with *domestic* allies but who can also make the case on their own, as illustrated by two examples from very different points in history. In the early 1940s, the Mexican government worked hand in glove with Mexican American civil rights groups to gain greater rights for persons of Mexican descent in Texas, especially equal access to public accommodations. Faced with resistance from state politicians, Mexico barred braceros from entering Texas, yielding a labor shortage that in turn activated growers, who in turn pressed state officials for concessions (Guglielmo 2006). Roughly sixty years later, as noted above and will be discussed at greater length in the next chapter, Mexico issued an identity card to provide undocumented Mexican immigrants in the United States with secure identification. Though restrictionists reacted with alarm, bankers, wanting the accounts and remittance services that could be accessed by clients possessing appropriate documentation, weighed in to ensure that the US government would allow the Mexican card to be accepted for banking purposes (Bakker 2011).

While sending states can thus activate host society interests to shackle the host state, additional opportunities stem from that state's pluralistic nature. Since incoherence is the common condition of *immigration* policy (Cornelius and Tsuda 2004), sending-state overtures can elicit a positive response from some, if not all, receiving-state actors. Police officials, for example, might see cooperation with consular officials as a means of facilitating order maintenance among a foreign-born population that would otherwise prefer to hide in the shadows; central bankers, anticipating the gains made if immigrants could be convinced to bank their savings and send them home via the financial system, an objective fully in line with sending-state goals, might think similarly. Like effects may result from differences across governmental levels, as local, regional, or state officials in areas of high immigrant density often see virtue in policies of *immigrant integration*, unlike national officials who are often more oriented toward *immigration control* (Kemp and Raijman 2004; Wells 2004; Friedmann and Lehrer 1997). Where the polity is also fragmented, as in the United States, sending states can exploit these points of cross-level divergence, linking with local or state officials who possess the authority, and sometimes the motivation, to expand many *immigrant rights*, albeit only those that fall short of national citizenship (Varsanyi 2007). Thus, in extending their reach onto *foreign* soil and partnering with *receiving-society* interests, home states can push back at efforts to diminish *aliens' rights*, expanding the liminal space between the boundaries of territory and citizenship, though also further embedding the *immigrants* in the *foreign* state where they have settled.

POLITICAL PARTICIPATION Movement to a *foreign* polity yields resources—insulation from the home state, greater freedom, influential allies—making for expanded political influence back *home*. As discussed in Chapter 5, *emigrant, homeland-oriented* political activism comes in numerous types, from ideologically motivated undertakings by exile elites to uncoordinated efforts by rank-and-filers seeking to help their hometowns. Whether involving state-seeking nationalism or regime-changing nationalism, either option typically generates "transplanted factions" (Ögelman 2003), which, though born out of *home* country politics, often engage in internecine combat on *host* country soil where *emigrants* are relatively free to behave as they please politically.

Today, the more common option involves attempts to participate in normal home country politics, an option facilitated by decolonization, the dismantling of multi-ethnic empires, and especially the last quarter century's wave of democratization. Hence, the agenda championed by politicized emigrants is more likely to be dominated by demands for long-distance political inclusion and participation, as described above.

The emigrants' quest for participation at *home* entails aligning the political boundaries of the sending state with the trans-state society resulting from migration. However, extending the polity across borders is impeded by the emigrants' foreign *location,* as indicated by the practical problems posed by emigrant voting, where the extraterritorial nature of the process is a threat to the integrity of the vote itself. From the standpoint of sending states, expatriate voting takes place in a *foreign,* "uncontrolled environment" (Baubock 2007: 2406) where *home* states can neither provide external voters with the same security available on their own territories nor furnish a mechanism for resolving disputes should extraterritorial votes or campaign practices be contested. These factors are particularly significant for democratizing societies, since expatriate voting systems require confidence that neither emigrant voters nor authorities will abuse the system, a level of trust that such countries often lack. Because expatriate voting can threaten the integrity of the entire electoral system, internal democratization therefore raises the bar: "the more sophisticated and exacting is the internal electoral regime, in terms of guarantees of security, confidence, and equity, the greater are the difficulties in replicating and controlling it abroad" (Navarro 2007: 251). Hence, protecting the interests of the people who voted to stay *home* may impede the political participation of those compatriots who voted for life *abroad.*

For sending states, in contrast, the type of *emigrant* politics that proves most attractive is the one that can be pursued through *immigrant* politics: the conversion of émigrés into potential lobbyists, an activity pursued with greatest success with receiving-state citizenship in hand. That objective is long-standing, one followed by Italy in the early 1900s when it wanted naturalized citizens to lobby against immigration restriction (Choate 2009), and again later in the interwar period, when consuls urged immigrants to become American citizens "to use their influence to build sympathy for the new and anti-socialist Italy and its fascist ruler" (Gabaccia 2000: 147). Today, the universal goal appears to be that of emulating the perceived success of America's "Jewish lobby." The objective is of obvious appeal to states sending migrants to the United States, as noted in Chapter 5. But the idea has traveled well beyond the Western Hemisphere, as Ostergaard-Nielsen (2003d: 124) found out when a Turkish national assembly member told her, "Everybody wants a Jewish lobby." Indeed, a nongovernmental Israeli organization, whose services are recommended by the International Organization of Migration, has now been set up to tutor emigration states on how best to connect with diasporas.

Linking *emigrant* and *immigrant* politics is a tricky, difficult game to manage. Immigration provides exposure to a different set of political institutions—more democratic, more accountable, more transparent, more reliable—potentially transforming emigrant political views and thus making them the vectors by which pressure for change flows from the country of destination to the country of origin. While an inability to protect nationals abroad is shameful, an inability to control emigrants is embarrassing, especially when the emigrants use the freedom gained from movement to *foreign* soil to demonstrate in front of embassies and consulates. As shown by the experience of Cuban Americans, *emigrants* can successfully pursue *immigrant* politics in order to bring homeland governments if not to heel, then at least to feel very great pain (Eckstein 2009). Neither ideological commitments nor material achievements of the Cuban American sort are required for similar results. When Mexico sought to raise the deposit paid by immigrants bringing home cars bought in the United States, the emigrants brought their own muscle to bear: after demonstrations in front of Mexican consulates and pressure from US congressional officials, Mexico backed down (Leiken 2000).

Moreover, both *emigrant* politics and *immigrant* politics have considerable potential to get out of hand. As noted in Chapter 5, a particular problem is that of ensuring that *homeland* connections persist without reminding *receiving-state nationals* of the *alien* attachments of the *foreign* and *foreign-born* people in their midst. *Immigrant* political actors may be quick to rally to help a homeland in distress, an activity that can also resonate with receiving-country publics; by contrast, lobbying activities that might cast them as sending-state tools, and thereby hamper efforts at *immigrant* integration, have far less appeal. Quite the same result can occur if *emigrant* home country engagement tips over into a pattern that might be perceived as *over*engagement; for sending states the problem is that, by virtue of the *emigrants'* presence on a *foreign* land, their manifestations of *home country loyalty* and agitation for *home country rights* can no longer be controlled. The overly active Turkish and Kurdish political associations in Western Europe are a good case in point: host authorities have either closed down or sharply circumscribed the scope of allowable public behavior.

Thus, *emigrant* politics runs the risk of reminding receiving-state nationals of the *foreign* presence in their midst. Just as foreign location can undermine *emigrants'* home country membership claims, even when sending-state status citizenship is retained, *immigrant* foreign involvements can have a like effect in the state of *residence,* putting membership in question for all, regardless of whether receiving-state status citizenship has been acquired or not.

## Conclusion

Common sense as well as much social science tell us that state, society, people, and population normally converge. In this frame, humans are sedentary by nature, not mobile. Hence, in a normal world, people will stay in place: "they," the foreigners, live "there" on foreign grounds; "we," the nationals, reside "here," on native soil. But the world rarely conforms to this particular model of normality. Rather, global inequalities draw persons from developing to developed countries, from states that can't take care of their people to states that can, making population movements across territorial boundaries an inherent part of the reality, to be expected regardless of what nationals and governments, whether in sending or receiving states, would prefer. In searching for the better life found in a foreign state, migrants don't arrive as solo adventurers but rather with attachments connecting them to both settlers and stay-at-homes. At once *immigrants* and *emigrants,* the migrants move social relations across state borders, yielding *intersocietal convergence.*

Having crossed a territorial border, the migrants find themselves *in* the country of destination but not *of* it. The newcomers do not belong; nonetheless, as *immigrants* they benefit from simple territorial presence, gaining opportunities for economic gain, access to superior public goods, and often an assurance of personal security not found at home. Those advantages spill over across boundaries since as *emigrants,* the new arrivals transfer some portion of the resources secured by displacement to members of the core familial network still living at home. But all that glitters is not gold: as *foreigners,* the migrants have to navigate unfamiliar terrain where the strangeness of the environment and their lack of know-how leave them exposed; as *aliens,* they stand outside the polity and lack the full protection enjoyed by citizens. Though immigrant workers may be wanted, immigrant residents are less often welcomed because many receiving-state nationals think that "they" should stay "there."

As aliens in the *receiving* state, the emigrants nonetheless remain citizens of the *sending* state. Paradoxically, the latter responds to the emigrants' prior decisions to express their discontent through exit rather than voice by following them, extending its infrastructure across territories. That extension occurs in reaction to the combination of resources and vulnerabilities produced by the migrants' relocation to a different state. On the one hand, sending states seek to capture some portion of the gains enjoyed by the *immigrants*—whether in the form of remittances, new knowledge, or new contacts—and ensure that they are exported home. Though the *emigrants'* extraterritorial presence precludes coercion, putting in place an infrastructure engaging with the diaspora provides the means to influence people who cannot be controlled while shoring up national loyalties eroded by the attractions that the *immigrants* discover in the new environment. On the other hand, the emigrants' need for help cannot be disregarded, all the more so because the many exchanges occurring across boundaries ensure that the fates of both emigrants and stay-at-homes are intertwined. And though in leaving, the emigrants shame their state, ignoring the problems of nationals *abroad* is a recipe for creating troubles at *home*.

*Of* the sending state, but not *in* it, a fraction of the emigrant population—small, but usually too large and too important to be neglected—seeks to engage with the polity left behind, whether at the local or national level, or both. While citizenship is portable, accompanying the emigrants as they move abroad, full citizenship rights prove stickier as they are typically attached to territorial presence. Consequently, the politically oriented emigrants may identify with the homeland political community but find themselves excluded from the homeland polity. Contending that the nation is deterritorialized, to be found not just in the homeland but wherever nationals reside, the emigrant activists seek to pull the polity onto foreign grounds.

Living "there," the emigrants present themselves as full-fledged members of the "we" remaining in the homeland and therefore deserving of full citizenship rights. As perceived from the sending state, those claims do not necessarily ring true. Personal experience convinces many of the stay-at-homes that the *emigrants* have become *immigrants*, not just residing in foreign lands but absorbing foreign ways as well. For state elites, the issue takes a different form because the emigrant demand for full citizenship rights as well as other privileges involves channeling resources to nationals often less needy than those who decided *not* to vote with their feet and who live in places where service provision greatly exceeds comparable costs back home. Moreover, the emigrants' extraterritorial location ensures that the sending state can only partly control the conditions of their political participation, thereby threatening the integrity of the electoral process itself.

Thus, the *emigrants* find that pulling the sending-state polity across borders proves difficult; as *immigrants*, by contrast, they discover that host country politics offers fewer obstacles. Opportunities for political participation exist even for those lacking receiving-state citizenship because the civic rights guaranteed by democratic states are not restricted to citizens but rather extend to all territorially present persons. Moreover, participation in the host country also provides an ideal means of pursuing homeland concerns, which is why sending states that allow emigrants to acquire receiving-state citizenship (and thus acquire dual citizenship) are simultaneously facilitating the emergence of ethnic lobbies that can mobilize in support of home state interests. However, nationals abroad cannot be controlled, so the pursuit of homeland politics can get out of control, confirming receiving-state nationals in their suspicion that "they"—the immigrants—have never cut their loyalty to the place and people found "there."

The parameters set by the scope conditions of this chapter—international migrations from poor(er) to rich(er) democratic states—explain why these unpredictable, inherently conflicted interactions consistently recur. Taking the long view allows one to leverage the insights gained by examining long-lasting (century or more) migrations, such as those from Italy or Mexico; by adding periods (the interwar and post–World War II guest worker years) usually excluded by the common approach of comparing migrations "now" (at the turn of the twenty-first century) and "then" (at the turn of the twentieth), one can expand the range of relevant cases. The continuities found across this long stretch of historical time also exclude the possibility that contemporary changes in telecommunications technology have transformed the interactions between emigrants and emigration states—as so often hypothesized in the literature.

But showing that *some* things stay roughly the same does *not* imply that *everything* stays the same. In passing, the chapter has noted some of the significant sources of change, most important, those related to the changing political organization of the globe (in particular, the decline of empires and other multiethnic states) and the spread of democracy, altering emigrants' goals as well as sending-state motivations. Were I instead aiming to explain variation over historical time, the chapter would have attended to a broader set of transformative factors, some linear in nature (the proliferation of emigration states or the growing involvement of international organizations), others contingent (the rise and decline of proletarian internationalism or the outbreak of international conflict).

In any case, accounting for change over time is a task for another project. The key point is that the phenomenon itself entails a persistent dilemma, one that immigrants, since they are also emigrants, cannot escape. Seeking to be both "here" *and* "there," "we" *and* "us," the people migrating across state boundaries engage in a quest with little chance of success. For the students of migration, by contrast, that dilemma is good news because complexity always makes for more interesting research. But to appreciate that dilemma and take advantage of its potential intellectual benefits, researchers need to go beyond the conventional intellectual division of labor between those who focus on *immigration* and those who focus on *emigration*. In the next two chapters, I will try to imitate those immigrants who are also emigrants, following them in their effort to straddle both sides, seeking to understand the forces that connect "here" and "there," "them" and "us," the same forces that also push them apart.

# CHAPTER SEVEN

# Politics across Borders

## Mexico and Its Emigrants

INTERNATIONAL MIGRATION is at once opportunity *and* dilemma, creating a conundrum that neither emigrants nor emigration states can escape. Migrants vote with their feet *against* the *home* state where they grew up and to which they belong, and *for* a *foreign* state, where the gains in security, stability, and standard of living outweigh the costs of rejection and exclusion. Yet physical distance doesn't yield separation, in part because both states and migrants think that it is possible to be at home while abroad. Emigration states look at the emigrants and see a collectivity that can be controlled and from which resources can be extracted. The emigrants, still connected to kin and communities, discover that residence *outside* the home state gives them leverage *within* the home state of a sort never enjoyed before. Whether India, Italy, Israel, Ireland, or what have you, there is no "emigration state" without a so-called diaspora that it is trying to mobilize; likewise, there are few emigrations without a core of activists seeking to transform the place that could not meet their needs but to which they nevertheless remain attached.

This chapter examines the interaction between states and emigrants abroad through a comparative case study of Mexico's large-scale effort to provide its emigrants with consular identification cards (the *matrícula consular*), on the one hand, and its experiment with expatriate voting in the 2006 presidential election, on the other. Having long approached its emigrants with a "policy of no policy," Mexico changed course in the late

1980s, following a strategy that involved significant investment, focused involvement with migrants at both rank-and-file and elite levels, and engagement with a broad range of US political actors. This new direction made Mexico a crucial actor in the world of sending states, disseminating and producing relevant information and linking concerned policy makers across countries. As interest in "diaspora engagement" has spread to international organizations and the development agencies and foreign ministries of developed states, Mexico has increasingly been profiled as an example for other emigration countries to follow.[1]

If Mexico provides a critical case, the two policies examined in this chapter are well-suited for studying the range of policies linking sending states with emigrants abroad. Both are common worldwide: electoral systems increasingly allow for expatriate voting; consular protection is a long-standing aspect of states' engagement with their nonresident citizens, albeit one of increasing intensity and importance. Both policies share a fundamental similarity in kind, as each is undertaken by one state in the territory of another. On the other hand, the two policies reflect the underlying split in the nature of the politics of emigration, as sending states respond both to *immigrants'* problems in the countries of residence *and* to *emigrants'* membership concerns in the state of origin. Consequently, as this chapter will show, each policy involved a different cross-border relational nexus, triggering the involvement of a distinctive set of actors whose engagement followed an equally distinctive sequence.

## Consular Identification Cards

Ever since the late nineteenth century, Mexico has provided consular identification cards to its nationals living abroad. For decades, Mexicans living in the United States who wanted to return to Mexico but lacked a passport would go to the local consulate, where they would be recorded in a book known as the consular register. Later, persons inscribed in the consular register received a document detailing identity characteristics, which subsequently came to include a photograph (Pradillo 2002). By 1987, a publication by the Ministry of Foreign Relations noted that the ever-growing presence of Mexicans in the United States had generated increasing demands for documents of all sorts—whether relating to those needed for activities undertaken in Mexico or for regularizing status in the United States (Flores Rivas 1987). As of 2000, roughly a million of the approximately ten million Mexican immigrants living in the United States possessed such a card, known as the *matrícula consular*.

In the aftermath of September 11, 2001, this protected but modest activity took on new importance. With the heightening of security preoccupations and ever-rising concerns over foreigners present on US soil, unauthorized immigrants suddenly faced new demands for identity documents. The attack on the twin towers also dashed until-then promising plans for a US-Mexico deal on immigration. With "amnesty founder[ing]," Mexican leaders began looking for ways to "integrate workers into US locales" (Porter 2002). As recounted by Jorge Castañeda, then the Mexican foreign minister charged with spearheading negotiations with the US over migration,

> Mexico's government changed tactics: it began to try to obtain rights for Mexicans via other mechanisms, certainly less satisfactory than a migration accord, but significant and with direct effects on the daily life of millions of compatriots in the United States. The heart of this tactical turn consisted, of course, in the expedition of the new matrícula and political negotiations with banks and local authorities in the United States by our consuls in order to achieve the recognition of this matrícula as an identity document. (Castañeda 2003)

Immigrants willing to pay $27 to obtain a *matrícula* crowded consulates around the country, with applications surging by late fall 2001 (Bazeley 2001). Shortly thereafter, Mexico introduced a new card, the *matrícula consular de alta seguridad,* with greatly enhanced security features. While big-city consulates issued cards in large volumes—with Chicago giving out as many as one thousand a day (*El Norte* 2002)—the foreign ministry organized traveling consulates to distribute the cards in the smaller destinations toward which Mexican immigrants had been gravitating since the early 1990s (de la Vega 2002). Almost 1.2 million consular cards were issued during 2002, more than twice the number obtained two years before (Secretaría de Relaciones Exteriores 2008: 239).

Mexico's strategy of "creeping legalization," as Casteñeda described it (2007: 146), built on its earlier decision to decentralize its diplomatic mission in the United States and "deliberately use [its consular offices] as channels to promote its interests" (González Gutierrez 1997: 50). Involving closer engagement with migrants, the strategy entailed two other, crucial prongs, one designed to exploit openings in the fragmented US political structure, the other to develop connections to Mexican Americans who could be converted into ethnic lobbyists. Having established ties to local stakeholders, whether in or outside government, and enjoying substantially augmented resources, the consulates quickly implemented the new tactic. As Casteñeda explains, "Every Mexican consul was instructed to negotiate with local banks, city officials, police departments, lawyers, etc.

to persuade them to accept or 'recognize' the ID as an official document" (2007: 146). Those negotiations quickly bore fruit, an outcome facilitated by support from immigrant advocacy and Mexican American organizations.

"What previously seemed impossible happened," noted a reporter for the Mexican newspaper, *La Reforma,* writing about the Orange County sheriff's department and its decision to accept the *matrícula* as a valid form of identification. Practical considerations linked to order maintenance—for example (Muñoz Bata 2001), identifying crime victims or issuing a citation for a traffic violation, rather than holding an unidentifiable person overnight in jail—led many police departments to endorse the *matrícula* as a valid form of identification (O'Neil 2003). Proactive consuls persuaded the financial sector, already interested in the rapidly expanding immigrant market, that the *matrícula* could prove advantageous. In a 2001 news release, the California regional president of Wells Fargo explained that "we were approached by the Consulate General of Mexico to help find solutions to the barriers that Mexicans are encountering when trying to open a checking or savings account at a US bank" (Wells Fargo 2001). That approach quickly yielded dividends: in November 2001, Wells Fargo began accepting the consular card as identification for new accounts (Wells Fargo 2001), a policy announced at Mexico's Los Angeles consulate and one that Mexico's then-consul in Los Angeles described as her greatest achievement (Dillon 2003; Arredondo 2003). Citibank and Bank of America soon followed suit (Gori 2002; Esterl 2003; Galan 2002). By fall 2003 customers using the *matrícula* had opened almost a quarter of a million accounts at Wells Fargo (Wells Fargo 2003). Following a 2004 closed-door meeting between top US bank leaders and then-president Vicente Fox, the banks gained permission to market their products throughout all of Mexico's consulates in the United States (Breitkopf 2004). Later, Bank of America began covering part of the costs of Mexico's mobile consulates in return for getting a venue for "bank employees to pitch its SafeSend remittance service and other banking products" (Lindemeyer 2005). Numerous local and state governments also moved toward acceptance. By 2005, the *matrícula* had been granted valid identification by 377 cities, 163 counties, and 33 states, as well as 178 financial institutions and 1,180 police departments (Bruno and Storrs 2005).

Proponents of reduced immigration, aware of and infuriated by Mexico's consular efforts, quickly pushed back. The Center for Immigration Studies (CIS), a restrictionist think tank in Washington, DC, lambasted the *matrícula* as an "ID for illegals." Insisting that the *matrícula* surreptitiously "advanced Mexico's immigration agenda" (Dinerstein 2003)—a claim later accepted by Jorge Castañeda (2007: 149)—the CIS sounded a security trope: despite safeguards, the matrícula was insecure, giving "both illegals and local law enforcement a way to ignore [the] troubling reality" of immigrants committing "criminal acts like crossing our border without permission, engaging in identity theft, and using fake, stolen, or borrowed Social Security numbers" (2003: 6). With CIS having framed the issue as a matter of ensuring domestic security against foreign threats, other players in the restrictionist network quickly took up the theme. Californians for Population Stabilization insisted that "*matrícula* cards sabotage national security efforts" (2003); the *National Review* warned of "Mexico's fake i.d.—and its terrorist implications" (Cooley 2004); the Federation for American Immigration Reform contended that "acceptance of the consular ID cards is placing critical national security matters in the hands of foreign governments" (2003). Restriction-oriented lawyers and academics founded a new organization, Friends of Immigration Law Enforcement, alerting state and municipal officials to the *matrícula's* purported security defects (*El Mural* 2002) and publishing model letters on its website, urging citizens to write to banks and public institutions to complain that acceptance of the *matrícula* is illegal (MALDEF [Mexican American Legal Defense and Education Fund] 2003). The *Washington Times,* the right-wing daily with close ties to conservatives on Capitol Hill, kept up a steady drumbeat of critical stories and editorials. Attempts by the foreign ministry's mobile consulates to distribute the *matrícula* periodically provoked controversy, with anti-immigrant groups in Oregon, Colorado, and California picketing in front of buildings where mobile consulates had set up shop (Millman 2006) and a Louisiana mayor forbidding use of a municipal building as a Mexican mobile consulate after the state's US senator had called for the immigration service to arrest undocumented immigrants who might visit the consulate in order to obtain a *matrícula* (Dinan 2006).

However, the most important reactions came from Washington, where the Bush administration could not decide whether to accept or reject the card. As with other immigration matters, the *matrícula* drove a wedge through Republican ranks. Then-senator Richard Lugar, a veteran Republican closer to the political center than most, urged acceptance on the grounds that "cards that simplify identification of immigrants and facilitate their contact with Americans and our institutions are a benefit to public safety, not a liability" (quoted in Swarns 2003). With the Republican Senate Campaign Committee, by contrast, paying for a television ad that portrayed *matrícula* cardholders as terrorist threats, Republican social conservatives predictably championed rejection.

With political leaders deadlocked, bureaucrats decided. The General Service Administration began a pilot program to accept the *matrícula* as valid identification for entering federal buildings but reversed course a month later, after twelve congressional representatives protested (Egelko 2003). By contrast, the Transportation Security Administration recognized the card as valid identification for passengers seeking to fly within the United States. The key mover, however, was the Treasury Department, required by the Patriot Act to prescribe minimum identification and verification standards for the customers of financial institutions, with particular attention to the identification requirements of foreign nationals. The Treasury Department's 2002 report found "significant impediments to domestic financial institutions' ability to identify, much less verify, the identity of foreign nationals" (United States Department of the Treasury 2002: 1). Putting the problem of unauthorized immigrants to the side, the Treasury noted that "no single, uniform identification document exists for all foreign nationals" (8); consequently, "any identity verification system for foreign nationals will have to rely, at least to some extent, on foreign documents" (9). The Treasury further noted that more restrictive identification requirements might hamper other department initiatives, such as those that encouraged "unbanked" persons to use mainstream financial institutions. Hence, the Treasury proposed rules setting minimum standards but with considerable flexibility, recommending that banks accept "the number and country of issuance of any other government-issued document evidencing nationality or residence and bearing a photograph or similar safeguard." In a footnote, it provided a further, crucial detail: "Thus, the proposed regulations do not discourage bank acceptance of the 'matrícula consular' identity card that is being issued by the Mexican government to immigrants" (16).

Controversy immediately followed. Testifying before the House Subcommittee on Immigration, convened by a high-profile, Republican advocate of immigration restriction, the Department of Homeland Security questioned acceptance, contending that cards could be fraudulently acquired and then used as breeder documents to acquire other forms of documentation, such as a driver's license (Verdery 2003). Testimony from the FBI's Office of Intelligence insisted that "it is the terrorist threat presented by the *Matrícula consular* that is the most worrisome . . . The ability of foreign nationals to use the *Matrícula Consular* to create a well-documented, but fictitious, identity in the United States provides an opportunity for terrorists to move freely within the United States" (McGraw 2003: 112). By contrast, the State Department provided supportive testimony, highlighting obligations incumbent under international law. Not only was the United States bound to allow foreign consuls to distribute identification cards to their citizens on US soil but the State Department itself issued similar cards to US citizens traveling abroad and therefore worried that "taking action against consular identification cards might foreclose our options to document or assist Americans overseas" (R. Jacobson 2003: 142).

The Treasury's recommendation, posted in the Federal Registry on July 1, 2003, generated over 34,000 comments (Bruno and Storrs 2005: 4). As described by the *American Banker* the banking industry went "on the offensive" (Jackson 2003), opposing any move to limit the card's use. Wells Fargo informed the Treasury that it had opened more than twenty-five thousand *InterCuenta Express* and *Dinero al Instante* accounts for Mexican immigrants looking for a convenient way to send remittances and praised the consular card's security features, which it described as "superior to many [US] state-issued driver's licenses and identification" (Esterl 2003). Ultimately, the Treasury opted not to recommend any further changes, much to the satisfaction of both banks and the Mexican government (Porter 2003).

The pragmatic arguments submitted by banking interests in favor of the *matrícula* crystallized the frame that supporters developed. Hearings conducted by a subcommittee of the Republican-controlled House Committee on Finance showed how both right and left sides of the congressional aisles lined up to refocus the debate toward mundane, local-level concerns and the positive consequences ramifying beyond immigrant populations. Congressman Chris Cannon, a conservative Utah Republican described by the *Washington Post* as Bush's "point man on immigration" (Milbank 2001), turned the usual security argument on its head, maintaining that "the absence of identification poses the real threat." By bringing immigrants, "legal and otherwise" into the banking system, he noted that "consular ID cards can deliver substantial economic benefits to both the holder of the card and to the US economy in general" (Cannon 2003: 8).

Similarly, liberal South Texas Democrat Rubén Hinojosa, author of a bill *requiring* banks to accept the *matrícula,* contended that the consular card would "infuse our banks, credit unions, and ultimately our economy with much-needed cash" (Hinojosa 2003: 4). Immigrant advocates and ethnic organizations rounded off the case by noting the public safety aspects: the National Council of La Raza maintained that "Mexican consular IDs are critical to public safety, crime prevention, and investigation," making "entire communities safer" (2003). Similarly, the Mexican American Legal Defense Fund, arguing that the *matrícula* was safer, easier to use, and more secure than a Mexican passport, also asserted that "acceptance of the Mexican consular ID has a proven track record of increasing public safety" (MALDEF 2003).

Though the Treasury's decision sealed this first phase of debate, the issue kept festering, along with the larger immigration dilemma. Republican proponents of restriction went furthest in 2004: the House Appropriations Committee approved language in its fiscal 2005 Treasury Department spending bill that would have prohibited banks from accepting consular cards as identification. Along with the White House, which was then fruitlessly pursuing a larger package of immigration reform, banks successfully fought back, preventing the House bill from going any further (*Congressional Quarterly Weekly* 2004). Later years saw continued but inconclusive skirmishing in both houses of Congress and in state legislatures.

Ultimately, the pattern entailed limited, patchwork, *de facto* acceptance. Although direct uses of the cards lay "in the very narrow band of public and private services for which high-quality identification is required, but proof of legal residency is not" (O'Neil 2003), they nonetheless produced sustained demand. Since the private sector discovered ways of turning the immigrants' liminality into a source of profit, institutional acceptance also gradually expanded. As of mid-2008, the Mexican Foreign Ministry reported that more than 7.5 million consular cards had been distributed since 2000, with almost 500,000 distributed during the first half of 2008 alone (Secretaría de Relaciones Exteriores 2008: 239). On the other hand, more ambitious hopes, entertained by the Ministry as well as immigrant advocates in the United States, seemed unlikely to be realized. While a few states had early allowed the *matrícula* to serve as proof of identification when applying for a driver's license, that option was eventually foreclosed. Passage of the REAL ID act, shepherded by proponents of reduced immigration, mandated a set of uniform, nationwide standards for acquisition of a driver's license; by requiring that applicants present "valid documentary evidence" of lawful presence in the United States (Federal Register 2008), the regulations ensured that the uses of the *matrícula* would remain highly circumscribed.

## Expatriate Voting

Though interest in expatriate voting dates back to the 1920s, the issue took on new salience in the 1980s, as Mexico's democratization opened up opportunities for migrant activists.[2] Renewed interested was triggered in 1988, when Cuahtémoc Cárdenas, having split from the ruling *Partido Revolucionario Institucional* and running an insurgent candidacy for president, looked for support in the United States. Migration-related spillovers of the same social crisis that fueled *cardenismo* in Mexico generated a US-based constituency. Consequently, *"cardenismo* built upon longstanding grievances and alienation, and was able to recover important themes that left-wing political organizers in the US had been proposing for years" (Dresser 1993: 96). In addition to supporters, the United States furnished a protected space, as explained by scholar-turned-politician Jesús Martínez Saldaña describing the activists who mobilized in Silicon Valley:

> An important resource for the *cardenista* forces of Silicon Valley and possibly other US regions was its autonomy from the Mexican state. Ever since the *porfiriato,* the Mexican government had participated in political spying and infiltration of Mexican organizations in the United States. With all certainty, that tradition continued . . . but migrant activists could count on more tolerance, better security, and also a less-censored press than in their homeland. (Martínez Saldaña 2002: 220)

Repeatedly demonstrating in front of consulates in Los Angeles and San Jose and confronting both consular officials and visiting political leaders, the vote activists made full use of the resources created by their extraterritorial location. Consequently, as described by the Mexican sociologist, Arturo Santamaría Gómez, "In few places in Mexico could one see members of the [opposition party] confront consular officials and government emissaries so openly. At the same time, few Mexican functionaries had ever performed in an environment where neither the press, nor the radio nor the television was supported and where one had to accept the critical and belligerent tone of one's opponents, without recourse to threats, bribery, corporatist control or other illegitimate means" (1994: 166–167).

Since the 1988 election results were so hotly contested, cross-border mobilization continued. Following the *cardenistas'* success in mobilizing a massive demonstration in Los Angeles, first Cárdenas' *Partido Revolucionario Democratico* (PRD) and then the ruling *Partido Revolucionario Institucional* (PRI) took their competition to the United States, seeking to win migrants' loyalties and, through the migrants, those of their kin back home, while also burnishing reputations among Chicano elites and gaining legitimacy in Washington.

As candidate, Cárdenas endorsed expatriate voting, giving it a prominence it had not previously enjoyed. More important, the growing influence of opposition parties from both right and left ultimately compelled the PRI to agree to sweeping electoral reforms, eventuating in the creation of the Federal Elections Institute (*Instituto Federal Electoral* [IFE]), "an independent entity, entirely autonomous from the federal Executive branch, which in turn lost any capacity to determine the Institute's composition" (Becerra et al. 1997: 34). Principally designed to increase electoral transparency and reduce the potential for manipulation, the final package approved in 1996 included a provision which "*de facto* opened the possibility of exercising the external vote" (Calderón Chelius 2003: 226) by eliminating the requirement that ballots be cast in the district to which the elector belonged. Implementation, however, was left to the future.

No sooner were expatriate voting rights enshrined by the electoral reforms of 1996 than the issue fell from view. Activists then sought to put it back on the agenda, holding mock elections in US cities; traveling to Mexico to lobby officials and gain media attention; forming an organized pressure group—the Coalition of Mexicans Abroad: Our Vote in 2000; and later holding a series of highly publicized meetings in the United States and Mexico, including encounters with officials of the newly created IFE and with Vicente Fox, then-governor of the state of Guanajuato but shortly thereafter president of Mexico (Saldaña and Pineda 2002). IFE's release of a report on the feasibility of expatriate voting provided additional momentum: the specialists who had been convened by IFE concluded that it was "technically possible to accomplish the 2000 Presidential election with the participation of Mexican voters in the exterior" (*Instituto Federal Electoral* 1998 [2004]: 21), though they also noted that implementation would be difficult and costly and stopped short of endorsing any specific plan (Woldenberg 2004). Nonetheless, release of the report led the more conservative *Partido Acción Nacional* to join the PRD in backing the extension of voting rights. Worried that immigrant voters would flock to the opposition, *Priista* leaders ensured that no change would be made by the 2000 presidential election.

That contest ended the PRI's decades-long monopoly on power, bringing to office Vicente Fox of the *Partido Acción Nacional,* who had campaigned as a champion of migrants' rights. Fox expanded preexisting programs of diaspora engagement, leading to closer contact with the US-based partisans of expatriate voting. For the most part, the latter involved a highly selective group of longtime US residents, hometown association and (Mexican) state federation leaders and entrepreneurs, professionals, journalists, and academics (Escamilla-Hamm 2009). Though each side was interested in co-opting the other, the government's program of diaspora engagement gave the activists a new, high-profile, legitimate platform: In 2004, the Consultative Council of the Institute of Mexicans Abroad endorsed not only expatriate voting but also an active effort at verifying the credentials of prospective immigrant voters (Instituto de los Mexicanos al Extranjero 2004; Hernandez 2005). Unlike the undocumented immigrants who could neither return home freely nor exercise full rights in the United States, the vote activists suffered no similar constraints. Benefiting from either legal permanent residence or US citizenship, they traveled to Mexico for lobbying and meetings with top government officials, to whom they submitted draft legislation, while simultaneously organizing US-side conclaves aimed at mobilizing immigrant supporters (Escamilla-Hamm 2009). As these efforts gained traction in the public realm, all the political parties prepared to line up in support. Between 1998 and 2004, the Mexican congress considered almost twenty bills, almost all favoring expatriate voting (McCann, Cornelius, and Leal 2009).

The expatriate voting rights approved in 2005 fell far short of activists' expectations. The legislation allowed Mexicans abroad to vote in presidential elections only, not state or local contests, as advocates had hoped; it prohibited candidates and parties from campaigning abroad, thus reducing participation; it mandated postal voting rather than voting at consulates, as many of the activists would have preferred; it limited participation to migrants already possessing the electoral credential, available only in Mexico, as opposed to the *matrícula consular,* available in the United States; last, it required eligible voters to send, via registered mail, a written request that they be included in a register of voters abroad, doing so in a three-and-a-half-month period, well before the most intensive period of campaigning would have begun. Activists in the United States did what they could to encourage the vote, using "their resources (e.g., skills, contacts, electronic networks, and infrastructure) to organize campaigns in communities across the United States in order to inform expatriates of the new legislation, facilitate voter registration, and get out the vote" (Escamilla-Hamm 2009: 111) and going so far as to organize a caravan that took residents of southern California to Tijuana to obtain a voting credential, an activity explicitly limited to those authorized to leave and reenter the United States (Truax 2005). Not surprisingly, only 40,786 emigrants registered to vote, 80 percent of whom later cast a ballot (Navarro Fierro and Carillo 2007).

A variety of factors, including the heavily undocumented nature of Mexican migration and the low socioeconomic background of the migrants depressed participation. While it is hard to quarrel with McCann, Cornelius, and Leal in concluding that "the legislation that allowed expatriates to vote ... made it practically difficult for them to do so" (2009: 145), asking about the available options and taking a second look at the identity of the relevant actors and the circumstances under which they intervened might explain why this particular path was chosen.

The key actors were to be found both south and north of the Rio Grande; US political and economic figures whose responses proved crucial in the deployment of the *matrícula* had no direct involvement in this debate. Nonetheless, the significance of territory and the migrants' location in a foreign land figured prominently in the competing frames developed by proponents and opponents of the expatriate vote movement.

The repertoire developed by vote movement activists connected nationalism to democratization, though with undertones reminding listeners of the migrants' economic contributions. Activists invoked membership, belonging, and loyalty to a deterritorialized Mexican nation. Analyzing the early stage of the vote movement, Perez-Godoy describes the claims as "integrationist," in the sense of constructing "a transnational community of Mexicans ... that extended beyond the territorial boundaries of the Mexican nation" (1998: 79). While the pro-vote activists referred to the migrants as "Mexicans in the diaspora," whom they describe as "transnational persons" (Coalición 2004: 354), their claims were not so much transnational as nationalist and patriotic, as summed up in a proposal submitted by a pro-vote coalition to the Mexican congress in 2003:

> The Mexicans that left the country never renounced their pride in their national origin or their rights and obligations ... The migrants have been admirable defenders of the language, the culture, and the civic traditions of the Mexican nation. (Coalición 2004: 353)

Proponents also contended that franchise extension was a matter of rights, inherent in the emigrants' Mexican citizenship, and one that would give them influence over consuls and other sending-state institutions that they encountered as migrants in the United States[3] while also consolidating Mexico's democratic transition. Buttressing these claims were reminders of the importance of the migrants' economic contributions, as underscored in the pro-vote coalition's proposal:

> The migrants directly sustain more than a million families that remain in Mexico, keep states and regional economies alive, and comprise the country's second most important source of currency. (Coalición 2004: 353)

By contrast, opponents of expatriate voting developed a frame that sought to discredit the migrants' membership claims by invoking the emigrants' foreign location and possibly foreign affiliation. Since expatriate voters would include naturalized US citizens, election results might be decided by "a group of foreign citizens, many of them living for years outside of Mexico, with a knowledge of the country not what it should be" (Carpizo and Valadés 1998: 109). Whereas the pro-vote activists presented themselves as true Mexicans, opponents suggested that they might instead be *norteamericanos,* with loyalties to that foreign country:

> Thus, millions of armed defenders of the North American flag would continue being Mexican citizens and voting in our Presidential election, doing so equally in a *barrio* of Los Angeles as in a base in Guantánamo. (Carpizo and Valadés 1998: 57)

Since US employers could easily sway the votes of vulnerable Mexican migrants, opponents further reasoned that franchise extension would provide yet another means of widening US interference in Mexican affairs.

Thus, in an echo of the restrictionists on the US side of the border, Mexican nationalists saw any extraterritorial influence as an infringement on national sovereignty. By contrast, political officials emphasized more pragmatic considerations related to matters of state. Consequently, Luis Derbez, foreign minister from 2003 to 2006 under Fox, insisted that the Mexican consular network lacked the capacity to serve as voting stations. Derbez also worried about repercussions in the United States:

> We cannot rule out the possibility that the celebration of Mexican elections in the US will reinforce the position of conservative US sectors and radicalize the anti-immigrant groups . . . Implementing a process of photocredentialization by millions of potential voters could have the collateral impact of eroding confidence in the *matrícula consular.* (quoted in Santamaría Gómez 2006: 103)

While elite views diverged from popular opinion, which favored the expatriate vote, they also resonated broadly: the same public that favored the vote also worried about the costs and potential for fraud involved in organizing elections in another country, as well as the possibility that the migrant vote might decide the election (Consulta Mitovsky 2004). Likewise, as shown by a variety of surveys, public opinion diverged from the emigrant vote activists in opposing campaigning abroad; in preferring that voting be limited to the presidential race (Centro de Estudios Sociales y de Opinión Pública [CESOP] 2006); and in rejecting, by a very large majority, the possibility that a dual national could be elected a federal deputy or senator, let alone president.[3]

Thus, the migrants' presence on the territory of another state provided both the leverage to exercise pressure *and* the basis by which their opponents constructed a counterframe. Paradoxically, Mexico's democratization, which initially facilitated the effort to expand the vote extraterritorially, also worked against that cause. As noted by IFE's expert commission, the costs and scale entailed in reproducing Mexico's voting system on US soil made that proposition a practical impossibility (Woldenberg 2004: 304–305). Consequently, any design of an expatriate electoral system would have to confront difficult choices: how to guarantee universal, equal, and secret suffrage; how to regulate party competition; how to prevent offenses against electoral law. Because expatriate voting would take place on the territory of a different, sovereign state, Mexico could neither provide external voters with the same security available on its own territory nor furnish a mechanism for resolving disputes should extraterritorial votes or campaign practices be contested (Nohlen and Grotz 2000, 2007). Each option involved its own set of trade-offs. Postal voting would reduce costs and yield the greatest coverage but would also entail greater security risks (*Instituto Federal Electoral* 1998 [2004]). Greater security could be achieved by voting in consulates or special election booths but at higher cost and to the detriment of voters living in areas of lower immigrant density. Moreover, the more ambitious the goals—such as expatriate voting for state as well as presidential elections—the higher the costs and the more difficult the logistical problems. While costs could be diminished by contracting electoral services to local electoral districts in the United States—as suggested by Illinois officials (*La Jornada* 2007)—collaborations of this sort put electoral management into the receiving state's control, raising just the issues of national autonomy and sovereignty flagged by vote opponents.

These factors took on particular significance in the Mexican context, tying the activists' hands. While the IFE was one of the few Mexican political institutions enjoying high confidence both among the public and across the parties (Camp 2007: 30), the problems inherent in expatriate voting threatened its integrity. Moreover, internal democratization raised the bar for external voting, since "the more sophisticated and exacting is the internal electoral regime, in terms of guarantees of security, confidence, and equity, the greater are the difficulties in replicating and controlling it abroad" (Navarro 2007: 251). Having framed the expatriate vote as an extension of Mexico's democratization, the activists could offer only solutions that would consolidate those gains, not weaken them. Hence, the issue of how external voters could prove eligibility turned out to be a fatal stumbling block.

Though described as "universal," in fact, all democratic suffrage systems restrict voting to a smaller class of eligible citizens. On home territory, age, mental ability, and residence comprise the criteria that electoral systems use for determining which nationals can enjoy the right to vote (Blais et al. 2001); once nationals cross the border, expatriate electoral systems also need to identify nationality, which is why documenting nationality is a standard feature of expatriate voting systems (Navarro 2007). Following the reform of Mexico's electoral system, persons wanting to cast a ballot *in* Mexico were required to present a tamperproof voter registration card, the *credencial para votar con fotografía* (CVPF), or electoral credential, to be checked against the electoral registry, which reproduced the photograph appearing on each credential (Becerra et al. 1997). Since the *credencial electoral* had only been introduced in the early 1990s, longer established immigrants were unlikely to have obtained it before leaving home. By the late 1990s, the credential was already functioning as a de facto identity card *in* Mexico, over time becoming almost universally possessed by Mexico's adult population.[4] Nonetheless, emigrants were likely to leave home without the credential in hand. As noted by Castañeda, "getting caught with documents, particularly authentic ones is perilous" for undocumented immigrants, which is why identifying documents are quickly disposed of, "in compliance with the coyote's instructions" (2007: 144). As the credential was of no use in the United States, migrants who brought it with them had no need to retain it.

As it gradually became clear that no one knew just how many migrants crossed the border with the *credencial electoral* in hand, all experts agreed that the great majority of migrants lacked a credential; hence, enfranchising the emigrants would necessarily entail a significant effort to check eligibility and provide proof of identity. However, the credential could be obtained only on site in Mexico. The activists advocated a registration process that would allow "potential voters to obtain a voter ID card without returning to Mexico" (Smith and Bakker 2008: 138), but that option lacked traction. Foreign ministry officials worried that any US-based effort to disseminate the electoral credential might raise questions about the *matrícula consular,* in whose credibility an enormous investment had been made (Truax 2005). Consuls in the United States insisted that they lacked the resources and funds needed to disseminate simultaneously an electoral card *and* furnish migrants with the *matrícula* (Garcia 2005). Accepting the more widely available *matrícula* would have been the more practical alternative, but it was one to which activists could not accede, worrying that acceptance of the *matrícula* would bring the government back into election administration, from which it had been removed by mid-1990s reform package (Urrutia 2004). Using consular offices for the purposes of issuing electoral credentials would have had the same effect, as the consulates were entities of the foreign ministry.

Publicly, the activists appeared to bow to the inevitable (Rodríguez Oseguera 2005), contending that, for all its disappointing results, the 2006 election was the first step in a broader expansion of emigrant voting rights. Once the dust settled, discussion resumed where it had last ended. "We need the credential," complained an immigrant activist in the aftermath of the 2006 election. "Having the right to vote does not do us any good if we cannot do it without the credential and we do not have access to it; it is as if someone loans you the car, but doesn't put in gasoline" (Truax 2007).

## Conclusion

Wherever they go, international migrants maintain their ties to the people left behind, whether through travel, communication, material support, or political involvement. These grassroots, wildcat migrant actions resulting from intersocietal convergence yield responses from sending states trying to influence, if not control, the behavior of nationals living abroad and turn their residence in a rich country to good account. With a century-long history of migration to the United States and roughly 10 percent of its population living outside its boundaries, Mexico has extended experience in responding to the spillovers of migration, which is why its engagement with Mexican emigrants has interested scholars and policy makers alike.

This chapter applies the framework developed in the previous chapter to gain traction on the politics of emigration by comparing two of its salient aspects: sending-state policies linked to the problems encountered by *citizens living abroad as aliens* and those related to efforts, whether initiated by states or by emigrants, to maintain *membership in the homeland* where the emigrants no longer reside. The literature insists that simultaneous embeddedness in two societies is a salient aspect of the immigrant reality, facilitated by the new, postnationalist, multicultural environment, which provides greater allowance for the retention and even the public expression of home country loyalties. But as both cases demonstrate, the relational nature of national identity, defined in contrast to alien states and people, ensured that claims made by *aliens* in their *place of residence* or by *citizens* residing in *alien places* would trigger hostile reactions.

The vigorous but highly selective campaign for the expatriate vote highlights the politics of *emigrant membership*. The *emigrant* activists presented themselves as displaced but true members of the Mexican nation, and also as Mexican citizens for whom the vote was a right. *Sotto voce,* they claimed that their remittances helped pay Mexico's bills. In their self-presentation, the activists appeared to be those very people "living lives across borders" identified by the scholarly literature on transnationalism. Mexican opponents of expatriate voting, however, saw things very differently, looking askance at the very idea that national loyalties could be shared. The ideologically minded, advancing views of nationhood that mirrored those put forth by the US critics of the *matrícula,* saw the activists as either *norteamericanos* or instruments of greater US influence. Pragmatically minded officials and bureaucrats, all too aware that their compatriots suffered from *nonincorporation* in the United States, were less concerned with emigrants' claims to belonging to a cross-border Mexican nation than with the negative reactions that expatriate voting might produce among the *norteamericanos* themselves.

By contrast, the case of the *matrícula consular* exemplifies the politics of *protecting citizens abroad.* In moving to the United States, Mexican *immigrants* discovered that arrival in a richer, freer country led neither to political incorporation nor to a basic, stable package of rights; moreover, they encountered a series of persistent, practical problems threatening their hopes for continued residence and also disrupting their ability to support close associates at home. In turn, these difficulties produced an opening for intervention by a sending state that otherwise had "little to offer its emigrants" (Fitzgerald 2009: 161). Though permitted, sending-state engagement was difficult to manage. As noted by Mexican diplomat, Carlos González Gutierrez: "A *sine qua non* of the consulates' activities is to ensure that nothing they do constitutes interference in the domestic matters of the host country" (1998: 63). That Mexico's advocacy of the *matrícula* provoked such antagonism shows that the bounds of "interference" lie in the eyes of the beholder. The appropriate line had long been crossed for the restrictionists, who used the *matrícula* to revive long-standing, still potent views of immigrants as foreign sources of threat. While defenders of the consular card rose in defense, they opted to avoid these membership issues, preferring instead to emphasize narrow, pragmatic concerns, thereby demonstrating the ideological potency of the traditional view of national sovereignty advanced by the restrictionists.

Concluding that "transnational involvement does not . . . impede immigrant integration" (Levitt and Jaworsky 2007: 137), the literature assumes that emigrants' aspiration to belong to both home *and* host countries will yield acceptance on receiving state soil, which is why it understands the politics of emigration as involving a dyadic interaction between emigrant activists and homeland political elites. However, the politics of the *matrícula consular* entailed a far more complex relational nexus, sweeping up migrants; homeland officials; and a highly conflicted, diverse set of host-state elites. As opposed to expatriate voting, the migrants did *not* undertake concerted action, a role seized by established, domestic groups with the capacity to intervene institutionally. On the other hand, the migrants engaged in large-scale parallel action: By quickly and massively applying for the *matrícula* and then putting it to use, they activated the interests of US-based entities, who then intervened to protect the *matrícula* for reasons of their own.

At first glance, Mexico's initial experience with expatriate voting may appear to fit the dyadic pattern involving interactions between emigrants, on the one hand, and home states, on the other. But as with the case of the *matrícula*, emigrant voting stimulated a broader set of negative reactions, most notably among civil society actors in Mexico, either for reasons of principle—thinking that residence abroad precluded membership in the home country polity—or for reasons of practicality—thinking that unpredictable emigrant votes could sway an election. Though the issue stirred no controversy in the United States, whether on the part of state officials or civil society actors, all parties attended to that possibility. Experience elsewhere, such as Germany, Australia, and even Canada, shows that proposals to encourage expatriate voting have elicited allergic responses from both host authorities and immigrant advocates, who see immigrant homeland involvement as impeding integration. Consequently, the politics of expatriate voting necessarily includes the host country, if not as an engaged player, then at least as a latent actor.

If both cases underscore the capacity deficit *inherent* in sending states' engagements with emigrants, the contrasting experience also underscores a source of fundamental *variation*. As we have seen, location matters, with foreign *origins* possibly discrediting the immigrants among the nationals in whose midst they live and foreign *residence* discrediting them among the nationals they left behind. No less important is the *place* toward which emigration policies are directed. The *matrícula consular* may not have delivered quite as much as Mexico's officials had hoped; still, it improved life for masses of *immigrants*, as indicated by the fact that millions so eagerly embraced it and then put it to good use. By intervening in the state where the *immigrants* actually lived, Mexico provided its *citizens abroad* with protection, giving them a practical tool well suited to the existing, on-site infrastructure, and one whose utility was appreciated by US financial institutions as well. Once having welcomed customers possessing the *matrícula*, banks and other like institutions then had a vested interest in its continued recognition; as noted in the Treasury report, so too did the US government because measures that brought unbanked persons into the financial system served other, valued policy ends. Similarly, what served Mexico well also converged with the ideal and material interests of immigrant rights advocates and ethnic organizations, who, working in parallel, and often in tandem with Mexican consuls, mobilized to get approval at the state and local levels, where they achieved significant success.

Further lessons can be found in the striking parallels to the "wanted but not welcomed" syndrome that characterizes Mexican migration overall, as the politics of the *matrícula* reproduced the strange bedfellows coalition characterizing the politics of immigration policy (Zolberg 1999; Tichenor 2002), with both right and left uniting in defense of the *matrícula's* acceptance. Likewise, the bureaucratic responses resemble the "smoke and mirrors," "border games" family of migration policies, not providing acceptance but not taking the hard, self-injurious steps that would have been entailed in outright rejection. However, contrary to scholars (Bakker 2011) who present the *matrícula* as an illustration of the "rescaling of citizenship," this case entailed no extension of *rights*—which, by definition, are universal, inviolate, and codified in law. Rather, the response by US authorities involved a series of pragmatic, ad hoc, uneven measures, of which the most important—intervention by the US Treasury—was purely discretionary and could be changed by a stroke of a pen from one minute to the next. The tacit but limited acceptance accorded the *matrícula* simply allowed all parties to continue with business as usual, making it easier for *immigrants* to adapt to their circumstances without in any way gaining membership or statutory enhancement of their status.

Thus, by attending to the needs of *immigrants* who were themselves needed by US domestic actors, Mexico found a productive avenue for engagement, albeit one that led to only mixed success. Even so, investments of this sort, which entail helping a population that "has decided to leave the country and settle permanently in the United States," add to the obligations of states "with so few resources and so many domestic problems" (1993: 225), to again cite Carlos González Gutierrez. But in contrast to the *matrícula consular* or other sending-state policies directed toward the state in which *immigrants* actually live, systems designed to facilitate *emigrant* voting entail a far more disadvantageous mix of costs and benefits. While a small group of activists campaigned intensely to gain expatriate voting rights, no such passion was evinced by the immigrant rank and file, who generally pay little attention to homeland political matters, as explained in Chapter 5.

Though activists and scholars often contended that the novelty of the 2006 election deterred participation, results from the presidential election of 2012 indicate otherwise: despite significant efforts by Mexico's electoral authority at building electoral awareness, the number of votes cast from the United States barely budged, rising by just over one thousand (*Instituto Federal Electoral* 2012). In thus detaching from homeland elections, Mexican immigrants in the United States have simply acted much like their counterparts elsewhere in the world. As noted by the *Handbook on Voting from Abroad*, "rates of registration and turnout among external voters are almost always lower than they are in-country" (Ellis and Wall 2007: 262). That pattern can be widely detected, whether the benchmark comes from long-established systems of expatriate voting, like France's or Sweden's, or from the newer systems, such as those that have sprouted elsewhere in Latin America (Ellis and Wall 2007; Navarro 2007). The same holds true even when the expatriate electoral system is relatively friendly—as demonstrated by the case of the 2004 election for president of the Dominican Republic, when migrants accounted for less than 1 percent of the vote (Itzigsohn and Villacres 2008: 672). Turnout levels drop even further when expatriates are allowed to vote at the substate level: of the roughly four million emigrants from the Mexican state of Michoacan living in the United States, fewer than 1,000 chose to register in 2007, when *Michoacanos* abroad were first allowed to vote in state elections (Espinoza Valle 2008).

Consequently, expatriate voting represents a "'boutique' form of engagement . . . open to only a select few" (Leal et al. 2012: 548). The activists, unlike the undocumented immigrants flocking to the consulates in search of protection, comprised an elite enjoying the freedom not just to press their demands by demonstrating in front of consulates but also to return to Mexico repeatedly for face-to-face lobbying of state officials. Those immigrants who opted to vote were no less selective, bearing little resemblance to the rank-and-file immigrant, and possessing especially strong ties to Mexico. As discovered by a survey of voters living in the United States conducted by Mexico's *Instituto Federal Electoral* (*Instituto Federal Electoral* 2006), 37 percent possessed a college degree and another 31 percent had completed some postgraduate work, 82 percent described themselves as "very interested" in Mexican politics (whereas only 12 percent of the almost 4,000 Mexican immigrants polled in the Latino National Survey told pollsters that they paid "a lot of attention" to Mexican politics), 40 percent had sent remittances to Mexico at least once in the previous three months, and 19 percent belonged to an immigrant organization (as opposed to 4 percent among those polled by the Latino National Survey).

Reconnecting with the homeland—whether to cast a ballot, to furnish talent or technical assistance gained from experience acquired abroad, or

to help out a community left behind—satisfies the patriotic or philanthropic wants of those *emigrants* who no longer require home state intervention for resolution of everyday needs associated with the *immigrant*
condition. Whereas sending-state policies designed to facilitate *immigrants' integration abroad* build on other processes that embed the newcomers in the place where they live, policies like the expatriate vote, which
reconnect *emigrants* with their *homeland,* are more likely to generate conflict. Like the vote activists, other reengaged emigrants—be they investors, inventers, or philanthropists—link up again with ideas and resources
that can threaten established interests—often of the very people who were
happy to see the emigrants go.

Moreover, catering to the wants of the small fraction of intensely politicized migrants entails the nontrivial costs of establishing an infrastructure *de novo,* in a place where the price of doing business exceeds the
comparable levels found at home. Mexico's initial experiment in expatriate voting proved highly costly, involving an expenditure of $27.7 mil-
lion, or $1,200 per expatriate vote cast (Ellis and Wall 2007: 262). While
startup operations are always expensive, Mexico's investment in external
voting in the 2012 election proved almost as costly as the 2006 effort,
yielding virtually no effect, as noted above (*Instituto Federal Electoral*
2012). Moreover, Mexico's experiences are paralleled elsewhere; thus, the
costs entailed in each Canadian expatriate vote are four times those dis-
bursed for in-country votes (Lesage 1998: 105), expenditures that are particularly striking because surveys indicate that Canadians abroad lack a
strong desire to vote (Zhang 2007). And whereas Canada and other developed states allowing external voting are rich countries whose expatriates
live abroad under conditions comparable to those at home, the same does
not hold for the emigration countries of the developing world. Moreover,
efforts by Mexico and other developing countries to invest in infrastruc-
tures facilitating emigrant voting effectively reallocate resources from
more deprived stay-at-homes to more prosperous migrants, living in more
secure societies with more abundant public goods.

The end results certainly left the vote activists frustrated. However,
their efforts did lead to an extension of the *rights* enjoyed by *emigrants,*
unlike the bureaucratic and inherently provisional decisions that allowed
*immigrants* to use the *matrícula* to solve some of their problems. That the
Mexican state bowed, at least in part, to the emigrants' demands is all the
more striking, given the relatively paltry number of emigrants who held
expatriate voting rights dear. In seeking to limit the practical impact of
the new legislation, Mexico acted much as sending states elsewhere: doing
what was needed to retain the emigrants' loyalty while minimizing the

likelihood that votes cast from abroad would alter electoral outcomes at home. Yet, as we have seen, symbolism did not come cheap.

The contrast between the two policies examined in this chapter reflects the duality at the heart of the migrant situation: *immigrants* are also *emigrants*. While sending states and emigrants *can* reach across borders to rebuild or expand membership in the political community left behind, those efforts take place in a territory that the home country cannot control and where—*relative to home state elites*—the movers possess resources never previously enjoyed. As foreigners, the *immigrants* seek acceptance on host country soil; as expatriates, the *emigrants* seek recognition on native grounds. However, neither option fully holds. For that reason, the interaction between sending states and nationals abroad yields conflict in receiving and sending societies alike. Although inherently constrained, sending states can exercise influence when intervening on the receiving-society side, where the embeddedness of *immigration* provides a source of leverage. By contrast, efforts to reengage the *emigrants* back home yield a much less favorable outcome.

Thus, while the possibility that immigrants "live lives across borders" may be a beautiful ideal, appealing to cosmopolitan intellectuals and resonating with their own experience of frequent and easy cross-border movements, the mass of migrants going from poor to rich countries face a different reality. Their world is one in which national boundaries are crossed with difficulty, only to settle down among unwelcoming strangers. Though often succeeding in their search for a better life in a different country, realizing the *immigrant* quest threatens to dash the *emigrant* dream because life abroad in a different society and distinctive polity impedes their efforts to sustain the connection to the people and places left behind.

# CHAPTER EIGHT

# Hometown Blues

## *Migrants' Long-Distance Pursuit of Development*

D ISPLACED FROM familiar ground and treated as strangers, migrants often discover a commonality in people originating from the same place. Since they may find comfort in the company of a familiar face, gain pleasure from reminiscing about times gone by, or derive satisfaction from the effort to make things better for the home and hometowners left behind, migrant hometowners repeatedly come together.

These connections and the organizations and activities that they spawn comprise a migration universal, to be found wherever and whenever long-distance migration occurs (Moya 2005). But today, emigrants' spontaneous efforts to use the resources captured in the rich place of residence in order to transform the poorer place of origin have gathered attention from new quarters, taking on unprecedented importance and attracting unparalleled interest.

The spotlight has been trained on humble hometown associations because policy makers worldwide increasingly think that migration might trigger development, thus conveniently sparing developed societies of the future immigrants that the former don't want. Motivating this view is increased awareness of the size of the remittance streams; seen as an effective means of reducing poverty *and* as a form of self-help, remittances have become the "new development mantra" (Kapur 2005). Whether the monies harvested by migration yield positive or negative effects is a question, however, to which research provides no firm answer. Thus, while remittances arriving in developing societies may cushion migrants' families against a variety of setbacks, their protective value depends on the nature of the shock: as soon as the great recession hit in 2008, widespread layoffs among the migrants shriveled the flow of monies heading to the developing world. Considerable evidence suggests that children in families receiving remittances, as opposed to those living without help from abroad, are more likely to continue with schooling, though the amounts of additional education obtained may be modest; since "remittances alone cannot remove the structural constraints to economic growth" (United Nations Development Program 2009: 79), rewards to small or modest gains in education are likely to be highly uncertain. Any economic gains to remittances also need to be balanced against the social and psychological costs that occur when migration splits families apart.

Exchanges between migrants and stay-at-homes can also yield the transmission of ideas, norms, expectations, skills, and contacts acquired in the society of destination. Capitalizing on the interest in worker remittances, some scholars have advanced the concept of "social" or "political" remittances to characterize these flows (Levitt 1998; Pérez-Armendáriz and Crow 2009). While the notion is intuitively appealing, it also entails a sleight of hand: worker remittances flow through the ties linking the senders of support abroad to specific recipients at home; by contrast, "social" or "political" remittances are generated when migrants export the new ideas, skills, and tastes gained from life abroad, which in turn diffuse well beyond the migrants' own egocentric networks. As expressed by a World Bank study, a hopeful view sees migrants serving as bridges, "providing access to market, sources of investment, and expertise" while also helping to "shape public debate, articulate reform plans and help implement reforms and new projects" (Kuznetsov and Sabel 2006: 3). Though transforming brain drain into brain gain is the most alluring way of activating the diaspora, there is considerable interest in the positive spillovers that could be harvested from the far more numerous low-skilled migrants.

The great bulk of migrant remittances result from the individual preferences of immigrants acting in parallel, uncoordinated fashion. But the very nature of migration leads migrants to engage in collective activities that might channel their resources in a very different way. After all, migration is a networked phenomenon in which connections between veterans and newcomers both provide the resources needed to move to a strange land and then get activated in order to help solve the problems associated with settlement: getting oriented, finding a place to live, getting a job, learning the skills needed to move ahead. While the most basic forms of help come from the closest of associates—namely, kin—other preexisting connections, in particular those to others with origins in the same place, get activated. Once together, the migrants often turn toward their hometown, pooling their earnings to improve conditions in the place left behind.

In putting their own hands into their pockets and taking out change to be given to others, the migrants effectively turn themselves into philanthropists. Though the monies that they can generate will never add up to the huge flow of resources heading from individual migrants to their families, even a small fraction could yield significant effects in the communities from which the migrants come.

From the standpoint of policy makers concerned with development, migrant philanthropy has other virtues: in particular, it appears to be a grassroots phenomenon, an important asset now that the prevailing wisdom suggests that economic performance and broader participation go hand in glove (Burgess 2005). No less interested in "collective remittances," sending-state officials realize that migrants are political actors, deploying resources that make it impossible for them to be ignored. As noted in Chapters 6 and 7, the migrants' extraterritorial location deprives sending states of their capacity to extract taxes from nationals abroad. Yet in banding together to help their hometowns, migrants are providing money for free, reason for cash-strapped governments in developing societies to find ways of keeping the flow moving.

Whether immigrants residing abroad can access the resources needed for the investments that their home communities require is open to doubt—especially at a time when the developed world is stuck in recession, a downturn that has struck the immigrants particularly hard. But on the grounds that prosperity is likely to return someday, this chapter puts that skepticism aside to ask instead, "How do the conditions inherent in the immigrant experience affect the potential for effective intervention back home?" On the one hand, as shown in Chapters 5, 6, and 7, movement to a rich country generates the resources that make homeland investment and engagement possible. On the other hand, as we have seen in Chapter 4, time and distance matter. Though initially connected, the immigrants detach; as their sojourn abroad increases, the immigrants increasingly take on the orientations of the people among whom they live.

In this chapter, I pursue this question by examining the migration universal of associations that bring together movers displaced from a common hometown abroad. Sociologically interesting, these hometown associations (HTAs) highlight the convergence of academic preoccupations and the real world, with scholars, international organizations, and sending-state actors all picking up their antennae, as noted above. Most important, they provide us with a strategic research site, allowing us to take apart the two very different aspects—namely, state and nation—that the popular transnational concept has so unfortunately conflated. In coming together with their fellow hometowners, the immigrants show their attachment to a social collectivity defined in terms of common origin in some other place. But that the long-distance identification of the migrant hometowners often takes the form of a "brotherhood of memory" (Weisser 1989) involving social support and the exercise of nostalgia among migrants living in the place of destination does not yet entail cross-state action that connects them to the stay-at-homes. Crucially, however, the upsurge of contemporary hometown-oriented activity, while also nostalgia-driven, involves cross-state spillovers, in which resources generated "here" are used for ends "there." As I will now show, the potential for home country involvement at once derives from and is shaped by the bounded, receiving-state resources that give the migrants new leverage not found before. Rather than linking immigrants and stay-at-homes in a single transnational community or social field, the cross-state activities undertaken by hometown associations yield not so much cross-state community but cross-state conflict, reproducing inequalities between migrants and the stay-at-homes in ways that reflect the inequalities between receiving and sending places.

## Hometown Associations:
### The Politics of Long-Distance Attachments

Hometown associations may be ubiquitous. But even if almost omnipresent, they are not necessarily all the same. Just what ends the associations promote—do they simply provide a space for socializing or do they fulfill some more instrumental end?—has long been a matter of dispute (Sassen-Koob 1979; Basch 1987.) The stimulus for associations derives from universal aspects of the migration process, yet scholars still debate the degree to which influences stemming from the sending, as opposed to the receiving, country shape the form and content of associational life. Though associations appear among both internal and international migrants, taking on similar forms and functioning in like ways, the question of whether the crucial influence stems from long or social distance on the one hand, or the crossing of a political border on the other, remains in play (as discussed in D. Fitzgerald 2008).

The ubiquity of the migrants' propensity for association might explain why the most influential studies of the phenomenon called transnationalism have instead focused on these cross-border, bilocal connections, linking particular places in sending and receiving states. Indeed, the most widely cited, influential empirical studies almost always involve research of this kind. Yet these sorts of localistic ties reappear in similar form just about everywhere that long-distance migration occurs, resulting from the stranger-native interaction, which is why a place-based identity is discovered only *after* dispersion *from* that place.[1] Consequently, *bilocalism* becomes an enduring source of identity and organization, reappearing in similar, if not identical, form among internal and international migrants alike.

To say that trans-state bilocalism strongly resembles intrastate bilocalism is not to say that they are the same. *Within* the national container, developed and developing states have often turned peasants into nationals, while intrastate regional differences have also declined. Both changes have reduced the displacing impact of internal migration, attenuating the impetus to seek solace in the company of those hometowners who have similarly converged on the big city. By contrast, the move across the national border generally remains a more deeply foreign experience, though less so in developing societies, where strangeness is still enough to bring contemporary migrants together with their fellow hometowners, as among Kurds in today's Istanbul (Celik 2005). Likewise, time-space compression has weakened intraborder localism, as internal migrants seeking to indulge hometown longings need no longer turn to one another but can instead return for a visit at relatively low costs (D. Fitzgerald 2008). Since distance, by contrast, is more likely to impede international migrants, who also need the right documents in order to return home, the bond to fellow hometowners in the place of destination is more likely to remain strong. Again, the difference is one of degree, not of kind, as illuminated by an article on the use of the Internet in the diaspora, the particular diaspora in question being that of contemporary Canadian migrants from the province of Newfoundland, displaced to the distant but oil-rich province of Alberta (Hiller and Franz 2004).

The key point is that sociological factors explain both why long-distance migration activates hometown ties *and* why border crossing usually generates hometown associations with greater intensity than the movements that take place within state boundaries. However, ties of this sort need not generate any further cross-border activity. Historically, hometown associations were mainly a tool by which the migrants solved their own problems, whether having to do with needs for sociability or the practical matters of pooling savings to provide burial insurance or medical funds, although crises at home episodically motivated some migrants to help out the communities they left behind (Soyer 1997).[2] Today, these same functions can be found among hometown associations formed by African migrants in Europe, which provide financial help at important life-cycle events—going so far as to pay for a deceased member's traditional funeral and burial in Africa and helping to defray the costs of sending the body back home—while also providing information about documents and visa procedure as well as some modest health care aid (Kerlin 2000; Mazzucato and Kabki 2009). In the contemporary United States, the search for familiar faces similarly continues to draw hometowners together; however, the locus of the activists' instrumental objectives appears to have changed, abandoning the goal of solving problems at the point of reception and focusing instead on sending places.

The migrants' spontaneous engagement with the places that they left behind has also activated a new set of players, transforming a topic of academic study into a matter of interest to policy makers and political officials. International organizations and development agencies, as Mazzucato and Kabki (2009) have pointed out, begin from the assumption that HTAs are democratic organizations, that they represent the interests of hometown residents, and that they maintain harmonious relationships with hometown residents. The fact that sending-state officials are no less interested in "collective remittances" suggests that a more skeptical view is warranted. As shown in Chapters 6 and 7, the migrants are political actors, deploying resources that make it impossible for them to be ignored. Unlike taxpayers, moreover, the migrants are willing to reach into their own pockets and provide money for free, reason for cash-strapped governments in developing societies to find ways of keeping the flow moving. Just how best to engage in "remittance capture" (Gamlen 2008) is a question with which sending states around the world are struggling, discarding old policies for new policies in the hope that some innovation will produce better results.

Thus far, no one has yet found a tool that would steer family remittances in ways that might directly trigger development; hence, interest has focused on how home state governments might stimulate migrant giving. Mexico's "Tres por uno" program, in which each HTA dollar raised for investment back home is matched by a dollar from the Mexican federal, state, and municipal government is perhaps the best known such effort; following this example, the governments of El Salvador, Somalia, Ecuador,

Colombia, and Peru have implemented programs of a similar type. Success in capturing HTA collective investments can also yield political gains for the political leaders who bring these benefits home, as noted by the authors of a UN Development Program report on Mexican migration who write that state "governors and political parties frequently try to influence the selection of projects and financing and to co-opt the migrant organizations" (Programa de las Naciones Unidas para el Desarrollo 2007: 95). Last, precisely because they are the most engaged with the homeland, the hometown activists can be a link by which home country states can exercise influence with those emigrants whose ties are otherwise attenuating. Indeed, the founding director of Mexico's Institute for Mexicans Abroad, a government agency, has seen engagement with hometown associations as a way to use "the natural mechanisms of organization among countrymen to strengthen their identity as members of the Mexican diaspora" (González Gutierrez 1999: 559).

As for social scientists, the thread leads from the ever-growing interest in the myriad connections that span migrant sending and receiving states. From this perspective, the hometown associations exemplify the emergence of "transnational communities" linking migrants here and there. In the most favorable view of the phenomenon, HTA engagement in hometown development denotes the advent of "migrant civil society" (as argued by Lanly and Valenzuela 2004), of which one component is "a common sense of membership in a shared political community," as argued by the political scientist Jonathan Fox (2005: 190).

Whether hometown associations can effect change in the communities from which the immigrants come and, if so, of what type, depends largely on the quality and content of the linkages connecting the migrants to one another; to the friends, families, and neighbors left at home; as well as to the other actors that have now engaged in the game. Scholarly views range the spectrum, with little consensus as to consequences, whether positive or negative, or the features that limit or propel successful associational activity. Indeed, the very same authors can present the phenomenon in two very different lights, sometimes emphasizing "the influence that home town civic committees can have on the power structure of places of origin" and insisting that "migrant transnational political activism is more likely to line up with the forces of change" (Portes 1999: 473–475), while in other statements noting how "a history of distrust and social fragmentation" can put associational "long term dynamism . . . in question" (Portes and Landolt 2000).

## The Receiving Context:
## Opportunities and Constraints

In assessing the factors affecting the HTA's functioning and impact, one can begin by noting that associational activity is on the rise. In Mexico, for example, the number of HTAs registered with the Mexican government increased from roughly 250 in 1995 to 1,662 in 2012, while projects funded by the "Tres por uno" program rose from 942 in 2002 to 14,636 in 2010. Notable levels of HTA growth have also been shown by immigrants from El Salvador and a range of countries in the circum-Caribbean.[3] On the other hand, HTA involvement, unlike remittance sending, is a distinctively minoritarian phenomenon. The Pew Hispanic Center's 2006 National Survey of Latinos, for example, provided ample evidence of lively home country connections, with half of the roughly two thousand foreign-born respondents sending remittances to relatives in their country of origin, 40 percent calling friends and relatives at least once a week, and two-thirds reporting at least one trip home after migration to the United States. By contrast, only 9 percent reported belonging to an immigrant civic, sport, or hometown association, with higher levels among Dominicans and Colombians, and lower levels among Mexicans, the overwhelmingly dominant group (Waldinger 2007a). Responses from a still larger, nationally representative sample of Mexican immigrants, the 2006 Latino National Survey, suggest an even lower membership rate (4 percent), even though the great majority of these immigrants also engaged in some form of regular, cross-border connection with relatives or friends in Mexico. Though the data source is a bit old and the survey drawn only from Colombian, Dominican, and Salvadoran respondents unevenly surveyed in a handful of cities, the picture emerging from examination of the random subsample of the survey collected from 1996 to 1998 by the Comparative Entrepreneurship and Immigration Project proves very revealing. Three-quarters of the sample *never* participated in *any* of the three types of organized hometown connections mentioned in the survey, whether involving sports clubs, HTAs, or collective remittances. By contrast, just over 4 percent checked off the boxes for each of these activities.

Moreover, when asked about their preferences, the immigrants show modest interest in the types of activities that HTAs mount and considerable skepticism toward the capacity of these organizations to fulfill their stated goals. Thus, a nationally representative survey of Mexican immigrants conducted by the Tomas Rivera Institute in 2003 found that 54 percent preferred to send funds directly to their own family and one-third lacked confidence that collective remittances would be used for the desired ends (Cortina et al. 2005). As always, behavior is revealing: though almost nine million Filipinos live and work abroad—roughly half of whom are permanent residents of a developed country and sent home $21.4 billion in individual remittances—the Filipino government's program to link migrant collective remittances to sending communities raised only $2.6 million in that same year (Licuanan et al. 2012).[4]

That the HTAs should engage such a small fraction of the immigrant population should really be no surprise. While socializing with familiar faces from back home can be satisfying, fulfilling that need rarely requires participation in a structured organization. As Patricia Zamudio explains in her study of Mexican migrants in Chicago,

> The *Huejuquillenses* in Chicago did not consider the organization of a club of *paisanos* a critical element in the preservation of both attachments and sense of community. The constant interaction of immigrants in Chicago with friends and relatives in Huejuquilla ensured the communication and diffusion of information. Those who were not able to travel due to lack of money or legal papers could share part of the everyday life of their relatives in Huejuquilla through the phone and through other immigrants who did a good job in "bringing" Huejuquilla to Chicago. (Zamudio 1999: 162–163)

That so many migrants, like those studied by Zamudio, arrive with little experience of organizational participation means that they also lack the motivations would make associational involvement attractive and the skills that would make it rewarding.

Consequently, the minority that engages in associational matters represents an immigrant elite. As described in a book on Mexican hometown associations published by the University of Guadalajara Press,

> In the great majority of cases, it is a matter of migrants of the first generation, well established in the United States (a decade or more after having migrated), who have already achieved a certain socio-economic level: many of them are owners of small businesses (insurance, real estate, Mexican restaurants); some are professionals (lawyers, social workers, doctors) or government employees. At the same time, the majority of leaders and members are men. (Escala-Rabadan 2004: 435)

The surveys tell a similar story. Analysis of the Pew Center Survey shows, not surprisingly, that higher incomes, more education, and greater time spent in the United States all increase the probability of associational membership. Likewise, Alejandro Portes's summary of the findings of the Comparative Entrepreneurship and Immigration Project tells us that cross-border activity is mainly the pursuit of solid, family men—educated, well-connected and firmly established in the host country. They, rather than the recently arrived and the downwardly mobile, organize cross-border enterprises; support political parties and civic committees in their countries; and lead the cultural festivities, sports and religious events linking each migrant diaspora with its respective nation. (Portes 2003)

As fund-raising typically involves family-oriented events, the associations do connect with immigrant youth. But as Ramakrishnan and Viramontes found in their research on Mexican HTAs in Los Angeles, "youth participation is relatively circumscribed, restricted mostly to playing for sports teams for boys, or participating in beauty pageants for girls" (2010: 159).

Thus, host country participation is highly selective, biasing HTA activities in a direction consistent with the interests of those who participate. In general, the associations have no paid staff, depending instead on the willingness and availability of volunteers to donate time, energy, and cash in the interest of some public good. It is not even clear that they have members either, a fact reflecting both the low level of organizational formality and the episodic nature of the HTAs' engagement with the larger, relevant collectivity. As noted by the Mexican study cited above, "membership" is rarely a clearly defined category, possibly pertaining to families or to individuals (Escala-Rabadan 2004). A public event may attract a few hundred people; more sustained efforts have difficulty attracting more than a handful, as suggested by this extract from an interview my colleagues and I conducted with a Salvadoran HTA leader in Los Angeles:

> **Case study evidence:** Describing the evolution of his association, one respondent told us that: "We began with 40 and we finished with 7, plus a son of the group whom we think of as part of our group. Two to three years after we began we invited all the members of the community to a carnival and the idea of that was to have food, give refreshments, the idea was to present ourselves to them and to renounce our posts and to invite them to participate, you understand? About 25 to 30 persons, families came, everything was nice and they were happy that we invited them . . . and no one wanted to do it . . . there are people who say "we want to participate" but we know that [they don't really want to do it].

With the rank and file disengaged, HTAs are easily susceptible to capture by those few with the deepest involvements.

Moreover, the ties binding hometowners together, such as residence in a common neighborhood or work in a similar occupation, tend to erode over time. Rather, the hometowners are often not a clearly bounded group, as residence in the United States has facilitated relationships of a much more diverse kind. Migration out of the hometown into the socially more varied immigrant world naturally generates marital options unavailable or hard to find at home, with a particularly common form involving "mixed marriages" to co-nationals from a different place of origin. Thus, as my collaborators and I discovered through fieldwork among Salvadoran associations in Los Angeles, associational events frequently engaged families, but the adults often had partners from a different hometown or national group. Likewise, the tight spatial and occupational groupings emphasized by the literature seemed to have loosened, a tendency already noticeable in the early 1990s, when Salvadoran participants in the soccer leagues no longer came from a single residential cluster in Los Angeles but commuted from a variety of places across the region. A decade later, observation of an association highlighted both geographic dispersion and social class diffusion: this association ran its social events in two different parts of town, as the more middle-class hometowners living in a suburban area no longer felt comfortable spending evenings in the inner city, where their less successful compatriots resided.[5]

If the activists comprise a selective group, agreement on goals and means often eludes the minority that opts for participation. The historical literature—perhaps because time facilitates distance from the subject matter—underscores the potential for conflict, an issue that contemporary scholars seem to underplay. As bilocalism competes with other loyalties that emphasize politics or ideology over affective ties, hometown associations need to find a way to unite right and left, believers and secularists, proletarians and entrepreneurs—which is why their *anti*political bias has often been so strong. Indeed, keeping principled differences at bay requires continuous work, as indicated by the three-point "philosophy" of an association of Salvadoran hometown associations—"no politics, no religion, no profit."

In addition to principled differences, self-interest yields ample reasons to fight. As the HTA context often provides opportunities for persons of very modest circumstances to gain recognition that they would rarely otherwise obtain, status seeking is often the source of friction and faction. The tendency toward secession, amply noted in the historical literature, was easy to detect in fieldwork that my collaborators and I conducted among Salvadorans in Los Angeles. Since the impediments to starting a rival group are low, and populations are often large enough to support more than one association from the same hometown, activists unhappy with their leaders have plenty of incentives to set up a rival group.

One alternative, of course, is rule by a self-perpetuating elite, noted in a UN Development Program report on immigration's impact on El Salvador, which recounts that "many groups suffer from little leadership rotation, including some that had the same president for more than a decade" (Programa de las Naciones Unidas para el Desarrollo 2005: 265). Indeed, this is the story recounted in Robert Smith's ethnographically rich account of immigrant bilocalism, *Mexican New York*. As he explains, the HTA of *Ticuanenses* living in New York is a player, perhaps the dominant force in the town from which the migrants began to leave decades before. Smith emphasizes the committee's role in displacing the local *cacique* from power and fostering democracy in Ticuani. What gets less attention is the fact that the committee itself appears guilty of *caciquismo*. As Smith explains, the committee "has been run by the same men for thirty years"—indeed with a single individual holding the presidency throughout that entire span of time (2005: 62), "whereas the municipio's leadership changes every three years" (2005: 57). While at least *some* of the migrant *Ticuanenses* dissent from the committee's priorities, there is little that they can do to make their opinions matter. Indeed, the unusually tight-knit nature of this population means that influence typically flows the other way, with the committee able to "create a socially coercive context" (2005: 64) that gets the migrant *Ticuanenses* to take cash out of their pockets in response to the committee's appeals.

Whether representative or not, *how* to get things done is often a struggle for the HTAs. The HTAs are indeed bottom-up, rank-and-file organizations, but this means that the leaders are volunteers for whom investment in the organization may entail a second, but unpaid, job, with time burdens that quickly mount. While they often have extensive personal connections among *paisanos* in the United States, "in most cases this personal asset is not transformed into a significant *organizational* social capital among these groups" (Escala-Rabadan et al. 2011: 49). Informality tends to prevail, in part because that is simply how things are done: even the most rudimentary organizational principles, such as setting regular meeting dates and times, may have to be learned. Keeping good books and maintaining them transparently are other seemingly simple devices for controlling funds and directing expenditures; they are also skills, of a nontrivial nature, that activists have to acquire. Moreover, accurate information about hometown needs is not easily obtained; having long lived abroad, the migrants themselves no longer have a finger on the local pulse. Although transparency is not always avoided, it is not always welcomed, as leaders seeking to hold on to positions of authority are often reluctant to invite accountability. Geographic factors come into play often, making collaboration with hometowners located in distant parts of the United States difficult. Informational barriers constrain not only coordination between migrants and stay-at-homes but also among the migrants themselves: associational activists are sometimes not even aware of one another's existence; accurate, up-to-date information needed to identify potential partners located elsewhere in the United States rarely exists. Even when outside resources are invested to facilitate coordination, the fragmented geography of immigrant settlement gets in the way, increasing the complexities and costs entailed in linking HTAs scattered across the United States (Pan American Development Foundation, 2005). Similarly, a history of ongoing contacts across the different nodes of immigrant concentration may not be enough, as evidenced by the experience of a long-established Salvadoran association whose affiliates in southern and northern California have seen priorities diverge. In effect, the hometown associations appear not so much transnational as doubly bilocalistic, with connections extending from a particular place in the home country to a particular place in the United States, and weak or nonexisting ties linking the hometowners residing in different parts of the migrant world. All these problems are aggravated by the complexities entailed in cross-border, long-distance cooperation. As Alison Paul and Sarah Gammage concluded from their study of Salvadoran hometown associations, "communicating and managing projects that cross national boundaries, that require working and coordinating with local governments, drawing up contracts, managing the flow of funds and supervising construction of implementation requires both time and skills" (2004: 15)—resources that are often in short supply.[6]

## Sending-Context Dilemmas

Not only do the HTA activists comprise a selective population with at best limited responsiveness to the broader migrant masses that they claim to represent, but the interaction with the stay-at-homes tends to reproduce the very inequalities between receiving and sending places that motivated the migration in the first place. Although the literature emphasizes the boundary-spanning aspects of immigrant "transnationalism," its preconditions are in fact the boundaries that separate receiving and sending communities. As I have argued throughout this book, movement to a new place gives the migrants freedom not possessed before; as emphasized above, residence in a rich country also means that even people of modest means have access to resources that can make a difference back home. For the same reason, therefore, they can exercise leverage in their dealings with home community interactants, a factor making for imbalance in the relationship between the two sets of hometowners and increasing the likelihood that the migrants will have access to home society influentials, which is not fully shared by the hometown rank and file. In addition to the strictly material, the migrants possess something else that the stay-at-homes don't share: namely, the experience of migration and exposure to a new way of life and its culture. While the HTA represents the power of continued home country attachment, those attachments are almost inevitably expressed in ways that reflect the changes that the migrants have undergone. As my collaborators and I heard from a long-time, left-leaning Salvadoran activist in Los Angeles, reflecting on his HTA experiences,

> Here we learned that the United States is a great country because even the most insignificant gringo, on Sunday, he will volunteer in some place, perhaps in his church, they'll say you have to sweep, you have to take care, you have to do this, here they will volunteer. There, no one wants to volunteer. They all say, "Give me." It comes from the United States.

While the analyst shouldn't accept this point of view as an accurate empirical description, one does have to acknowledge its existence: though speaking community, the hometowners here and there are really no longer the same.

In our research on Salvadoran associations, my collaborators and I found that initiatives began in the United States. However, the impulse can also come from the other direction. That pattern has become increasingly common as sending communities have become aware of the resources that HTAs could unlock, and local officials have realized that HTA-sponsored projects could leverage government funds. Indeed, some research on Mexico's "Tres por uno" program underscores the role played by local political leaders in spurring the formation of HTAs and influencing the process by which government funded projects are approved (Aparicio and Meseguer 2012).

Nonetheless, the fundamental choices are usually for the migrants, *not* the stay-at-homes, to decide: which goals are to be met, how help is to be delivered, to whom assistance should be provided. Likewise, the question of how, if at all, to involve the stay-at-homes—whether as partners, advisers, or simply as the more or less passive recipients of help—is a matter for the migrants to determine. Imported predilections toward clientelism combined with the significant difficulties and costs entailed in cross-border coordination often work against effective coordination with a representative cross-section of stay-at-homes, increasing the likelihood that hometown kin comprise the key interlocutors. Of course, even when hometown involvement is actively sought, developing collaborative relationships proves difficult, as was the case among the Salvadoran associations studied by Sarah Gammage:

> The channels of communication relied disproportionately on family members and friends, and were for the most part informal and sporadic. Consultations were brief and narrow. The chief limitation was time and resources. Few members of the leadership could stimulate wide consultative and participatory processes to identify and rank priorities in their home town. Needs were assessed instinctively with some consultation with authority figures such as priests, pastors, the leadership of ADESCOs [local development organizations], and occasionally the mayor. The HTAs frequently relied upon these authority figures to mediate HTA and community expectations, to interpret needs and speak for the community. The leadership would verify the claims that these authority figures made with family members and friends, but largely used these authority figures as intermediaries or proxies in their home town communities. (Gammage 2005: 13)

The migrants' goals are affected by any number of factors, starting with their desire to do good for their hometown and hometowners. But HTA views of how best to do good are largely ad hoc, with few undertaking systematic assessments of community needs and many prioritizing according to the potential for raising funds state-side, which provides the channel through which migrant preferences enter (Gammage and Paul 2004). In turn, those preferences frequently lead to visible physical investments, such as the construction of roads or recreational facilities or the renovation of a church. Thus, one study of "Tres por uno" expenditures in the Mexican states of Jalisco and Zacatecas found that almost half of the investments went for roads, with another 33 percent devoted to rebuilding squares and churches, and constructing rodeo rings—that is to say, projects unlikely to improve material well-being (Kijima and González-Ramirez 2012: 296).

While investments of many types may be commendable, they often fail to converge with the preferences of the stay-at-homes. For example, a World Bank study of Mexican hometown associations found that few hometowners thought that productive or entrepreneurial projects were of great importance, but "leaders and members of hometown associations tended to hold the opposite point of view" (Torres and Kuznetsov 2006: 117). Moreover, circumstances are such that the assistance from outside is too late and too little to undo the pressures that have produced migration. Consequently, the migrants often end up providing "mausoleums of nostalgia," shoring up physical structures in communities, like the small Salvadoran town below, that can no longer hold on to their own people:

> To walk the streets of the village is to be struck by the changes that the cash infusion has wrought . . . the village is at least an hour's bumpy drive from the nearest asphalt road. Yet over the past six years, many streets in the village have been paved . . . Farmers who once slept in huts of mud and sticks have built spacious, if modest, houses of cement block painted in bright hues of orange and turquoise. On the main square, near a gleaming whitewashed church, stands a two-story community center with glass windowpanes where children receive computer training several times a week, one of more than a dozen projects, along with the village's roads, that were at least partially funded with $125,000 raised by a charitable association of Piedras Blancas natives in the United States. Still, for all the improvements, the village's most noticeable feature is the silence that has fallen over it ever since an economic downturn . . . during the 1980s prompted the first massive wave of migration. During the day, the stillness is interrupted only by the chirp of crickets and the soft footfall of an occasional stray dog. In the evenings, a street corner that old-timers say once echoed with the cries of dozens of men playing soccer matches after work is now the site of a subdued card game played by a few farmhands from neighboring Nicaragua and Honduras—who have taken over some of the jobs left by the Salvadoran men who have departed. (Aizenman 2006)

As the role of the stay-at-homes is often limited to oversight and logistics, HTA goals are also often not fully realistic and therefore not fully consistent with the preferences of the stay-at-homes or local officials. Lacking the capacity to assess costs fully, ambitious projects can easily exceed resources, with the result that investments fail to eventuate in completion. Even when projects are brought to fruition, the HTAs tend to underestimate long-term costs of maintaining investments in physical goods, as noted in a recent World Bank study that found many of the projects financed by Mexican migrants suffer from lack of sustainability (Torres and Kuznetsov 2006). Symbolizing that problem are the many ambulances donated by migrants to their home communities, which all too often end up sitting immobilized because there are no funds for maintenance or, for that matter, the skilled personnel needed for operation.

Implementation is ultimately affected by conditions and people on the ground—a crucial factor affecting the balance of influence between locals and the migrants residing abroad. While scholarships are a common form of HTA support, the behavior of scholarship students is far more difficult to monitor from afar than on site. After all, the very same conditions that make the beneficiaries eligible for support—namely, poverty—are also likely to inhibit regular attendance or adequate school performance. The involvement of locals can be an effective check increasing the likelihood that the migrants' investments are actually fulfilled as originally intended—but only if the migrants are ready to work with a group of "stay-at-homes."

Moreover, while the HTAers want to do good, it is not clear that they *only* want to do good: physical investments are preferred, in part because they are tangible products, reminding the stay-at-home public of the good that the HTAers have done. Of course, control over resources is always a source of power. However, the very nature of the investments made by HTAs increases the likelihood that the benefits will accrue to only some part of the public. For example, in one remittance-dependent sending community in El Salvador, emigrants in Washington helped fund a half-million-dollar football stadium in the town center, even though many of the outlying areas were "still without bare necessities such as potable water and electricity" (Itzigsohn and Villacres 2008: 679). In this case, the bias favored one part of the locality over another; however, the biases can be narrowed still further, directing resources toward the people most closely connected to the migrants abroad. Whether involving a road, a drain, or a water pipe, public goods of this type can be diverted to private ends. Consequently HTA goal setting has not been immune to the influence of naked self-interest, which can yield hometown investments that suit the migrants but not necessarily the stay-at-homes, as suggested by the example found in a UN report on migration's impact on El Salvador:

> In the case of small infrastructure [works], such as paving of a road, excavation of wells, the investment is such that it has the potential to be appropriated by particular elites, excluding the benefits from other members of the community. Concretely, in one of the cantons, the population lacks potable water at home. The committee in the United States organized events to raise money and channeled the funds to dig a well, via persons of confidence and close relatives, with the goal of providing water to the entire community. However, that well was exactly dug on the land of one of the fathers of the president of the committee in the United States. After a little time, the water pressure fell and it was not possible to distribute water to the entire community; the well was still being used, but only for the family of the leader of the committee. (Programma de las Naciones Uunidas para el Desarollo 2005: 274–275)

While those who hold the resources do not always engage in equally self-seeking behavior, the literature provides ample evidence of imbalance in the relationship between migrant hometown activists and stay-at-homes. As previously mentioned, Peggy Levitt's (2001b) book, *The Transnational Villagers,* includes a chapter focusing on a development committee started by the migrants. Levitt depicts the committee as a grassroots effort yielding positive effects: investment in hometown public goods; the fostering of social capital, in part by stimulating broader participation, in both home- and host towns; and increased hometown government accountability, as migrants' dollars and pressure gave stay-at-homes greater leverage over state officials. The details of the account, however, point in a different direction. Notwithstanding the many informal exchanges that had regularly passed through the migrant circuit, migrants were at first skeptical of organized efforts to assist development in Miraflores, in part because previous such ventures had taken advantage of migrant contributors seeking to do good (187). As of the publication of Levitt's book, the development committee had developed procedures that were unusually standardized for organizations of this type—in part, because an individual involved in an earlier fund-raising activity had been able to take private control of property bought with collective funds (189–190). In the end, as Levitt notes, the inherent inequalities between the *Mirafloreños* in Boston and those still living in the Dominican Republic skewed the development committee's activities and objectives, with decision making gravitating to the Bostonians, whose priorities increasingly diverged the *Mirafloreños* still living in Miraflores.

Quite a similar story emerges from Robert Smith's account of the balance of power between the Mexican New Yorkers and the stay-at-homes. The local *caciques,* explains Smith, "face demands from well-funded migrants" (2005: 79), who can take advantage of changes in the Mexican political system to make their opinions heard and have their dollars "neutralize . . . the *caciques'* local advantage of wealth" (83). Migrant donations, for example, helped a challenger mobilize a caravan in *ranchos* that had previously supported the *cacique,* contributing in 1999 to the challenger's electoral success. However, the hometown committee in New York, split between supporters of the *cacique* and supporters of the challenger, remained neutral in the election; afterward it refused to support the new mayor's projects, with the result, as Smith explains, of "denying him access to *Ticuanense* dollars in New York City and making it impossible to do large-scale projects" (84). According to Smith, the new mayor, who saw the committee president as "the New York counterpart to the Tiquani *cacique*" (85), interpreted the committee's action as punishment for ending their arrangement with the long-reigning *cacique*. And as Smith's book shows, municipal politics is not an exception but rather the rule as differences in the resources linked to place of residence consistently divide and oppose the *Ticuanenses* living in New York from their counterparts who have yet to leave home.

## Conclusion

The hometown association, as shown in this chapter, is the quintessential form of immigrant long-distance attachment: immigrants' predilection for seeking the company of their fellow hometowners is a phenomenon familiar to every student of immigration. In extending their scope from sociability in the new land to development in the old country, the HTAs of the contemporary period further demonstrate that many migrants are far from uprooted. Instead, flows of various sorts continue to move across borders, and social relations in the new home remain structured by connections brought from the old. For these reasons, the study of hometown associations also highlights the two quite separate dimensions that the "transnational" concept unfortunately conflates, namely, attachment to a social collectivity identified with the place left behind, which the migrants can pursue through mutual aid or nostalgic get-togethers, and cross-state social action, in which the migrants generate flows that converge back on the place from which they came.

Focusing on an explicitly cross-border expression of immigrants' home country ties, this chapter provides little support for the view that sending and receiving communities are encompassed by transnational social fields in which persons participate and belong to a common social world, regardless of physical location. Rather, the real estate agent's maxim of "location, location, location" proves decisive.

With action shifting to the trans-border axis, in turn triggering responses from other actors, the migrants' ability to exercise leverage back home derives from the bounded, territorial resources that they access by virtue of cross-border movement from poor to rich states. To a large extent, that potential derives from the same conditions that motivated the migration in the first place: by collecting funds in countries where wages are high in order to support changes in countries where costs are low, small contributions from low-wage migrant workers are enough to give hometown activists the resources they need to make a difference back home. Moreover, even among the most disadvantaged migrants, not all the migrants stay at the bottom; many instead experience upward movement, with some of the more successful migrants putting their means, as well as their contacts, at the disposal of the trans-state activists.

Asking just how the hometowners "here" and "there" can actually collaborate, and which of the hometowners on either side of the divide participate in the process, moves the obstacles to cross-state cooperation into clearer relief. Not everyone can go from "here" to "there" and back with equal ease: the stay-at-homes are largely precluded from on-site intervention with the HTAers living in the new land. Among the migrants, only a selective minority participates in associational matters. As travel back to the hometown requires legal and economic resources that all too many migrants don't yet possess, the crucial interlocutors comprise a still smaller group. Indeed, among respondents surveyed randomly by the Comparative Entrepreneurship and Immigration Project directed by Alejandro Portes, 90 percent *never* returned to their hometowns to participate in fiestas or celebrations and only 2 percent did so regularly. While individual communication with close relatives may be easier in the era of the cell phone and Internet than it was in the day of the transatlantic letter, distance and geographical separation still matter, producing high transaction costs that impede effective contact between migrant activists and hometown communities.

Moreover, the migrants' efforts are structured by the translocal, *not* transnational, nature of the ties linking them to the people and places back home. While the HTAers are unquestionably motivated by a desire to help, they want to furnish assistance to their own hometown, not some other locality, no matter how needy. As discovered by a USAID program set up to facilitate interventions by Salvadoran HTAs, three-quarters of the HTAs contacted wanted to channel support to their own communities exclusively (Pan American Development Foundation 2005: 6). But since emigration is selective, with the regions with the highest levels of outmigration usually *not* the poorest, and the remittances that the emigrants later send helping to reduce poverty levels, the communities that benefit from the emigrants' collective remittances are rarely those that are most in need of the philanthropy that could be raised by the compatriots now residing in the richer countries of the developed world. Thus, whereas the Salvadoran government wanted US-based HTAs to prioritize localities with the lowest level of educational achievement, that territorial focus largely left out those communities with established HTAs in the United States.[7] Research has repeatedly, though not always, picked up that mismatch between emigrant preference and stay-at-home need. In the Filipino case, migrant donations get channeled to high emigration zones, which means that they largely stay clear of the country's poorer areas because emigration is highest in the Philippine's most developed provinces (Licuanan et al. 2012). The bias may not be quite as great in Mexico, where emigration does not stem from the country's most developed regions; nonetheless, research shows that the collective remittances generated by the "Tres por uno" program are more likely to go to medium, rather than high, poverty towns (Aparicio and Meseguer 2012).

That the migrants present themselves as hometowners, moreover, does not mean that they are actually one and the same. As many scholars have noted, the impetus for hometown-oriented activity frequently derives from rejection in the new land. However, the satisfaction sought from intervention in the community left behind often bespeaks unequal, not collaborative, relationships with the stay-at-homes, with the migrants committed to goals that are tenuously related to the priorities of the communities from which they come.

In the end, this effort to focus on the specifically trans-border dimension of immigrants' homeland affections does show that trans-state connections are an inherent aspect of international migration, albeit in varied and unpredictable ways. As international migration escapes sending states' efforts to constrain exit and receiving states' efforts to control entry, it generates ideational, cultural, economic, and political spillovers that in turn yield significant effects in points of origin as well as destination. The content and form of those feedbacks, however, are not determined in advance. More important, those spillovers are both shaped and constrained by the bounded nature of the environment into which the migrants have come. While communities of all kinds are internally differentiated, characterized by inequalities of myriad sorts, the cleavages in the cross-state communities studied here are distinctive in that they coincide exactly with the borders of national states. It is by moving across borders into the territory of a rich state that the migrants have gained opportunities to affect change back home, doing so in ways that reflect, and largely reinforce, the inequalities between sending and receiving societies.

# CHAPTER NINE

# Conclusion

## *Foreign Detachment*

O N July 4, 1984, the *Wall Street Journal* called for a laissez-faire immigration policy, allowing labor to flow as freely as goods. Saluting immigrants, the editors asked whether anyone would "want to 'control the borders' at the moral expense of a two-thousand-mile Berlin Wall with minefields, dogs and machine-gun towers?" Answering no, they proposed a constitutional amendment: "There shall be open borders."

The *Journal* has kept beating that drum, reflecting the views of American business, which generally believes that the more immigrants, the better. Most Americans, however, see the matter differently. For the last decade or more, Republicans have been striving to heighten the already high barriers at the US-Mexico border, while pushing to reduce rights and entitlements for immigrants living on US soil. Not wanting to appear soft, Democrats have played along, with deportations reaching an all-time high under a president eager for Latino votes.

Similar challenges appear elsewhere. After 1945, western Europe looked for workers abroad, only later to learn it had instead received people. Struggling to integrate the guest workers' children and grandchildren, the Europeans are now striving to tap into global flows of highly skilled labor while simultaneously keeping unwanted, low-skilled newcomers off the old continent.

How to respond to international migration is not a dilemma for the residents of the rich countries alone. Bad as things are at the US-Mexico border, the Mexico-Guatemala border is a circle closer to hell; for decades a country of *emigration* and then a country of *transit migration* (by Central Americans), Mexico is now becoming a country of *immigration*, creating a furor that even gringos can understand. Further afield, migration to South Africa from Zimbabwe and Angola has triggered xenophobic violence, adding to the burdens of the post-apartheid transition.

Notwithstanding the obstacles put in their place, the people from abroad continue to move, crossing borders to find a place where life can be better. They do so for good reason: since migration involves changing a poorer for a richer place, migration is good for the migrants. In fact, the poorer the migrants' point of origin, the more they gain from migration. On average, migrants from the poorest to the Organization for Economic Cooperation and Development (OECD) countries experience a fifteenfold increase in income, a sixteenfold decrease in child mortality, and roughly a doubling of child school enrollment. By crossing boundaries, the migrants achieve what the natives of the rich countries enjoy not out of merit but by the luck of birth in a wealthy place. As development economist Lant Pritchett notes in his provocatively titled *Let Their People Come,* "Nearly all the differences in wages between individuals in rich and poor countries are explained by the *location* of the work, not their personal characteristics" (2006: 20). Hence, a Salvadoran high school graduate in the United States makes as much as his US-born counterpart but almost nine times as much as a similarly educated compatriot living back home.

Migration isn't good only for the migrants: it does good things for kin and communities left behind. Moving to rich countries, the migrants consume at higher rates, gaining access to everyday comforts that the people of the developed world take for granted, all the while saving money that they send home, at a volume greatly exceeding the level of official aid and often comprising more than 10 percent of the GDP in many developing countries.

While migration helps the migrants, it does little if any damage to the people among whom they settle. Increased migration has little impact on destination country per capita income, and any of the slightly detectable effects appear to be positive. Migrant workers are most likely to compete with prior migrants, making aggregate labor market effects small or nil.

And yet the people of the receiving countries want migration to stop. The reasons are multiple, but ultimately they are all informed by a single view of the world. In that optic, people, state, and society are one and the same thing. We, let's call them the United Statesians, are the people both *of* the United States and *in* the United States. US society is found "here," where "we" live; similarly, the borders of US society extend to the territorial boundary but not one inch further. "They," the foreigners, live "there," in foreign places. "We" and "they," "here" and "there" shall forever remain distinct.

This view claims to represent the world both as it is and as it should be. Perhaps the world should be one where we, and only we, live here, and they, and only they, live there. Yet whatever one thinks about how the world *should* be, reality persistently takes a different form.

And so what social scientists and men and women in the street take for granted isn't really what they should expect. Rather, networks of goods, ideas, and (most important for this book) people regularly and normally spill across territorial lines. Consequently, international migration means cross-border connections, now the subject of a burgeoning, ever more lively scholarly literature. For most scholars, the concept of transnationalism provides the prism for understanding the ways in which international migration brings here and there together. In a sense, the fascination with transnationalism has been a scholarly boon, pushing researchers to shift their intellectual stance. Instead of standing with one's back at the borders, looking at the "immigrants" and the ways in which they become like the people among whom they now live, the transnational perspective has refocused attention on the connections between places of origin and destination and the factors that make distant places so often interlaced.

But the problem is that the transnational perspective provides only a way of seeing, not a way of understanding. Knowing that migration builds circuits through which people, resources, ideas, and influence subsequently cross borders is a good place to start. But to move further, one needs other tools, those that I have tried to provide in this book. At once immigrants *and* emigrants, aliens *and* citizens, foreigners *and* nationals, the migrants are caught in a dialectic of constant tension. In searching for the good life—often in opposition to the preferences of both receiving and sending states—international migrants also pull one society onto the territory of another, generating *intersocietal convergence*. In propelling them onto a different environment, that very same search changes the migrants in fundamental ways, gradually producing *intersocietal divergence*. But the passage from one stage to another does not entail a process of linearly declining home country ties, since in the short- to medium-term, settlement actually increases the migrants' capacity to engage with the people and communities left behind.

Cross-border ties typically spring from the connected survival strategies pursued by both migrants and their closest relatives at home. In developing societies, *emigration* is often undertaken without the goal of *immigration:* rather, relocating to a developed society takes place so that emigrants can gain the access to the resources that can be found only there. In turn, those gains get channeled back home in order to stabilize, secure, and improve the options of the kin network remaining in place. Relocation to a richer state yields the potential for enjoying the fruits of its wealth. However, the emigrants are also *foreigners* not knowing the ropes and *aliens* lacking the full protections granted citizens, and therefore encounter risks and uncertainties of myriad sorts. When trouble strikes—a job gets lost, a fine has to get paid—or when opportunity arises—a document must be produced to acquire a more secure status—the emigrants have no choice but to turn to the stay-at-homes for help. As assistance from the latter is often the condition of exit—grandparents taking care of children or siblings looking after property—the emigrants' dependency on the stay-at-homes gives the former all the more reason to attend to the needs of the latter. These intertwined survival strategies of emigrants and stay-at-homes yield continuing exchanges of money, support, information, and ideas; as migrant populations grow, those exchanges broaden and deepen, producing an infrastructure that facilitates and reinforces these bidirectional flows.

In today's world, moreover, these decisions to build family economies across borders reflect the additional impact of receiving states' ever intensifying effort to police national boundaries. While leaving home for life abroad requires both finances and social capital, those resources no longer suffice; migrants need to find a way through or around control systems. Since not every family member can penetrate borders with equal ease, those most able to cross go first. Consequently, other kin members are left home to wait, remaining there until a visa allows for legal passage or resources permit yet another unauthorized crossing.

The political and social logic of international migration thus produces international families. Consequently, while no longer *in* the society of origin the migrants remain *of* it, living in a *zone of intersocietal convergence,* a conceptual space in which home and host societies overlap. The very logic of the migrants' project then steadily pushes them inward, away from the outer edge of the zone of intersocietal convergence where they began. After all, the immigrants encounter a *foreign* environment, which has to be *learned.* Unlike natives, for whom the complexities of everyday life are invisible and unconsciously navigated with tacit skills acquired from day one, immigrants need to pick up basic competencies: how to make change; how to move around in the new, puzzling world; how to find the foods to which one is accustomed and to learn which of the new possibilities are pleasing; how to transmit and receive information reliably when the other party to the conversation speaks only the native tongue. Hence, behavioral changes are immediate, potentially involving small, almost imperceptible, virtually costless steps, each one of which makes the next advance a bit easier. Thus, the cumulative, continuous nature of the process renders the strange familiar, while yielding results that validate the original search for the better life. As time passes, one steers one's way through the formerly foreign world without thought, using newly acquired skills to demonstrate competence in ways that bring recognition and reward and yield exposure to an entirely different mix of people than those known before leaving home.

Transitioning from the outer toward the inner bounds of the zone of intersocietal convergence transforms the migrants, making them less like the people left behind and more like the people among whom they have settled, changes that in turn yield paradoxical consequences. As the migrants gain greater control over their new environment, learning how to navigate and manage it and thereby capture more of the resources found around them, their potential for making a difference back home grows. With greater stability migrants can also invest in maintaining the connection, whether by traveling home with greater frequency or engaging in activities oriented to the hometown community or even national polity. For much the same reasons, the migrants trigger the attention of home states, which reach out across boundaries to nationals abroad, seeking to gain their share over the human and financial resources generated by the migrants' move to another country.

However, greater capacity also transforms the relationships crossing boundaries. Over time, the initial, rough equilibrium between the flows emanating from new and old homes falters, as advantage shifts to the migrants. Consequently, the migrants gain leverage, with the resulting power asymmetries affecting their interactions with the stay-at-homes. That greater leverage lets them engage in community matters from afar, as we have seen in Chapter 8. And, as shown in Chapters 5, 6, and 7, it also facilitates the migrants' emergence as political actors with the capacity to both help and harm home state interests, giving sending states further incentive to expand their geographic scope, thereby gaining the infrastructural capacity needed to connect with and influence citizens abroad.

Thus, *intersocietal convergence* gradually gives way to *intersocietal divergence*. As the balance in the duality between *emigrant* and *immigrant* shifts from the former to the latter, the migrants find themselves not simply *in* the society of reception but increasingly *of* it as well. Residence in a rich country yields qualitative as well as quantitative changes, turning the migrants, if not into new people, then into people very different from those who left home. Identity, as the dictionary defines it, means the condition of being the same. But sameness ends once the migrants leave kin, hometown friends, and compatriots behind, which is why their identity is rapidly in flux. Migration engenders a change in the interior of the person, one both entailing and resulting from practical adaptations to a different social structure. As a result, the migrants develop a new set of wants, needs, and expectations that are no longer fully compatible with the ways of life and modes of behavior back home. Those changing orientations generate conflict in the cross-border relationship.

Moreover, the locus of the migrant's key connections also tends to shift over time, though that transition may be highly protracted. Regardless of the motivation leading any one family or individual to leave home, the core familial network almost always moves gradually, erratically, and incompletely: some significant other is usually to be found at home. Because other commitments, such as property ownership, keep emigrants rooted in the place from which they began, inertia exercises considerable weight.

Nonetheless, as the sojourn abroad persists, the social center of gravity is apt to cross the border, at which point the motivation to keep up cross-border ties falters. The needs of life in the place where the migrant actually lives soak up an increasing share of disposable income, reducing the resources available to remaining relatives at home, even as those ties become increasingly fraught. Because physical *re*location yields *dis*location, managing those relationships becomes all the more difficult. No longer in their proper, accustomed place, the migrants find that distance can be compressed, but it can be shrunk only so far. As shown in Chapter 4, technology, geography, the exigencies of daily life, and the very global inequalities that motivate migration all conspire to prevent the migrant from being "here" and "there" at the same time.

Distance impinges with particular force on the selective group of emigrants who seek engagement not just with the core members of their familial network but with the broader community from which they departed, the story told in Chapter 8. Wanting to do something good, the emigrant activists find that doing so proves problematic, in part because the complexities of cross-border coordination are daunting, especially for hard-working immigrants with limited technical skills trying to be cross-border citizens in their limited spare time. Cross-border activists may often claim that "the absent are always present" but delivering on that promise typically exceeds the emigrants' capacity. Instead, these efforts at homeland-oriented civic activity demonstrate how different the migrants are from the communities and people to which they are still attached and how often cross-border civic coordination founders on the shoals of dispersion, distance, and disconnection.

While *cross-border* contacts and connections to the *homeland* come under pressure, *cross-ethnic* contacts in the *host country* grow ever more prevalent, yielding ties to nationals whose social worlds are largely, if not entirely, encompassed by national borders, and which, in turn, tend to absorb interest and time at the expense of long-distance, cross-border relationships. Of those relationships, the most important are the most intimate, producing the households in which the next generation will grow up. While migrants who move as a couple typically share a connection to a specific *place* of origin within the *country* of origin, those who move as unattached adults encounter a much broader range of possibilities. Sometimes the ties furnished by hometown networks furnish a spouse, but that hardly exhausts the range of options. Marriages leading to the crossing of lines—whether simply involving two different places from the same country of origin or a more radical shift across national, ethnic, linguistic lines—change the household context in ways that weaken the signals and resources needed to transmit cross-border connections to the next generation. Consequently, boundaries that may have been important before migration and that may remain salient in the places from which the migrants came no longer have the same meaning in the place where the migrants now live.

Thus, movement across the zone of intersocietal convergence both strengthens *and* weakens the linkages that cross borders. As host country ties grow increasingly dense and in-place connections extend to host country nationals and other persons *outside* the zone of intersocietal convergence, *intersocietal divergence* becomes the prevailing pattern. But as international migration is an inherently political dimension, the facts that foreigners are also home country nationals and aliens are also home country citizens affect the motivation to keep up cross-border ties and the means by which they are pursued.

*Every* immigrant starts out as an alien *within* the society of reception but *outside* its polity. With the exception of the stateless, *every* emigrant remains a citizen *outside* the society of origin and only sometimes within its polity. In a sense, every state is also a sending state, as in a globalized world, citizens abroad comprise too large a fraction to be ignored. Hence, predominantly emigration and predominantly immigration states find themselves in a situation of some symmetry, which is why both parties have an interest in letting the other extend across boundaries to connect with citizens, wherever they are.

*In* the receiving state but not *of* it, the migrants confront a mixture of resources and vulnerabilities, benefiting from the wealth and freedom of the new environment but never fully free from the risk of rejection or the more devastating threat of ejection. *Of* the receiving state but not *in* it, the migrants' cross-border activities and engagements promote a deterritorialized vision of a national community extending across state boundaries. Living abroad, however, the migrants' foreign location undermines their legitimacy as political actors back home. For developing states, servicing the needs of citizens abroad entails allocating resources from those who chose to stay to those who chose to exit; however, the latter are too connected to the homeland to be ignored. Moreover, a failure to respond to the *immigrants'* problems feeds back in the form of political difficulties back home. As we have seen, building up the external state infrastructure to meet emigrants' needs has the advantage of reinforcing loyalties while also reinforcing an activity in which state and emigrant interests converge: namely, the sending of remittances. But as Chapter 7 has shown, states can do only so much for people who reside on the territory of another state, whose nationals already regard foreign-origin residents possessing persistent foreign loyalties with suspicion.

International migration inherently produces *intersocietal* convergence without necessarily producing a corresponding *interpolity* convergence. In leaving the home state, emigrants retain citizenship but *not* all citizenship rights. Crossing the territorial boundary usually takes the emigrants outside the home polity, which then proves off-bounds to those no longer living on home grounds. Chapters 5 and 7 demonstrated that residence abroad hardly precludes political activity oriented toward the home state, in part because the wealth accessible in the developed world is a source of political capital that the migrants can use to influence conditions in the country where they no longer live. No less important are the consequences that result from moving into a different political jurisdiction, as crossing political boundaries also lets the emigrants escape the home state's coercive power. However, that evasion allows for political freedom only when territorial presence is a source of destination society *civic* rights. Where those conditions hold—as in most democracies—emigrants gain the capacity to organize, protest, raise funds, and lobby, even if destination-society citizenship and full political rights remain out of reach. When combined, the freedoms and economic resources made possible by emigration have the potential to pack a powerful punch, forcing home state officials to listen to and sometimes accommodate people they would have despised had the emigrants not been able to leave home.

As we have seen, homeland politics leaves the mass of rank and file largely indifferent. To begin with, emigration is a form of voting with one's feet: *against* the state of origin and *for* the state of destination. Postmigration political involvement offers few incentives, especially for the many migrants who never engaged before departing. The key impediments derive from the extraterritorial context itself, which lacks a political infra-structure capable of connecting migrants to the homeland polity, quite in contrast to the situation in the new environment, where on-site opportu-nities for participation are broadly on offer, even for those lacking full legal status.

Nonetheless, some fraction of the emigrants—usually small but often too big to be ignored—wants full citizenship rights and therefore tries to pull the home country polity across boundaries so that it extends to the foreign territories where the departed nationals can be found. As indi-cated by the growing number of countries that allow for some form of expatriate voting, cross-territorial polity extension is increasingly com-mon, albeit to a limited degree. For the most part, that phenomenon involves the politics of recognition, not the politics of redistribution, as home states have limited capacity to respond to the number one concerns of their citizens abroad—which have to do with matters of immigration, *not* emigration. For that reason, the extension of voting rights often entails little more than a costly exercise in symbols, proving of little interest to the rank-and-file immigrants pursuing their search for a better life. Moreover, neither sending-state elites nor ordinary sending-state citizens find the demands for extraterritorial political participation fully con-vincing. As experienced from the sending side, the same people who claim to be *emigrants* appear often to be acting like *immigrants;* that they also live in *foreign places* provides further reason to think that they are unlikely to share the interests and needs of those people still living on *native grounds.*

*Home country polity extension* entails *interpolity convergence* only when full citizenship rights for *emigrants* are coupled with full citizenship rights for *immigrants*—an outcome that requires immigrants to traverse the internal, formal boundary of receiving-state citizenship. Citizenship, as Rogers Brubaker famously pointed out, is simultaneously inclusive *and* exclusive, binding together the citizens and keeping out the foreigners. Crossing the territory doesn't necessarily yield eligibility for receiving-state citizenship; only certain classes of legally present persons can apply and even they have to meet certain preconditions. Once immigrants are eligible for citizenship, it often proves hard to acquire, entailing expendi-ture of effort and savings, with unpredictable outcome and reward of uncertain value. And since citizenship is tied to national identity, the acquisition of a new citizenship is a matter of the heart, not just the brain. If, as so many scholars have argued, the nation is understood and felt as the family writ large, then abandoning one nationality and replacing it with another may seem like an act of betrayal in which one turns one's back on one's family as well one's country. Hence, the emotive pull of home country citizenship may add to the material and cognitive costs imposed by receiving-state citizenship requirements, with the result that the transition from *emigrant* to *immigrant* may nonetheless leave substantial numbers remaining as *aliens* in the state where they actually live. Ironically, therefore, those with the strongest affective tie to the homeland may have the least capacity to pursue those connections effectively because moving back and forth across the national border is easiest for those who have already acquired receiving-state citizenship.

While democratic states vary in the degree to which they facilitate or impede naturalization, they all provide a door through which long-term foreign residents can become citizens of the country where they actually reside. The combination of host country citizenship *acquisition* and home country citizenship *retention* yields a convergence of polities paralleling the convergence of societies that results from the extension of social networks across boundaries. While sending states are not particularly keen on the polity's cross-territorial extension, they see virtue in the acquisition of host country citizenship, which by furthering immigrant integration into the destination society increases emigrants' capacity to transmit resources, whether remittances, ideas, or innovations, back home and allows the immigrants to speak out for home country interests in ways not possible when still standing outside the polity. For these reasons, sending states increasingly offer emigrants the option of dual citizenship, as the right to retain home country citizenship removes the stigma of disloyalty and thus relaxes the inner emotional constraint impeding immigrants from becoming nationals of the place where they live.

The civic rights accorded by democratic societies technically allow any emigrant to pursue homeland politics on alien soil, but only with the acquisition of receiving-state citizenship does the door open wide. In that pursuit, the selective, often unrepresentative, group of *emigrant* activists frequently takes the path of *immigrant* politics, as mobilizing resources in the destination country is best done with the political skills required by that environment. To exercise influence, homeland activists inevitably engage with mainstream political figures, in the process gaining the skills and building the host society political network needed to do so with success. Learning how to play the political game facilitates entry into the receiving-state polity, which in turn yields greater influence; thus activists initially motivated by homeland concerns often move deeper into host country politics, whose rewards are also hard to ignore. The shift from emigrant to immigrant politics takes a variety of forms, with political structure, political culture, and historical experiences widening or narrowing the options. In a polity like that of the United States, immigrant politics is particularly attractive, as the political culture validates the pursuit of homeland politics and the political system makes it possible. Though certain limits cannot be crossed, emigrant politics yields a predominantly integrative impact. Paradoxically, homeland activism becomes an apprenticeship in host country politics.

Thus, in the end, the very same decisions that produce intersocietal *convergence* eventually yield intersocietal *divergence*. To be sure, separation does not necessarily entail detachment. On the contrary, for the most part, the migrants are actually in-between: *in* the country of immigration but *of* the country of emigration, *foreigners* where they reside but *immigrants* whenever they return home. Even if many migrants and, even more so, their descendants drift away from any homeland attachment, that origin remains meaningful to some and sufficiently so to entail investment of energy and time. But engagement with the homeland is ultimately shaped by migration and habituation to the expectations and rhythms of a physically separate, economically richer, culturally distinctive place. Consequently, the interactions between migrants and their descendants, on the one hand, and homeland leaders and everyday people, on the other, fall subject to tensions that coincide with territorial divides.

## Crossing Boundaries: A Look Ahead

While international migration is good for the migrants, its revival has also been good for migration scholarship. The continuing flows of people across borders and the endless controversies provoked by this phenomenon have spurred a burgeoning of migration scholarship transforming a once peripheral, somnolent area into an exceptionally lively interdisciplinary field. Yet for all the research effort poured into this topic, migration scholarship has not reached its full potential. The central handicap stems from the field's distinctive division of labor, with one literature situated at the point of origin studying *emigration* and the other at the point of destination studying *immigration*. The sociology of *emigration* demonstrates how the people crossing borders actively shape their own destinies, doing what neither home nor host state wants, getting ahead by making effective use of the resource that they almost all possess—one another. The sociology of *immigration* explains why a move to the territory of another richer state simultaneously improves the migrants' lives but transforms them in ways that they could not have expected, often producing distance from the people, places, cultures, and loyalties left behind. The problem is that these two separate sociologies describe the same people, thus failing to see the internal tensions and contradictions arising among people who are simultaneously immigrants *and* emigrants.

That defect can be rectified by following the approach adopted in this book: namely, to focus on the cross-border dimension, thereby defining international migration as a distinctive field of study, encompassing but going beyond "immigration" and "emigration" as conventionally defined. The cross-border nature of the phenomenon reminds us that the immigrants who are also emigrants are also *foreigners* from *foreign* places. Whereas social science shows that international migration is a normal event, repeatedly bringing one society onto the territory of another state, nationals have a different view, believing that state, society, and territory *should* be one and the same. Disturbed by the influx of foreigners, many nationals respond with hostility: some insist that boundaries *around* the state be tightened; others demand that boundaries of the political community *within* the state be narrowed; some are more accepting but expect the newcomers to take on the native code and switch loyalties from home to host societies. Those reactions, comprising an inherent part of the phenomenon, shape and circumscribe both the *emigration* options of those seeking to leave home and the *immigration* options of those who have ventured to a different land in search of a better life.

With the cross-border dimension in view, one no longer sees emigration through the perspective of the people of the developed world, who, wanting immigration reduced, believe that their states' policies have failed. Rather one also considers the developing world perspective, from which standpoint the migration controls imposed by the United States and the other rich democracies are all too effective. Doors to international trade in goods and services have opened wide, leading differences in international prices for goods to drop: a Big Mac bought in a developed country is not even twice the cost of the Big Mac purchased in countries at the 20th percentile. By contrast, differences in international wages have grown immensely, making gains to migration ever greater than before. Current wage ratios between numerous pairs of possible origin and destination countries (e.g., Vietnam and Japan at 1:9) are far higher than the "historical ratios between the mass senders and the United States" (Pritchett 2006: 20). Although migration entails social and psychological costs deterring many potential movers, evidence indicates ample readiness to migrate. The Gallup poll estimates that 700 million people wish to migrate *permanently:* among them, 6.2 million Mexicans and fully *half* of the respective populations of El Salvador, Haiti, and Ethiopia. Letting the world's poor move would appear to have immensely beneficial effects:

according to one analysis, free migration could as much as *double* world income (Pritchett 2006: 32). One need not go so far: if rich countries would let their labor force rise by a mere 3 percent, the gains to poor country citizens would exceed the costs of foreign aid by a factor of almost five (World Bank 2006: 5).

However, "let them stay *there;* do *not* let them come *here*" is the developed world's fundamental goal; far from inept, the United States and the other rich democracies do a remarkably effective job of facilitating cross-border movement by citizens of wealthy countries while forcing people from the developing world to queue up for visas or climb over walls. Consequently, migrants' decision making is inherently related to the policy decisions and preferences of the nonmovers in the developed world, making the determinants of emigration inextricably linked to the politics of migration restriction.

Focusing on the inter*national* dimension of the phenomenon also highlights the difficulties that the researchers of *immigration* encounter in identifying the population *into* which the immigrants and their offspring are meant to assimilate. The "mainstream" is apparently the concept of the day; however, as it also implies the existence of a sidestream, one also needs to explain who gets into the sidestream, who stays there, and why. Alas, the conventional approach provides no such account. Politically, the population described as the mainstream is divided, whether by ideology, class, region, religion, or some material interest. Moreover, assimilation into the mainstream and a corresponding diffusion of identity is *not* what nationals want. Rather, they clamor that foreigners become nationals—in the US case, "Americans"—replacing the particularism imported from abroad with the particularism found in their new home.

As emphasized throughout this book, the immigrants are not just foreigners; they are also *aliens*, a condition shared by *every* foreigner crossing national boundaries, whether as legal permanent resident, temporary worker, tourist, or undocumented immigrant. *Social* boundaries may be blurry, but *legal* boundaries surrounding the myriad formal categories of alien are bright. While the import of alien status varies by citizenship regime, exercising least weight where citizenship is a birthright, nowhere is its significance trivial. Naturalized citizens currently comprise one-third of all foreign-born people living in the United States; another third are legal permanent residents; another third belongs to some other, more tenuous legal status. Undocumented immigration in Europe is lower, but naturalization barriers are higher. While immigrant offspring born in the United States are citizens, many young immigrant offspring *growing up* in the United States are born abroad. No small fraction is undocumented;

many more have undocumented parents or siblings. Consequently, the brightest boundaries are not imported and have nothing to do with ethnicity; rather, they are fundamentally political, made *in* and *by* receiving states, exercising long-term consequences at the individual level and beyond. Beginning outside the body politic, migrants have limited ability to influence "who gets what," let alone "who is what," making it easy for nationals to ignore the needs and preference of those who have no organized voice.

Hence, the scholarly path ahead entails attending to the links between "here" and "there" while also highlighting the cross-state and political aspects that distinguish *international* migration from other forms of long-distance movement. International migrants do not move under circumstances of their own choosing; rather, they contend with states trying to control movement across both the *external* borders of the territory *and* the *internal* borders of membership and citizenship. Consequently, politics and policy shape migrant options, yielding bright, formal, relatively unyielding boundaries. In seeking to sort and sift, states respond to their citizens, whose preferences for a bounded community—not just a prejudice but also an ideal—put them at the heart of the phenomenon. Therefore, the study of international migration encompasses receiving as well as sending contexts, focusing both on the processes that recurrently produce population movements across states *and* the mechanisms by which nation-states attempt to keep themselves apart from the world.

Notes
References
Acknowledgments
Index

# Notes

## 1. Immigrants, Emigrants, and Their Homelands

1. In addition to the Wyman book, which is cited above, this paragraph-long condensation of the history rests on a number of works, most notably Cinel (1991), Choate (2009), Gabaccia (2000), and Ramirez (1991).

## 2. Beyond Transnationalism

1. This first generation of transnational studies did generate some research on ethnicity and transnational relations, most notably Stack's (1979) study of "ethnic conflict in an international city," as well as a related anthology (1981), which the current generation of scholarly transnationalists has ignored. Taking aim at the state centrism of the international relations literature, Stack argues that the cross-state networks of migrants help transfer international conflicts (and cross-state loyalties) into the domestic political system. This emphasis on the conflict-producing consequences of international migration provides an important corrective to the views of the current generation of scholarly transnationalists. On the other hand, Stack confused the long-distance modes of *nationalism* that cross state boundaries with those forms of trans-state activity and association that go *beyond* nationalism—thus exactly foreshadowing the pitfalls on which the next generation of scholarly transnationalists would stumble.

2. The scholarly debate has indeed moved far from the formulation taken by the initial transnational perspective on migration, which asserted that the home country connections of contemporary international migrants took an unprecedented form. Concerns generated by research on the international migrations of

the contemporary era directed historians to patterns of which they had been aware but perhaps not fully attentive. The social scientists have agreed that connections between here and there were indeed seen before—though most still insist that there is something distinctive about the host/home linkages of today. More important, there is a steady stream of publications seeking to make systematic past/present comparisons. For further discussion, see Foner 2000, Morawska 2001, and Waldinger 2008.

3. The complaint is nothing new. Writing in the early 1970s, Samuel Huntington contended, " 'Transnationalism' is a term which suffers from being 'in' in social science. . . . It has achieved popularity at the price of precision" (1973: 334).

4. Indeed, one scholar (Nimtz, 2002) calls Marx and Engels the "prototypical transnational actors," a description that, while replacing the still-serviceable label of internationalism with one of more recent vintage, nonetheless underscores the fundamental incompatibility of the two notions of transnationalism that circulate in the academic literature.

5. On Africa, see Claire Mercer, Ben Page, and Martin Evans, "Unsettling Connections: Transnational Networks, Development and African Home Associations," *Global Networks* 9, 2 (2009), 141–161.

## 3. The Dialectic of Emigration and Immigration

1. Thus, the Ecuadorian immigrants to New York City studied by Pribilsky all arrived with prior experience of wage labor and a cash economy. "Nevertheless, the kinds of money-management skills necessary to generate income far and above that needed to live in the United States were qualitatively different from the tasks to which most migrants were accustomed" (212).

## 4. Cross-Border Ties

1. Calculated from the Americas Barometer Merged 2004–2012 data file; downloaded from http://www.vanderbilt.edu/lapop/index.php. The text reports the fraction of respondents reporting that "close relatives who previously lived in this house" now live in the United States only *and* in the United States and other countries. Data weighted to equalize size across countries.

2. US Bureau of Transportation Statistics, passenger arrival/departure numbers. http://www.bts.gov/publications/national_transportation_statistics/#chapter_1.

3. Calculations from Pew Global Attitudes Project: Spring 2007 Survey, downloaded from http://pewglobal.org/category/data-sets/. Developing countries defined as all those countries classified by United Nations Development Project as "high human development" or lower. Countries include Argentina, Bangladesh, Bolivia, Brazil, Bulgaria, Chile, China, Egypt, Ethiopia, Ghana, India, Indonesia, Ivory Coast, Jordan, Kenya, Kuwait, Lebanon, Malaysia, Mali, Mexico, Morocco, Nigeria, Pakistan, Palestinian Territories, Peru, Russia, Senegal, Tanzania, Turkey, Uganda, Ukraine, and Venezuela.

4. Calculated from the Americas Barometer Merged 2004–2012 data file; downloaded from http://www.vanderbilt.edu/lapop/index.php. Data in the text

refers to those respondents surveyed in 2008 or 2010 and who reported that "close relatives who previously lived in this house" now live in the United States only. Data weighted to equalize size across countries.

5. Calculated from the Detroit Arab American Survey (Baker et al. 2003). Data weighted.

6. Thirty-nine-year-old, Spanish-dominant, primary schooled, Mexican-born woman without children or property in the home country, residing in the United States for fifteen years, still possessing Mexican citizenship, and living in a household where annual income is under $30,000.

7. Calculated from Pew Hispanic Institute 2010 National Survey of Latinos; weights applied.

8. Calculated from 2006 National Survey of Latinos, Pew Hispanic Institute.

9. World Bank, World Development Indicators.

10. Calculated from the Americas Barometer Merged 2004–2012 data file; downloaded from http://www.vanderbilt.edu/lapop/index.php. Data in the text refers to those respondents surveyed in 2008 or 2010.

11. This section draws on Thomas Soehl and Roger Waldinger, "Making the Connection: Latino Immigrants and Their Cross-Border Ties," *Ethnic and Racial Studies*, vol. 33, no. 9 (2010): 1489–1510.

## 5. Engaging at Home from Abroad

1. Calculated from Latino National Survey (Fraga et al. 2006) and National Asian American Survey (Ramakrishnan et al. 2008).

2. The remainder of this section draws on findings reported in "The Bounded Polity: The Limits to Mexican Emigrant Political Participation" (coauthored with Thomas Soehl), *Social Forces*, vol. 91, no. 4 (2013): 1239–1266 and "Emigrants and the Body Politic Left Behind" (with Thomas Soehl and Nelson Lim), *Journal of Ethnic and Migration Studies*, vol. 38, no, 5 (2012): 711–36.

3. This paragraph and the one to follow summarize results more fully reported in Waldinger and Soehl (2013).

## 6. Emigrants and Emigration States

1. Calculated from MIREM-RDP, © EUI, Database on Return Migrants to the Maghreb; public use data downloadable from http://www.eui.eu/Research/Library/ResearchGuides/Economics/Statistics/DataPortal/DReMM.aspx.

## 7. Politics across Borders

1. Extensive international consultation and networking characterized Mexico's approach in both the buildup to and the aftermath of the 2006 expatriate vote. In 1998, for example, the *Instituto Federal Electoral* convened an International Seminar on Expatriate Voting, featuring representatives from over twenty countries (*Instituto Federal Electoral*, "Informe de la Comisión de Especialistas," in *El voto de los mexicanos en el exterior*, ed. Gonzalo Badillo Moreno [Michoacán:

Gobierno del Estado de Michoacán, 1998 {2004}]). Later, with the International Institute for Democracy and Electoral Assistance, it was a cosponsor and co-publisher of the *Handbook* on *Voting from Abroad* (Andrew Ellis et al., *Voting from Abroad: The International IDEA Handbook* [Stockholm: International IDEA, 2007]). In 2004 and 2005, Mexico's Foreign Ministry convened two international conferences on "State-Diaspora Relations," with policy makers and academics from a broad range of countries, including Turkey, Morocco, India, Haiti, El Salvador, and others, and later published the proceedings of the meetings.

2. Unless otherwise indicated, this section draws from the following sources: Alcocer, 2005; Calderón Chelius, 2003 and 2007; Dresser, 1993; Martínez Saldaña, 2002; Perez Godoy, 1998; Santamaría Gómez, 1994 and 2006; Smith, 2008; and Smith and Bakker, 2008.

3. My own tabulations from the survey, *Mexico, las Americas y el mundo,* conducted by the Mexican research center CIDE, 79 percent of the Mexican respondents to the 2008 survey opposed the election of dual nationals as senator or deputy and 83 percent opposed the election of dual nationals as president.

4. As of 2006, 95 percent of Mexicans age eighteen or over were inscribed in the electoral registers, of whom 99 percent possessed an electoral credential (*Instituto Federal Electoral,* 2006).

## 8. Hometown Blues

1. In nineteenth-century Paris, for example, the migrants from the Auvergne and the Limousin were perceived as foreigners; indeed, the provincials in Paris lived together in "ghettos," with "eyes remained fixed on home society" (Weber 1976: 192), just as would the Poles, Italians, and Jews who succeeded them. For villagers not yet nationalized, like the shepherds or peasants from northwestern Italy at the turn of the last century who moved to either Turin or Marseilles, international differed little from internal migration, both connecting to satellite communities in otherwise equally alien environments (Milza 1993). In the late nineteenth and early twentieth centuries, internal migrants within China formed native-place associations that were organized and functioned in much the same way as those created by their countrymen who instead went overseas (McKeown 2001). The examples can be multiplied almost endlessly.

2. As noted by Daniel Soyer in his book on Jewish immigrant associations, the *landsmannshaftn* threw themselves into efforts to provide relief to their home communities in Poland and Russia during and especially after World War I. While those activities tailed off once the war-induced crises abated, many associations continued to provide financial support to hometown institutions (1997: 199). By contrast, Donna Gabaccia contends that, among the southern Italians, the emigrants only occasionally invested in communal institutions (2000: 97).

3. Number of Mexican HTAs from http://www.ime.gob.mx/Directorio Organizaciones/, accessed February 26, 2014; number of funded projects from *Sedesol: The 3X1 Project for Migrants 2011,* www.au.int/en/sites/default/files /Mexico_2.pdf, accessed February 26, 2014.

4. Data on remittances from World Bank, *Migration and Remittances Factbook 2011*, http://issuu.com/world.bank.publications/docs/9780821382189/7?e=0, accessed October 15, 2013.

5. Our observations find an echo in Thomas Lacroix's study of Moroccan hometown associations in France, where he found that the "maintaining of a village identity has been challenged by the process of integration. With family reunification and upward social mobility, immigrants gradually moved to new neighbourhoods and cities in search of better living conditions. The process dismantled the spatial concentration of village groupings. In parallel, the transformation of power relations between migrants and villages, the process of individualisation and the loss of social homogeneity among migrants put an end to the original raison d'être of hometown organisations. Their members have followed divergent life trajectories. Some have become successful entrepreneurs while others have worked their whole life in the same factory. Diverging political alignments have created new fault lines, often widening existing factional rivalries. The identity of hometowners became more complex, more attuned with the evolution of their life trajectory in the country of settlement. In this process of spatial, social and political diversification, a large number of village organisations have either disappeared or been reinvented in order to survive." (Lacroix, 2011: 12)

6. A somewhat similar observation is made by Mercer, Page, and Evans (2009) in their study of African associations: "Though some information travels quickly and effectively between some people, the connections with home can also be weak, depending on intermittent phone calls, email postings and nuggets of information. Such contacts as there are often depend on chance (for example, the chance of having a member who is visiting) and their relationships with home branches or linked associations are often not formalized. The experience of the water project in particular suggests that proximity still matters when it comes to improving the home place" (155).

7. Yoko Kajima and Horacio González-Ramirez, "Has the Program 3×1 for Migrants Contributed to Community Development in Mexico? Evidence from Panel Data of 2000 and 2005," *Review of Development Economics*, 16(2), 291–304.

# References

Adamson, Fiona. 2004. "Displacement, Diaspora Mobilization, and Transnational Cycles of Political Violence." In *Maze of Fear: Security and Migration After September 11th,* John Tirman, ed., 45–58. New York: New Press.

Aizenman, N. C. 2006. "Vibrant Village Quieted As Salvadorans Go North." *Washington Post,* May 8.

Alarcon, Rafael, Luis Escala Rabadan, and Olga Odgers Ortiz. 2012. *Mudando el hogar al norte: trayectorias de integración de los inmigrantes mexicanos en Los Ángeles.* Tijuana, MX: El Colegio de la Frontera Norte.

Alba, Richard, and Victor Nee. 2003. *Remaking the American Mainstream: Assimilation and Contemporary Immigration.* Cambridge, MA: Harvard University Press.

Alcocer, V. Jorge. 2005. *El voto de los mexicanos en el exterior.* Mexico, DF: Nuevo Horizonte.

Anderson, Benedict. 1998. "Long-Distance Nationalism." In *The Spectre of Comparisons: Nationalism, Southeast Asia and the World,* Benedict Anderson, ed., 58–74. London: Verso.

Aparicio, Francisco Javier, and Covadonga Meseguer. 2012. "Collective Remittances and the State: The 3×1 Program in Mexican Municipalities." *World Development* 40 (1): 206–222.

Arendt, Hannah. 1951. *The Origins of Totalitarianism.* New York: Harcourt.

Arias, Patricia. 2009. *Del arraigo a la diáspora: Dilemas de la familia rural.* Mexico, DF: Miguel Angel Porrua.

Aron, Raymond. 1966. *Peace and War: A Theory of International Relations.* Garden City, NY: Doubleday.

Arredondo, Maria Luisa. 2003. "Embajadora Martha Lara, cónsul general de México en la matrícula consular fue un acierto." *La Opinión*, April 27.

Babiano, Jose, and Ana Fernandez Asperilla. 2009. *La patria en la maleta: Historia social de la emigración española a Europa*. Madrid: Fundación Primero de Mayo.

Baker, Wayne, Ronald Stockton, Sally Howell, Amaney Jamal, Ann Chih Lin, Andrew Shryock, and Mark Tessler. 2003. Detroit Arab American Study (DAAS). ICPSR04413-v2. Ann Arbor, MI: Interuniversity Consortium for Political and Social Research [distributor], 2006-10-25. doi:10.3886/ ICPSR04413.v2.

Bakker, Matt. 2011. "Mexican Migration, Transnationalism, and the Rescaling of Citizenship in North America." *Ethnic and Racial Studies* 34 (1): 1–19.

Balboni, Mariana, Sebastián Rovira, and Sebastián Vergara, eds. 2011. *ICT in Latin America: A Microdata Analysis*. Santiago, Chile: United Nations.

Baldassar, Loretta, Raelene Wilding, and Cora Baldock. 2007. *Families Caring Across Borders: Migration, Ageing and Transnational Caregiving*. Basingstoke, Hampshire, England: Palgrave Macmillan.

Basch, Linda. 1987. "The Vincentians and Grenadians: The Role of Voluntary Associations in Immigrant Adaptation to New York City." In *New Immigrants in New York City*, Nancy Foner, ed., 159–193. New York: Columbia University Press.

Basch, Linda, Nina Glick Schiller, and Cristina Szanton Blanc. 1994. *Nations Unbound: Transnational Projects, Postcolonial Predicaments, and Deterritorialized Nation States*. New York: Gordon and Breach.

Baubock, Rainer. 2003. "Toward a Political Theory of Migrant Transnationalism." *International Migration Review* 37 (3): 700–723.

———. 2007. "Stakeholder Citizenship and Transnational Political Participation: A Normative Evaluation of External Voting." *Fordham Law Review* 75: 2393–2447.

Bayes, Jane H., and Laura González. 2012. *Organizing the Mexican Diaspora: Can it Strengthen North American Integration?* Working Paper, Digital Commons Florida International University. Downloaded February 26, 2014. http://digitalcommons.fiu.edu/cgi/viewcontent.cgi?article=1011&context= ippcs_colloquia.

Bazeley, Michael. 2001. "Mexican Consulates Face Deluge Seeking ID Cards." *San Jose Mercury News*, November 11.

Becerra, Ricardo, Pedro Salazar, and José Woldenberg. 1997. *La reforma electoral de 1996: Una descripción general*. Mexico City: Fondo de Cultura Económica.

Berg, Ulla Dalum, and Carla Tamagno. 2006. "El Quinto Suyo from Above and from Below: State Agency and Transnational Political Practices among Peruvian Migrants in the US and Europe." *Latino Studies* 4 (3): 258–281.

Blais, Andre, Louis Massicotte, and Antoine Yoshinanka. 2001. "Deciding Who Has the Right to Vote: A Comparative Analysis of Election Laws." *Electoral Studies* 20: 41–62.

Bloemraad, Irene. 2007. "Much Ado About Nothing? The Contours of Dual Citizenship in the United States and Canada." In *Dual Citizenship in Global Perspective: From Unitary to Multiple Citizenship*, Thomas Faist and Peter Kivisto, eds. London: Palgrave Macmillan.

Borkert, Maren, Pietro Cingolani, and Viviana Premazzi. 2009. *The State of the Art of Research in the EU on the Uptake and Use of ICT by Immigrants and Ethnic Minorities*. IMISCOE Working Paper 27.

Bosniak, Linda. 2006. *The Citizen and the Alien: Dilemmas of Contemporary Membership*. Princeton, NJ: Princeton University Press.

Bourne, Randolph. 1916. "Trans-national America." *Atlantic Monthly* 118 (1): 86–97.

Breitkopf, David. 2004. "Getting High-Powered Help in Mexican Outreach." *American Banker*, June 24, 7.

Brubaker, Rogers, ed. 2006. *Nationalist Politics and Everyday Ethnicity in a Transylvanian Town*. Rutgers, NJ: Princeton University Press.

Bruno, Andorra, and K. Larry Storrs. 2005. *Consular Identification Cards: Domestic and Foreign Policy Implications, the Mexican Case, and Related Legislation*. Washington, DC: Congressional Research Service, Report for Congress, RL 32094.

Buhle, Paul, and Dan Georgakas, eds. 1996. *The Immigrant Left in the United States*. Albany, NY: SUNY Press.

Burgess, Katrina. 2005. "Migrant Philanthropy and Local Governance." In *New Patterns for Mexico: Observations on Remittances, Philanthropic Giving, and Equitable Development*, Barbara Merz, ed. Cambridge, MA: Harvard University Press.

Caffarena, Fabio. 2012. "Introduzione/Introducción." In *Scritture migranti: Uno seguardo italo-spagnolo*, Fabio Cauffarena and Laura Martinez Martin, eds. Milan: Franco Angeli.

Calavita, Kitty. 1992. *Inside the State: The Bracero Program, Immigration, and the I.N.S.* New York: Routledge.

Calderón Chelius, Leticia. 2003. "Votar en la distancia: experiencia de una ciudadanía en movimiento." In *Votar en la Distancia*, Leticia Calderón Chelius, ed., 19–52. Mexico City: Instituto Mora.

———. 2007. "En Busca del Voto Perdido: Análisis del Resultado del Voto en el Exterior en la Elección Presidencial Mexicana de 2006." In *Invisibles? Migrantes internacionales en la escena politica*, Cecilia Imaz Bayona, ed., 199–215. Mexico: UNAM.

Californians for Population Stabilization. 2003. "Matrícula Controversy Heats Up." *CAPS News* 44 (1): 3.

Camp, Roderick. 2007. *Politics in Mexico: The Democratic Consolidation*. New York: Oxford University Press.

Cancian, Sonia. 2010. *Families, Lovers and Their Letters: Italian Postwar Migration to Canada*. Winnipeg: University of Manitoba Press.

Cannon, Chris. 2003. "Statement." *Hearings*, Subcommittee on Financial Institutions and Consumer Credit, Committee on Financial Services, 108th Congress. Washington, DC: Government Printing Office.

Carpizo, Jorge, and Diego Valadés. 1998. *El voto de los mexicanos en el extranjero.* Mexico City: Universidad Nacional Autónoma de México.

Castañeda, Jorge. 2003. "La matrícula consular: Hay que buscar aliados." *La Opinión* August 17, 1D.

———. 2007. *Ex Mex: From Migrants to Immigrants.* New York: New Press.

Celik, Ayse Betul. 2005. "'I miss my village:' Forced Kurdish Migrants in Istanbul and Their Representation in Associations." *New Perspectives on Turkey* 32: 137–163.

Centro de Estudios Sociales y de Opinión Pública (CESOP). 2006. *Perspectiva Ciudadana* Num. 2, Cámara de Diputados, LIX Legislatura. Accessed December 14, 2009. (May). www.diputados.gov.mex.

Chavez, Jorge M., and Doris Marie Provine. 2009. "Race and the Response of State Legislatures to Unauthorized Immigrants." *The ANNALS of the American Academy of Political and Social Science* 623: 78–92.

Chen, Yong. 2000. *Chinese San Francisco, 1850–1943: A Trans-Pacific Community.* Stanford, CA: Stanford University Press.

Choate, Mark. 2009. *Emigrant Nation: The Making of Italy Abroad.* Cambridge, MA: Harvard University Press.

Cinel, Dino. 1991. *The National Integration of Italian Return Migration, 1870–1929.* New York: Cambridge University Press.

Citrin, Jack, and John Sides. 2008. "Immigration and the Imagined Community in Europe and the United States." *Political Studies* 56 (1): 33–56.

Clavin, Patricia. 2005. "Defining Transnationalism." *Contemporary European History* 14 (4): 421–439.

Coalición por los Derechos Políticos de los Mexicanos en el Extranjero. 2004. "Propuesta ciudadana de inciativa de ley que reforma artículos y adiciona un libro noveno al código federal de instituciones y procedimientos Electorales." In *El voto de los mexicanos en el exterior,* Gonzalo Badillo Moreno, ed., 351–363. Michoacán: Gobierno del Estado de Michoacán.

Cochrane, Feargal. 2007. "Irish-America, the End of the IRA's Armed Struggle and the Utility of 'Soft Power.'" *Journal of Peace Research* 44 (2): 215–231.

*Congressional Quarterly Weekly.* 2004. "2004 Key Votes: A Mix of Hits and Misses for Republican Leadership." December 11.

Consulta Mitovsky. 2004. *El voto de los mexicanos en el extranjero.*

Cook-Martin, David. 2013. *The Scramble for Citizens: Dual Nationality and State Competition for Immigrants.* Palo Alto, CA: Stanford University Press.

Cooley, James A. 2004. "Quienes Son? No Sabemos. Mexico's Fake I.D.—And Its Terrorist Implications." *National Review Online.* Accessed September 2, 2009. http://www.nationalreview.com/comment/cooley200404210915.aspH.

Cordeiro, Albano. 2005. "Le non-exercise des droits politiques par les Portugais de France." *Hommes et Migrations,* July–August, Number 1256.

Cornelius, Wayne, and Takeyuki Tsuda. 2004. "Controlling Immigration: The Limits of Government Intervention." In *Controlling Immigration: A Global Perspective,* Wayne Cornelius, Takeyuki Tsuda, Philip Martin, and James Hollifield, eds., 3–50. Stanford, CA: Stanford University Press.

Cortina, Jerónimo, Rodolfo De la Garza, and Enrique Ochoa-Reza. 2005. "Remesas: límites al optimism." *Foreign Affairs en Español* 5 (3): 27–36.

Dalacoura, Katerina. 2001. "Islamist Movements as Non-State Actors and Their Relevance to International Relations." In *Non-state Actors in World Politics*, Daphne Josselin and William Wallace, eds., 235–50. New York: Palgrave.

Daniels, Michael. 2007. " 'Ethnic' Routes—Growth Market for Airlines: Cheap Travel for Immigrants; For Hungary's Wizz Air, Focus Is on Trips Home; Cork-Katowice for $26." *Wall Street Journal*, March 7, A.1.

de Haas, Hein. 2007. *Between Courting and Controlling: The Moroccan State and 'Its' Emigrants*. Working Paper No. 54, Centre on Migration, Policy and Society, University of Oxford.

de la Fuente, Graciela. 2011. "Las TIC en medio de las relaciones: manejo de la distancia y la proximidad en las familias transnacionales." *Digithum*, May 13, 21–38.

de la Vega, Norma. 2002. "Mexican Consulate's Mobile Office Overwhelmed In Vista." *San Diego Union-Tribune*, March 12.

Diggins, John P. 1972. *Mussolini and Fascism; the View From America*. Princeton, NJ: Princeton University Press.

Dillon, Sam. 2003. "Mexican Consulate in Los Angeles Exudes Power and Energy." *New York Times*, March 15.

Diminescu, Dana. 2008. "The Connected Migrant: An Epistemological Manifesto." *Social Science Information* 47: 565–579.

Dinan, Stephen. 2006. "Vitter Rebuffed in Demand for Carding Matrícula Sites." *Washington Times*, November 17.

Dinerstein, Marti. 2003. *IDs for Illegals: The "Matrícula Consular" Advances Mexico's Immigration Agenda*. Washington: Center for Immigration Studies.

Douki, Caroline. 2011. "Protection sociale et mobilité transatlantique: Les migrants Italiens au début du XXe siècle." *Annales. Histoires, Sciences Sociales* 66 (2): 375–410.

Dreby, Joanna. 2010. *Divided by Borders: Mexican Migrants and Their Children*. Berkeley: University of California Press.

Dresser, Denise. 1993. "Exporting Conflict: Transboundary Consequences of Mexican Politics." In *The California-Mexico Connection*. Abraham Lowenthal and Katrina Burgess, eds., 82–113. Stanford, CA: Stanford University Press.

Dufoix, Stéphane. 2002. *Politiques d'exil : Hongrois, Polonais et Tchécoslovaques en France après 1945*. Paris: Presses Universitaires de France.

———. 2003. *Les Diasporas*. Paris: Presses Universitaires de France (2008 English translation, *Diasporas*, University of California Press).

Eckstein, Susan. 2009. *The Immigrant Divide: How Cuban Americans Changed the US and Their Homeland*. New York: Routledge, 2009.

Egelko, Bob. 2003. "Mexican ID Cards Under Fire—Feds Suspend Pilot Program in S.F." *San Francisco Chronicle*, January 25.

Ellis, A., and A. Wall. 2007. *Voting from Abroad: The International IDEA Handbook*. Stockholm: International IDEA.

*El Mural*. 2002. "Alientan el rechazo de matrícula en EU." December 15, 19.

*El Norte*. 2002. "Inicia consulado programa piloto en Chicago." Jul. 1.

Escala-Rabadan, Luis. 2004. "Migración y formas organizatives en los Estados Unidos: Los clubes y federaciones de migrantes mexicanos en California." In *Clubes de migrantes, oriundos mexicanos en los Estados Unidos: La political transnacional de la nueva sociedad civil migrante,* Guillaume Lanly and M. Basilia Valenzuela V. eds., 425–454. Guadalajara: Universidad de Guadalajara.

Escala, Luis, Gaspar Rivera-Salgado, and Rigoberto Rodriguez. 2011. "Is More Necessarily Better? Leadership and Organizational Development of Migrant Hometown Associations in Los Angeles, CA." *Migraciones Internacionales* 6 (2): 41–73.

Escamilla-Hamm, Patricia. 2009. "How Transnationalism Facilitates the Participation of Mexican Immigrants in US Politics." *Migracion y desarollo* 12: 89–114.

Espinoza Valle, Victor Alejandro. 2008. "Ciudadanía, nacionalidad y democracia politica: El voto de los mexicanos en el extranjero." Accessed January 28, 2013. http://www.wilsoncenter.org/sites/default/files/Art%25C3%259Dculo Ciudadania,nacionalidadydemocraciapolitica.pdf.

Esterl, Mike. 2003. "US Banks Worry Patriot Act Will Cost Them Mexican Clients." *Wall Street Journal,* September 18, B3F.

Esteves, Rui, and David Khoudour-Castéras. 2009. "A Fantastic Rain of Gold: European Migrants' Remittances and Balance of Payments Adjustment During the Gold Standard Period." *Journal of Economic History* 69 (4): 951–985.

Fairlie, R. W., R. A. London, R. Rosner, and M. Pastor. 2006. *Crossing the Divide: Immigrant Youth and Digital Disparity in California.* Santa Cruz, CA: Center for Justice, Tolerance, and Community.

Faist, Thomas. 2000. "Transnationalization in International Migration: Implications for the Study of Citizenship and Culture." *Ethnic and Racial Studies* 23: 189–222.

Fassin, Didier. 2011. "Policing Borders, Producing Boundaries: The Governmentality of Immigration in Dark Times." *Annual Review of Anthropology* 40: 213–226.

*Federal Register.* 2008. "Minimum Standards for Driver's Licenses and Identification Cards Acceptable by Federal Agencies for Official Purposes; Final Rule." 73, 19 (January 29).

Federation for American Immigration Reform. 2003. "Matrícula Consular ID Cards." Accessed September 2, 2009. http://www.fairus.org/site/PageServer?pagename= iic_immigrationissuecenters6520H.

Fitzgerald, David. 2004. "Beyond 'Transnationalism': Mexican Hometown Politics at an American Labor Union." *Ethnic and Racial Studies* 27 (2): 228–247.

———. 2008. "Colonies of the Little Motherland: Membership, Space, and Time in Mexican Migrant Hometown Associations." *Comparative Studies in Society and History* 50 (1): 145–169.

———. 2009. *A Nation of Emigrants: How Mexico Manages Its Migration.* Berkeley: University of California Press.

———. 2012. "A Comparativist Manifesto for International Migration Studies." *Ethnic and Racial Studies* 35 (10): 1725–1740.

Fitzgerald, Patrick. 2008. "Exploring Transnational and Diasporic Families through the Irish Emigration Database." *Journal of Intercultural Studies* 29 (3): 267–281.

Fletcher, Peri. 1999. *La casa de mis sueños: Dreams of Home in a Transnational Mexican Community.* Boulder, CO: Westview.

Flores Rivas, Edgardo. 1987. "La institución consular conforma a la práctica mexicana." In *El Servicio Exterior Mexicano,* 60–77. México, DF: Secretaria de Relaciones Exteriores.

Fox, Jonathan. 2005. "Unpacking Transnational Citizenship." *Annual Review of Political Science* 8: 171–201.

Fraga, Luis R., John A. Garcia, Rodney Hero, Michael Jones-Correa, Valerie Martinez-Ebers, and Gary M. Segura. 2006. "Latino National Survey (LNS)." ICPSR20862-v6. Ann Arbor, MI: Inter-university Consortium for Political and Social Research [distributor], 2013-06-05. doi:10.3886/ICPSR20862.v6.

Friedmann, John, and Ute Angelika Lehrer. 1997. "Urban Policy Responses to Foreign In-migration: The Case of Frankfurt-am-Mein." *Journal of the American Planning Association* 63 (1): 61–78.

Fullilove, Michael. 2008. *World Wide Webs: Diasporas and the International System.* Lowy Institute Paper 22.

Gabaccia, Donna. 2000. *Italy's Many Diasporas.* London: UCL Press.

Gabaccia, Donna, Dirk Hoerder, and Adam Walaszek. 2007. "Emigration and Nation Building during the Mass Migrations from Europe." In *Citizenship and Those Who Leave: The Politics of Immigration and Expatriation,* Nancy L. Green and François Weil, eds., 63–91. Urbana, Illinois: University of Illinois Press.

Galan, Veronica. 2002. "Acepta Citibank Cuentas De Ilegales." *El Norte,* March 19, 3.

Gamlen, Alan. 2008. "The Emigration State and the Modern Geographical Imagination." *Political Geography* 27 (8): 840–856.

Gammage, Sarah. 2005. "Crowding in Collective Remittances: Lessons Learned from State-HTA Collaborations in El Salvador." Destination DC Working Paper, 7.

Gans, Herbert. 1979. "Symbolic Ethnicity: The Future of Ethnic Groups and Culture in America." *Ethnic and Racial Studies* 2 (9): 1–20.

Garcia, Adriana. 2005. "Inquieta Voto En El Exterior A Cónsules." *El Norte,* January 1.

Gerber, David A. 2000. "Epistolary Ethics: Personal Correspondence and the Culture of Emigration in the Nineteenth Century." *Journal of American Ethnic History* 19 (4) (Summer): 3–23.

Giglia, Angela. 2001. "Uso de los medios de comunicación y expresión de las emociones en sujetos transnacionales: Una exploración." *Perfiles Latino-americanos,* June 18.

Glick Schiller, Nina. 1999. "Transmigrants and Nation-States: Something Old and Something New in the US Immigrant Experience." In *The Handbook of*

*International Migration: The American Experience,* Charles Hirschman, Josh DeWind, and Philip Kasinitz, eds., 94–119. New York: Russell Sage.

Glick Schiller, Nina. 2003. "The Centrality of Ethnography in the Study of Transnational Migration: Seeing the Wetlands Instead of the Swamp." In *American Arrivals,* Nancy Foner, ed., 99–128. Santa Fe, NM: School of American Research Press.

Glick Schiller, Nina, Linda Basch, and Cristina Blanc-Szanton, eds. 1992. *Towards a Transnational Perspective on Migration: Race, Class, Ethnicity, and Nationalism Reconsidered.* New York: New York Academy of Sciences.

González, Gilbert. 1999. *Mexican Consuls and Labor Organizing.* Austin: University of Texas Press.

González Gutierrez, Carlos. 1993. "The Mexican Diaspora in California: Limits and Possibilities for the Mexican Government." In *The California-Mexico Connection,* Abraham Lowenthal and Katrina Burgess, eds., 221–238. Stanford, CA: Stanford University Press.

———. 1997. "Decentralized Diplomacy: The Role of Consular Offices in Mexico's Relations with Its Diaspora." In *Bridging the Border: Transforming Mexico-US Relations,* Rodolfo de la Garza and Jesús Velasco, eds., 40–68. Boston, MA: Rowman and Littlefield.

———. 1999. "Fostering Identities: Mexico's Relations with Its Diaspora." *The Journal of American History* 86 (2): 545–567.

———. 2006a. "Del acercamiento a la inclusión institucional: La experiencia del instituto de los mexicanos en el exterior." In *Relaciones estado-diáspora: La perspectiva de América Latina y el Caribe,* Carlos González Gutierrez, ed., Vol. 1, 181–220. Mexico, DF: Porrua.

———. 2006b. "Introducción: El Papel de los Gobiernos." In *Relaciones Estado-diáspora: La perspectiva de América Latina y el Caribe,* Carlos González Gutierrez, ed., Vol. 2., 13–42. Mexico, DF: Porrua.

Goodman, Gary, and John Hiskey. 2008. "Exit without Leaving: Political Disengagement in High Migration Municipalities in Mexico." *Comparative Politics* 40: 169–188.

Goodman, Sara Wallace. 2010. "Integration Requirements for Integration's Sake? Identifying, Categorising and Comparing Civic Integration Policies." *Journal of Ethnic & Migration Studies* 36 (5): 753–772.

Gori, Graham. 2002. "A Card Allows US Banks to Aid Mexican Immigrants." *New York Times,* July 6.

Gosse, Van. 1996. " 'El Salvador is Spanish for Vietnam': A New Immigrant Left and the Politics of Solidarity." In *The Immigrant Left in the United States,* Paul Buhle and Dan Georgakas, eds., 301–329. Albany, NY: State University of New York Press.

Grazzi, Mateo. 2011. "Patterns of Internet use." In *ICT Latin America: A Micro-data Analysis,* Balboni, Mariana, Sebastián Rovira, and Sebastián Vergara, eds. United Nations. ECLAC.

Grazzi, Matteo, and Sebastian Vergara. 2011. *ICT Access in Latin America: Evidence from Household Level.* http://EconPapers.repec.org/RePEc:pra: mprapa:33266.

Green, Nancy L. 2012. "Americans Abroad and the Uses of Citizenship: Paris, 1914–1940." *Journal of American Ethnic History* 31 (3): 5–32.

———. 2005. "The Politics of Exit: Reversing the Immigration Paradigm." *Journal of Modern History* 77 (2): 263–289.

Gregg, Heather. 2002. *Divided They Conquer: The Success of Armenian Ethnic Lobbies in the United States*. Rosemarie Rogers Working Paper #13, Inter-University Committee on International Migration.

Guarnizo, Luis E. 2001. "On the Political Participation of Transnational Migrants: Old Practices and New Trends." In *E Pluribus Unum? Contemporary and Historical Perspectives on Immigrant Political Incorporation*, Gary Gerstle and John H. Mollenkopf, eds., 213–263. New York: Russell Sage.

Guarnizo, Luis, Alejandro Portes, and William Haller. 2003. "Assimilation and Transnationalism: Determinants of Transnational Political Action among Contemporary Migrants." *American Journal of Sociology* 108: 1211–1248.

Guevarra, Anna Romina. 2010. *Marketing Dreams, Manufacturing Heroes: The Transnational Labor Brokering of Filipino Workers*. New Brunswick, NJ: Rutgers University Press.

Guglielmo, Thomas A. 2006. "Fighting for Caucasian Rights: Mexicans, Mexican Americans, and the Transnational Struggle for Civil Rights in World War II Texas." *Journal of American History* 92 (4): 1212–1237.

Guillen, Pierre. 1982. "L'antifascisme: Facteur d'integration des Italiens en France entre les deux guerres." In *L'emigrazione Socialista nella lotta contro il Fascismo*, 209–220. Milan: Sansoni.

Gupta, Akhil, and James Ferguson. 1992. "Beyond 'Culture': Space, Identity, and the Politics of Difference," *Cultural Anthropology* 7 (1): 6–23.

Halliday, Fred. 2001. "The Romance of Non-State Actors." In *Non-state Actors in World Politics,* Daphne Josselin and William Wallace, eds., 21–40. New York: Palgrave.

Hamel, Jean-Yves. 2009. *Information and Communication Technologies and Migration*. Human Development Research Paper 2009/39. Accessed June 15, 2010. http://hdr.undp.org/en/reports/global/hdr2009/papers/HDRP_2009 _39.pdf.

Hamilton, Nora, and Norma Chinchilla. 2001. *Seeking Community in a Global City: Guatemalans and Salvadorans in Los Angeles*. Philadelphia, PA: Temple University Press.

Hansen, Randall. 2009. "The Poverty of Postnationalism: Citizenship, Immigration, and the New Europe." *Theory and Society* 38 (1): 1–24.

Hansen, Randall, and Jobst Kohler. 2005. "Issue Definition, Political Discourse and the Politics of Nationality Reform in France and Germany." *European Journal of Political Research* 44 (5): 623–644.

Harrington, Mona. 1980. "Loyalties: Dual and Divided." In *Harvard Encyclopedia of American Ethnic Groups*, Stephan Thernstrom, ed., 676–686. Cambridge, MA: Harvard University Press.

Hazan, Miriam. 2006. *Incorporating in the United States and Mexico: Mexican Immigrant Mobilization and Organization in Four American Cities*. PhD dissertation, University of Texas, Austin.

Heinze, Andrew. 1990. *Adapting to Consumption: Jewish Immigrants, Mass Consumption and the Search for American Identity.* New York: Columbia University Press.

Hernandez, Sergio. 2005. "Urge IME a aprobar voto en el exterior." *El Norte,* May 15.

Hernández-León, Rubén. 2008. *Metropolitan Migrants: The Migration of Urban Mexicans to the United States.* Berkeley: University of California Press.

Hiller, Harry, and Tara Franz. 2004. "New Ties, Old Ties and Lost Ties: The Use of the Internet in Diaspora." *New Media and Society* 6 (6): 731–752.

Hinojosa, Rubén. 2003. "Statement." *Hearings,* Subcommittee on Financial Institutions and Consumer Credit, Committee on Financial Services, 108th Congress. Washington, DC: Government Printing Office.

Hobsbawm, Eric J. 1988. "Working-Class Internationalism." In *Internationalism in the Labour Movement,* Frits van Holthoon and Marcel van der Linden, eds., 1–18. V. I. Leiden, Netherlands: E. J. Brill.

———. 1994. *The Age of Extremes: A History of the World, 1914–1991.* New York: Pantheon.

Hollinger, David. 1995. *Postethnic America.* New York: Basic.

Howard, Marc. 2009. *The Politics of Citizenship in Europe.* New York: Cambridge University Press.

Howe, Irving. 1976. *World of Our Fathers.* New York: Harcourt.

Huntington, Samuel P. 1973. "Transnational Organizations in World Politics." *World Politics* 25.03: 334–368.

———. 2004. *Who Are We? The Challenge to America's National Identity.* New York: Simon and Schuster.

Instituto de los Mexicanos en el Exterior. 2004. *Mexicanos en el exterior,* 1, 9.

*Instituto Federal Electoral.* 1998 [2004]. *Informe de la comision de especialistas.* In *El voto de los mexicanos en el exterior,* Gonzalo Badillo Moreno, ed., 19–106. Michoacán: Gobierno del Estado de Michoacán.

———. 2006. *Avances y retos del proyecto del voto de los mexicanos residentes en el extranjero.* Presentation to the 7th Meeting of the Consejo Consultativo del Instituto de los Mexicanos en el Exterior.

———. 2012. *Informe final del voto de los mexicanos residentes en el exterior: Proceso electoral federal 2012.* http://www.votoextranjero.mx/c/document _library/get_file?uuid = fce8dbba-63e7-4e1e-946e-e09fd59de581&groupId = 10157.

Iskander, Natasha. 2010. *The Creative State: Forty Years of Migration and Development Policy in Morocco and Mexico.* Ithaca, NY: Cornell University Press.

Itzigsohn, Jose, and Silvia Giorguli Saucedo. 2002. "Immigrant Incorporation and Sociocultural Transnationalism." *International Migration Review* 36 (3): 766–798.

Itzigsohn, Jose, and Daniela Villacres. 2008. "Migrant Political Transnationalism and the Practice of Democracy: Dominican External Voting Rights and Salvadoran Home Town Associations." *Ethnic and Racial Studies* 31 (4): 664–686.

Jackson, Ben. 2003. "Foreign I.D. Ban Seen Damaging Immigrant Biz." *American Banker,* July 24.

Jacobson, David. 1996. *Rights Across Borders: Immigration and the Decline of Citizenship.* Baltimore, MD: Johns Hopkins University Press.

Jacobson, Roberta S. 2003. "Statement." *Hearings,* Subcommittee on Immigration, Border Security, and Claims, House Committee on the Judiciary, 108th Congress. Washington, DC: Government Printing Office.

Jessup, Philip. 1956. *Transnational Law.* New Haven, CT: Yale University Press.

Joppke, Christian. 2010. *Citizenship and Immigration.* Cambridge, England: Polity.

Josselin, Daphne, and William Wallace, eds. 2001. *Non-state Actors in World Politics.* New York: Palgrave.

Kaiser, Karl. 1971. "Transnational Relations as a Threat to the Democratic Process." *International Organization* 25 (3): 706–720.

Kapur, Devesh. 2005. "Remittances: The New Development Mantra?" In *Remittances: Development Impact and Future Prospects,* Samual Munzele Maimbo and Dilip Ratha, eds., 331–361. Washington, DC: World Bank.

Kapur, Devesh, and Kevin McHale. 2005. *Give Us Your Best and Brightest: The Global Hunt for Talent and Its Impact on the Developing World.* Washington, DC: Center for Global Development.

Kearney, Michael. 1995. "The Local and the Global: The Anthropology of Globalization and Transnationalism." *Annual Review of Anthropology* 24: 547–565.

Keck, Margaret, and Kathryn Sikkink. 1998. *Activists Beyond Borders: Advocacy Networks in International Politics.* Ithaca, NY: Cornell University Press.

Kemp, Adrianna, and Rebeca Raijman. 2004. " 'Tel Aviv Is Not Foreign to You': Urban Incorporation Policy on Labor Migrants in Israel." *International Migration Review* 38 (1): 26–51.

Kenny, Kevin. 2003. "Diaspora and Comparison: The Global Irish as a Case Study." *Journal of American History* 90 (1): 134–162.

Kerlin, Michael D. 2000. "New Agents of Socio-Economic Development: Guinea-Bissauan Hometown Associations in Portugal." *South European Society & Politics* 5 (3) (Winter 2000): 33–55.

Khagram, Sanjeev, and Peggy Levitt. 2005. "Toward a Field of Transnational Studies and a Sociological Transnationalism Research Program." Accessed July 28, 2007. http://www.transnational-studies.org/pdfs/transnational_field.pdf?abstract_id=556993.

Kijima, Yoko, and Horacio González-Ramirez. 2012. "Has the Program 3× 1 for Migrants Contributed to Community Development in Mexico? Evidence from Panel Data of 2000 and 2005." *Review of Development Economics* 16 (2): 291–304.

King, David, and Miles Pomper. 2004. "The US Congress and the Contingent Influence of Diaspora Lobbies: Lessons from US Policy toward Armenia and Azerbaijan." *Journal of Armenian Studies* 3 (1): 72–98.

Kivisto, Peter. 2001. "Theorizing Transnational Immigration: A Critical Review of Current Efforts." *Ethnic and Racial Studies* 24 (4): 549–577.

Koopmans, Ruud, Paul Statham, Marco Giugni, and Florence Passy. 2005. *Contested Citizenship: Immigration and Cultural Diversity in Europe.* Minneapolis: University of Minnesota Press.

Kurien, Prema. 2004. "Multiculturalism, Immigrant Religion, and Diasporic Nationalism: The Development of an American Hinduism." *Social Problems* 51 (3): 362–385.

Kuznetsov, Yevgeny, and Charles Sabel. 2006. "International Migration of Talent, Diaspora Networks, and Development: Overview of Main Issues." In *Diaspora Networks and the International Migration of Skills,* Yevgeny Kuznetsov, ed., 3–20. Washington, DC: World Bank.

Lacroix, Thomas. 2011. "Integration, transnationalism and development in a French-North African context," Paper presented to the 2011 Norface Conference on Migration, Economic Change and Social Challenge, http://halshs .archives-ouvertes.fr/docs/00/82/03/94/PDF/Lacroix_2011_norface_conf _paper.pdf

Laglagaron, Laureen. 2010. *Protection through Integration: The Mexican Government's Efforts to Aid Migrants in the United States.* Washington, DC: Migration Policy Institute.

*La Jornada.* 2007. "Piden al IFE credencial para votar en el extranjero," July 28.

Lanly, Guillaume, and M. Basilia Valenzuela V. 2004. "Introducción." In *Clubes de migrantes, oriundos mexicanos en los Estados Unidos: La political transnacional de la nueva sociedad Civil migrante,* Lanly and Valenzuela, eds. Guadalajara: Universidad de Guadalajara.

Leal, David L. 2002. "Political Participation by Non-Citizen Latinos in the United States." *British Journal of Political Science* 32: 353–370.

Leal, David L., Byung-Jae Lee, and James A. McCann. 2012. "Transnational Absentee Voting in the 2006 Mexican Presidential Election: The Roots of Participation." *Electoral Studies* 31 (3): 540–549.

Leiken, Robert. 2000. *The Melting Border: Mexico and Mexican Communities in the United States.* Washington, DC: Center for Equal Opportunity.

Lesage, Carol. 1998. "Organización y logística en Canadá." *Conferencia trilateral sobre el voto en el extranjero. Mexico: Tribunal electoral del poder judicial de la federación,* Instituto Federal Electoral, 101–108.

Levitt, Peggy. 1998. "Social Remittances: Migration Driven Local-Level Forms of Cultural Diffusion." *International Migration Review* 32 (4): 926–948.

———. 2001a. "Transnational Migration: Taking Stock and Future Directions." *Global Networks: A Journal of Transnational Affairs* 1 (3): 195–216.

———. 2001b. *The Transnational Villagers.* Berkeley: University of California Press.

Levitt, Peggy, and Rafael de la Dehesa. 2003. "Transnational Migration and the Redefinition of the State: Variations and Explanations." *Ethnic and Racial Studies* 26 (4): 587–611.

Levitt, Peggy, and Nina Glick Schiller. 2004. "Transnational Perspectives on Migration: Conceptualizing Simultaneity." *International Migration Review* 38 (3): 1002–1039.

Levitt, Peggy, and B. Nadya Jaworsky. 2007. "Transnational Migration Studies: Past Developments and Future Trends." *Annual Review of Sociology* 33: 129–155.

Levitt, Peggy, and Mary C. Waters, eds. 2002. *The Changing Face of Home: The Transnational Lives of the Second Generation.* New York: Russell Sage.

Lewis, David Levering. 1984. "Parallels and Divergences: Assimilations Strategies of Afro-American and Jewish Elites from 1910 to the Early 1930s." *Journal of American History* 71 (3): 543–564.

Liang, Zai. 2001. "Rules of the Game and Game of the Rules: The Politics of Recent Chinese Immigration to New York City." In *Migration, Transnationalization, and Race in a Changing New York,* Hector Cordero-Guzman et al., eds., 131–145. Philadelphia, PA: Temple University Press.

Licoppe, Christian. 2004. " 'Connected Presence': The Emergence of a New Repertoire for Managing Social Relationships in a Changing Communication Technoscape." *Environment and Planning D: Society and Space* 22: 135–156.

Licuanan, Victoria, Toman Omar Mahmoud, and Andreas Steinmayr. 2012. *The Drivers of Diaspora Donations for Development: Evidence from the Philippines.* Kiel Institute for the World Economy, Working Paper, No. 1807.

Lindemeyer, Isabelle. 2005. "Remittance Lift for B of A by Mexican Government." *American Banker,* July 11.

Livingston, Gretchen. 2011. *Latinos and Digital Technology, 2010.* Report of the Pew Hispanic Center. http://www.pewhispanic.org/2011/02/09/latinos-and-digital-technology-2010/.

Lopez, Mark Hugo, Ana González-Barrera, and Eileen Patten. 2013. *Closing the Digital Divide: Latinos and Technology Adoption.* Washington: Pew Hispanic Center. Accessed January 28, 2014. http://www.pewhispanic.org/files/2013/03/Latinos_Social_Media_and_Mobile_Tech_03-2013_final.pdf.

Lopez, Sarah. 2010. "The Remittance House: Architecture of Migration in Rural Mexico." *Buildings and Landscapes* 17 (2): 33–52.

Luconi, Stefano. 2007. "The Impact of Italy's Twentieth-Century Wars on Italian Americans' Ethnic Identity." *Nationalism and Ethnic Politics* 13 (3): 465–491.

Lyons, Terence, and Peter Mandaville, eds. 2011. *Politics from Afar: Transnational Diasporas and Networks.* New York: Columbia University Press.

Maciel, David. 2000. *El bandolero, el pocho y la Raza: Imágenes cinematográficas del chicano.* Mexico: Siglo XXI Editores/CONACULTA.

Mahler, Sarah J. 2001. "Transnational Relationships: The Struggle to Communicate across Borders." *Identities Global Studies in Culture and Power* 7 (4): 583–619.

MALDEF (Mexican American Legal Defense and Education Fund). 2003. "Acceptance of Mexican Consular IDS Is Not Only Legal—It Improves Public Safety and Enhances the Economy." *Hearings,* Subcommittee on Financial Institutions and Consumer Credit, Committee on Financial Services, 108th Congress. Washington, DC: Government Printing Office.

Mann, Michael. 1993. *The Sources of Social Power,* Vol. II, Cambridge, England: Cambridge University Press.

Martínez Saldaña, Jesús. 2002. "Participación política migrante: Praxis cotidiana de Ciudadanos Excluidos." In *La dimensión politica de la migración mexicana,* Leticia Calderón Chelius and Jesús Martínez Saldaña, 159–331. Mexico City: Instituto Mora.

Martínez Saldaña, Jesús, and Raúl Ross Pineda. 2002. "Suffrage for Mexicans residing abroad." In *Cross-Border Dialogues: US-Mexico Social Movement Networking.* David Brooks and Jonathan Fox, eds., La Jolla, CA: University of California, San Diego, Center for US-Mexican Studies.

Massey, Douglas, Jorge Durand, Rafael Alarcon, and Humberto González.1987. *Return to Aztlan.* Berkeley: University of California Press.

Mathew, Biju, and Vijay Prashad. 2000. "The Protean Forms of Yankee Hindutva." *Ethnic and Racial Studies* 23 (3): 516–534.

Mattelart, Tristan. 2009. "Les Diasporas à l'heure des technologies de l'information et de la communication: petit état des savoirs." *tic&société* 3: 1–2.

Mayer, Philip. 1962. "Migrancy and the Study of African Towns." *American Anthropologist* 64 (3): 576–592.

Mazzolari, Francesca. 2009. "Dual Citizenship Rights: Do They Make More and Richer Citizens?" *Demography* 46 (1): 169–191.

Mazzucato, Valentina. 2009. "Informal Insurance Arrangements in Ghanaian Migrants' Transnational Networks: The Role of Reverse Remittances and Geographic Proximity." *World Development* 37 (6): 1105–1114.

Mazzucato, Valentina, and Mirjam Kabki. 2009. "Small Is Beautiful: The Micropolitics of Transnational Relationships Between Ghanaian Hometown Associations and Communities Back Home." *Global Networks* 9 (2): 227–251.

Mazzucato, Valentina, and Djamila Schans. 2011. "Transnational Families and the Well-Being of Children: Conceptual and Methodological Challenges." Journal of Marriage and Family 73.4: 704–712.

McCann, James, Wayne A. Cornelius, and David Leal. 2007. *Transnational Political Engagement and the Civic Incorporation of Immigrants in the United States.* Paper presented at the XXVII International Congress of the Latin American Studies Association, September 5–8, 2007, Montreal, Canada.

———. 2009. "Absentee Voting and Transnational Civic Engagement among Mexican Expatriates." In *Consolidating Mexico's Democracy,* Jorge Dominguez and Chappell Lawson, eds. Baltimore, MD: Johns Hopkins University Press.

McGraw, Stephen. 2003. "Statement." *Hearings,* Subcommittee on Immigration, Border Security, and Claims, House Committee on the Judiciary, 108th Congress. Washington, DC: Government Printing Office.

Mejia-Estévez, Silvia. 2009. "Is Nostalgia Becoming Digital? Ecuadorian Disapora in the Age of Global Capitalism." *Social Identities* 15 (3): 393–410.

Melissen, Jan, and Ana Mar Fernandez. 2011. *Consular Affairs and Diplomacy.* Boston, MA: Martinus Nijhoff.

Mendelsohn, Ezra. 1993. *On Modern Jewish Politics.* New York: Oxford University Press.

Michaels, Daniel. 2007. " 'Ethnic' Routes—Growth Market for Airlines: Cheap Travel for Immigrants; For Hungary's Wizz Air, Focus Is on Trips Home; Cork-Katowice for $26." *Wall Street Journal,* March 7, A1.

*Migration News.* 1996. "Immigrant Beatings, Numbers and Naturalization." 3, 5. Accessed February 26, 2014. http://migration.ucdavis.edu/mn/more .php?id=939_0_2_0.

Milbank, Dana. 2001. "Bush Goes Slow on Immigrant Amnesty—Resistance in Congress Forces Gradual Steps." *Washington Post,* August 20.

Miller, Arpi. 2011. " 'Doing' Transnationalism: The Integrative Impact of Salvadoran Cross-Border Activism." *Journal of Ethnic and Migration Studies* 37 (1): 43–60.

Miller, Daniel, and Mirca Madianou. 2011. "Mobile Phone Parenting: Reconfiguring Relationships between Filipina Mothers and Their Children in the Philippines." *New Media & Society* 13: 457–470.

Miller, Mark. 1981. *Foreign Workers in Western Europe: An Emerging Political Force.* New York: Praeger.

Millman, Joel. 2006. "Consulates in US Hit the Road to Help Far-Flung Paisanos; Workers Off the Beaten Track Need Diplomatic Aid; Mr. Castillo's Remittances." *Wall Street Journal,* November 29.

Milza, Pierre. 1993. *Voyage en Ritalie.* Paris: Payot.

Morawska, Ewa. 1985. *For Bread with Butter: The Life-worlds of East Central Europeans in Johnstown, Pennsylvania.* New York: Cambridge.

———. 2001. "Immigrants, Transnationalism, and Ethnicization: A Comparison of This Great Wave and the Last." In *E Pluribus Unum? Contemporary and Historical Perspectives on Immigrant Political Incorporation,* Gary Gerstle and John H. Mollenkopf, eds., 175–212. New York: Russell Sage.

———. 2003. "Immigrant Transnationalism and Assimilation: A Variety of Combinations and the Analytic Strategy It Suggests." In *Toward Assimilation and Citizenship: Immigrants in Liberal Nation-States,* Christian Joppke and Ewa Morawska, eds., 133–76. New York: Palgrave.

———. 2005. "The Sociology and History of Immigration: Reflections of a Practicioner." In *International Migration Research: Constructions, Omissions, and Promises of Interdisciplinarity,* Michael Bommes and Ewa Morawska, eds., 203–242. Aldershot, England: Ashgate.

Mormino, Gary, and George E. Pozzetta. 1987. *The Immigrant World of Ybor City: Italians and Their Latin Neighbors in Tampa, 1885–1985.* Urbana: University of Illinois Press.

Moya, Jose C. 1998. *Cousins and Strangers: Spanish Immigrants in Buenos Aires.* Berkeley: University of California Press.

———. 2005. "Immigrants and Associations: A Global and Historical Perspective." *Journal of Ethnic and Migration Studies* 31 (5): 833–864.

Muñiz, Brenda. 2003. "The Role of Matrícula Consular at Financial Institutions." Statement submitted by the National Council of La Raza to the *Hearings,* Subcommittee on Financial Institutions and Consumer Credit, Committee on Financial Services, 108th Congress. Washington, DC: Government Printing Office.

Muñoz Bata, Sergio. 2001. "Frontera invisible/ Recuperan su nombre y su origen." *La Reforma,* November 29.

National Audit Office. 2005. *Consular Services to British Nationals Abroad.* London: National Audit Office.

Navarro, Carlos. 2007. "El voto en el extranjero." In *Tratado de derecho electoral comparado de América Latina,* Dieter Nohlen et al., eds., 224–252. Mexico City: Fondo de Cultura Económica.

Navarro Fierro, Carlos, and Manuel Carillo. 2007. "Mexico: Safeguarding the Integrity of the Electoral Process." In *Voting from Abroad: The International IDEA Handbook,* IDEA, 189–192. Sweden: International IDEA.

Nimtz, August. 2002. "Marx and Engels: The Prototypical Transnational Actors." In *Restructuring World Politics: Transnational Social Movements, Networks, and Norms,* Sanjeev Khagram, et al., eds., 245–268. Minneapolis: University of Minnesota Press.

Nohlen, Dieter, and Florian Grotz. 2000. "External Voting: Legal Framework and Overview of Electoral Legislation." *Boletín Mexicano de Derecho Comparativo* 99: 1115–1145.

———. 2007. "The Legal Framework and an Overview of Election Regulation." In *Voting from Abroad: The International IDEA Handbook,* IDEA, 65–76. Sweden: International IDEA.

Nosthas, Ernesto. 2006. "Acciones del gobernó salvadoreño en torno a la migración." In *Relaciones estado-diáspora: La perspective de América Latina y el Caribe,* Carlos González Gutierrez, ed., Volume 1, 365–74. Mexico, DF: Porrua.

Nye, Joseph S. Jr., and Robert O. Keohane. 1971. "Transnational Relations and World Politics: An Introduction." *International Organization* 25 (3): 329–349.

Ó Dochartaigh, Niall. 2009. "Reframing Online: Ulster Loyalists Imagine an American Audience." *Identities: Global Studies in Culture and Power* 16: 102–127.

Ögelman, Nedim. 2003. "Documenting and Explaining the Persistence of Homeland Politics among Germany's Turks." *International Migration Review* 37 (1): 163–193.

Okano-Heijmans, Maaike. 2011. "Changes in Consular Assistance and the Emergence of Consular Diplomacy." In *Consular Affairs and Diplomacy,* Jan Melissen and Ana Mar Fernández, eds., 21–42. Leiden, Netherlands: Martinus Neijhoff.

O'Neil, Kevin. 2003. "Consular ID Cards: Mexico and Beyond, Migration Information Source." April 1. Accessed on January 23, 2009. http://www .migrationinformation.org/feature/print.cfm?ID=115H.

Ono, Hiroshi, and Madeline Zavodny. 2008. "Immigrants, English Ability and the Digital Divide." *Social Forces* 86 (4): 1455–1479.

Orozco, M. 2005. "Transnationalism and Development: Trends and Opportunities in Latin America." *Remittances: Development Impact and Future Prospects,* 307–330.

Ostergaard-Nielsen, E. 2003. "International Migration and Sending Countries: Key Issues and Themes." In *International Migration and Sending Countries,*

*Perceptions, Policies and Transnational Relations,* E. Ostergaard-Nielsen, ed., 3–33. New York: Palgrave Macmillan.

———. 2003a. "The Politics of Migrants' Transnational Political Practices." *International Migration Review* 37 (3): 760–786.

———. 2003b. "Turkey and the 'Euro-Turks': Overseas Nationals as an Ambiguous Asset." In *International Migration and Sending Countries: Perceptions, Policies, and Transnational Relations,* Eva Ostergaard-Nielsen, ed., 77–98. London: Palgrave.

Painter, Joe, and Chris Philo. 1995. "Spaces of Citizenship: An Introduction." *Political Geography* 14 (2): 107–120.

Pan American Development Foundation (PADF). 2005. *Increasing the Impact of Community Remittances on Education in El Salvador.* Washington, DC: Pan-American Development Foundation.

Panayi, Panikos, ed. 1993. *Minorities in Wartime: National and Racial Groupings in Europe, North America, and Australia During the Two World Wars.* Providence, RI: Berg.

Paschalidis, Gregory. 2009. "Exporting National Culture: Histories of Cultural Institutes Abroad." *International Journal of Cultural Policy* 5 (3): 275–289.

Paul, Alison, and Sarah Gammage. 2004. *Hometown Associations and Development: The Case of El Salvador.* Destination DC Working Paper, No. 3. Women's Studies Department, George Washington University and Center for Women and Work, Rutgers, The State University of New Jersey. Washington, DC.

Paul, Rachel Anderson. 2000. "Grassroots Mobilization and Diaspora Politics: Armenian Interest Groups and the Role of Collective Memory." *Nationalism and Ethnic Politics* 6 (1): 24–47.

Paz, Octavio, ed. 1994. *The Labyrinth of Solitude.* New York: Grove Weidenfeld.

Peñaloza, Lisa. 1994. "Atravesando Fronteras/Border Crossings: A Critical Ethnographic Exploration of the Consumer Acculturation of Mexican Immigrants." *Journal of Consumer Research* 21 (1): 32–54.

Peres, W., and M. Hilbert. 2009. *La sociedad de la información en América Latina y el Caribe: Desarrollo de las tecnologias y tecnologias para el desarrollo.* ECLAC Institutional Book, N. 98 (LC/G.2363-P), Santiago, Chile.

Pérez-Armendáriz, Clarissa, and David Crow. 2009. "Do Migrants Remit Democracy? International Migration and Political Beliefs and Behavior in Mexico." *Comparative Political Studies* 42 (9): 1–28.

Perez Godoy, S. Mara. 1998. *Social Movements and Internacional Migration: The Mexican Diaspora Seeks Inclusión in Mexico's Political Affaire, 1968–1998.* Unpublished PhD dissertation, University of Chicago.

Perkins, Richard, and Eric Neumayer. 2010. *The Ties That Bind: The Role of Migrants in the Uneven Geography of International Telephone Traffic.* Working paper, Department of Geography and Environment, London School of Economics and Political Science.

Perla, Hector. 2008. "Grassroots Mobilization against US Military Intervention in El Salvador." *Socialism and Democracy* 22 (3): 143–159.

Piore, Michael. 1979. *Birds of Passage.* Cambridge, England: Cambridge University Press.

Plutzer, Eric. 2002. "Becoming a Habitual Voter: Inertia, Resources, and Growth in Young Adulthood." *American Political Science Review* 96: 41–56.

Poinard, Michel. 1988. "La politique d'un pays d'origine : le Portugal." *Revue européenne des migrations internationales* 4 (1–2): 187–202.

Popkin, Eric. 2003. "Transnational Migration and Development in Postwar Peripheral States: An Examination of Guatemalan and Salvadoran State Linkages with Their Migrant Populations in Los Angeles." *Current Sociology* 51 (3–4): 347–374.

Porter, Eduardo. 2002. "Mexico Pushes ID for Migrants—Aim Is to Integrate Workers into US Locales as Amnesty Founders." *Wall Street Journal*, October 25.

———. 2003. "Banks Can Accept Foreign IDs." *Wall Street Journal*, September 19, A12.

Portes, Alejandro. 1997. "Immigration Theory for a New Century." *International Migration Review* 31 (4): 799–825.

———. 1999. "Conclusion: Towards a New World: The Origins and Effects of Transnational Activities." *Ethnic and Racial Studies* 22 (2): 463–477.

———. 2003. "Conclusion: Theoretical Convergencies and Empirical Evidence in the Study of Immigrant Transnationalism." *International Migration Review* 37 (3): 874–892.

Portes, Alejandro, Luis E. Guarnizo, and Patricia Landolt. 1999. "The Study of Transnationalism: Pitfalls and Promise of an Emergent Research Field." *Ethnic and Racial Studies* 22 (2): 217–237.

Portes, Alejandro, William J. Haller, and Luis Eduardo Guarnizo. 2002. "Transnational Entrepreneurs: An Alternative Form of Immigrant Economic Adaptation." *American Sociological Review* 67 (2): 278–298.

Portes, Alejandro, and Patricia Landolt. 2000. Social Capital: Promise and Pitfalls of Its Role in Development." *Journal of Latin American Studies* 32 (2).

Portes, Alejandro, and Rubén Rumbaut. 2006. *Immigrant America* (3rd edition). Berkeley: University of California Press.

Pradillo, Augustin. 2002. "La matrícula consular: Un rostro con identidad." *La Opinión*, July 9.

Pribilsky, Jason. 2007. *"La Chulla Vida": Gender, Migration and the Family in Andean Ecuador and New York City*. Syracuse, NY: Syracuse University Press.

Price, Richard. 2003. "Transnational Civil Society and Advocacy in World Politics." *World Politics* 55 (4): 579–606.

Pritchett, Lant. 2006. *Let Their People Come: Breaking the Gridlock on Global Labor Mobility*. Washington, DC: Center for Global Development.

Programa de las Naciones Unidas para el Desarrollo. 2005. *Informe sobre el desarrollo humano en El Salvador: Una mirada al nuevo nosotros. El impacto de las migraciones*. San Salvador, El Salvador: PNUD.

———. 2007. *Informe sobre desarrollo humano: México, 2006–2007*. Mexico City: PNUD.

Rabadán, Luis Escala, Gaspar Rivera-Salgado, and Rigoberto Rodríguez. 2011. "Is More Necessarily Better? Leadership and Organizational Development of Migrant Hometown Associations in Los Angeles, California." *Migraciones Internacionales* 6 (2): 41–73.

Ramakrishnan, S. Karthick, Jane Junn, Taeku Lee, and Janelle Wong. 2008. National Asian American Survey, 2008. ICPSR31481-v2. Ann Arbor, MI: Inter-university Consortium for Political and Social Research [distributor], 2012-07-19. doi:10.3886/ICPSR31481.v2.

Ramakrishnan, S. Karthick, and Celia Viramontes. 2010. "Civic Spaces: Mexican Hometown Associations and Immigrant Participation." *Journal of Social Issues* 66 (1): 155–173.

Ramirez, Bruno. 1991. *On the Move: French Canadian and Italian Migrants in the North Atlantic Economy, 1860–1914*. Toronto, Canada: McClellan and Stewart.

Ramirez, G. Jacques. 2007. "'Aunque sea tan lejos nos vemos todos los días': Migracion transnacionaly uso de nuevas tecnologias de comunicacion." In *Los Usos de Internet: comunicación y sociedad*, 7–64, Volume 2. Quito, Ecuador: FLACSO.

Richman, Karen. 1992. "'A *Luvalas* at Home/A *Lavalas* for Home': Inflections of Transnationalism in the Discourse of Haitian President Aristide." *Annals of the New York Academy of Sciences* 645: 189–200.

Risse-Kappen, Thomas. 1995. "Bringing Transnational Relations Back In: An Introduction." In *Bringing Transnational Relations Back*, Thomas Risse-Kappen, ed., 3–36. Cambridge, England: Cambridge University Press.

Rodríguez Oseguera, Primitivo. 2005. "Asi se gano el voto!" *Mexicanos sin Fronteras*, 14–20.

Rojas, Francisca. 2010. *New York Talk Exchange: Transnational Telecommunications and Migration*. PhD dissertation, Massachusetts Institute of Technology, Cambridge, Mass.

Rosenberg, Clifford. 2006. *Policing Paris: The Origins of Modern Immigration Control between the Wars*. Ithaca, NY: Cornell University Press.

Rosenstone, Steven J., and John Mark Hanson. 1993. *Mobilization, Participation, and Democracy in America*. New York: Macmillan.

Rosental, Paul-Andre. 2011. "Migrations, souveraineté, droits sociaux. Protéger et expulser les étrangers en Europe du XIXe siècle à nos jours." *Annales. Histoires, Sciences Sociales* 66 (2): 335–373.

Rouse, Roger. 1991. "Making Sense of Settlement—Class Transformation, Cultural Struggle, and Transnationalism among Mexican Migrants in the United States." In *Towards a Transnational Perspective on Migration: Race, Class, Ethnicity, and Nationalism Reconsidered*, Nina Glick Schiller, Linda Basch, and Cristina Blanc-Szanton, eds., 25–52. New York: New York Academy of Sciences.

———. 1995. "Questions of Identity: Personhood and Collectivity in Transnational Migration to the United States." *Critical Anthropology* 15 (4): 351–380.

Salyer, Lucy. 1995. *Laws Harsh as Tigers: Chinese Immigrants and the Shaping of Modern Immigration Law*. Chapel Hill: University of North Carolina Press.

Santamaría Gómez, Arturo. 1994. *La politica entre Mexico y Aztlan*. Culiacán Rosales: Universidad Autonoma de Sinaloa.

———. 2006. *Emigrantes Mexicanos: Movimientos y elecciones transterritoriales*. Culiacán Rosales: Universidad Autonoma de Sinaloa.

Sargent, Carolyn, Samba Yatera, and Stephanie Larchanché-Kim. 2005. "Migrations et nouvelles technologies." *Hommes et migrations* 1256: 131–14.

Sassen-Koob, Saskia. 1979. "Formal and Informal Associations: Dominicans and Colombians in New York." *International Migration Review*: 314–332.

Saunier, Pierre-Yves. 2009. "Transnationalism." In *The Palgrave Dictionary of Transnational History*, Arika Iriye and Pierre-Yves Saunier, eds., 1047–1055. New York: Palgrave.

Sayad, Abdelmalek. 1991. *L'Immigration ou les paradoxes de l'aterité*. Paris: Raison d'agir.

Schuetz, Alfred. 1944. "The Homecomer." *American Journal of Sociology* 50 (5): 369–376.

Scopsi, Claire. 2004. "Représentation des TIC et multiterritorialité : Le cas des télé et cyber boutiques de Château-Rouge, à Paris." In *Technologies de la Communication et Mondialisation en Afrique*, Anne Cheneau-Loquay, ed. Paris: Karthala.

Secretaria de Relaciones Exteriores. 2008. *Segundo informe de labores*. Mexico City: Gobierno de los Estados Unidos de México.

Shain, Yossi. 1999. *Marketing the American Creed Abroad: Diasporas in the US and Their Homelands*. New York: Cambridge University Press.

Sierra Blas, Verónica. 2004. "Puentes de papel: Apuntes sobre las escrituras de la emigración." *Horizontes Antropológicos* 10 (22): 121–147.

Sinke, Suzanne. 2006. "Marriage Through the Mail: North American Correspondence Marriage from Early Print to the Web." In *Letters Across Borders: The Epistolary Practices of International Migrants*, Bruce Elliot, David Gerber, and Suzanne Sinke, eds., 75–96. New York: Palgrave.

Sirkeci, Ibrahim, Jeffrey Cohen, and Dilip Ratha. 2012. *Migration and Remittances during the Global Financial Crisis and Beyond*. Washington, DC: World Bank.

Sklair, Leslie. 2001. *The Transnational Capitalist Class*. Oxford: Malden, MA: Blackwell.

Smith, Michael Peter, and Matt Bakker. 2008. *Citizenship Across Borders: The Political Transnationalism of "El Migrante."* Ithaca, NY: Cornell University Press.

Smith, Robert C. 2006. *Mexican New York: Transnational Lives of New Immigrants*. Berkeley: University of California Press.

———. 2008. "Contradictions of Diasporic Institutionalization in Mexican Politics: The 2006 Migrant Vote and Other Forms of Inclusion and Control." *Ethnic and Racial Studies* 31 (4): 708–741.

Smith, Tom. 1994. *What Do Americans Think About Jews?* New York: American Jewish Committee.

Smith, Tony. 2000. *Foreign Attachments: The Power of Ethnic Groups in the Making of American Foreign Policy*. Cambridge, MA: Harvard University Press.

Soehl, Thomas, and Roger Waldinger. 2010. "Making the Connection: Latino Immigrants and their Cross-Border Ties." *Ethnic and Racial Studies* 33 (9): 1489–1510.

Soyer, Daniel. 1997. *Jewish Immigrant Associations and American Identity in New York, 1880–1939*. Cambridge, MA: Harvard University Press.

Soysal, Yasemin. 1994. *The Limits of Citizenship*. Chicago, IL: University of Chicago Press.

Stack, John F., Jr. 1979. *Ethnic Conflict in an International City*. Westport, CT: Greenwood.

———. 1981. *Ethnic Identities in a Transnational World*. Westport, CT: Greenwood.

Swarns, Rachel. 2003. "Old ID Card Gives New Status to Mexicans in US" *New York Times*, August 25.

Taylor, J. Edward, and Philip L. Martin. 2001. "Human Capital: Migration and Rural Population Change." In *Handbook of Agricultural Economics*, 458–503. Amsterdam: Elsevier.

Tichenor, Daniel. 2002. *Dividing Lines: The Politics of Immigration Control in America*. Princeton, NJ: Princeton University Press.

Torpey, John. 1999. *The Invention of the Passport: Surveillance, Citizenship, and the State*. Cambridge, England: Cambridge University Press.

Torres, Federico, and Yevgeny Kuznetsov. 2006. "Mexico: Leveraging Migrants' Capital to Develop Hometown Communities." In *Diaspora Networks and the International Migration of Skills*, Yevgeny Kuznetsov, ed., 99–128. Washington, DC: World Bank.

Truax, Eileen. 2005. "Caravana por el voto postal." *La Opinión*, November 22.

———. 2007. "Mexicanos exigen credencial al IFE." *La Opinión*, July 22.

United Nations. 2005. *Vienna Convention on Consular Relations*. New York: United Nations.

United Nations Development Program. 2009. *Overcoming Barriers: Human Mobility and Development*. New York: United Nations.

United States Department of the Treasury, 2002. *Report to Congress in Accordance with Section 326b of the USA PATRIOT Act*, October 21.

Urrutia, Alfonso. 2004. "Demandan organizaciones de mexicanos en el extranjero derecho al voto en 2006." *La Jornada*, February 16.

Varsanyi, Monica. 2007. "Documenting Undocumented Migrants: The Matrículas Consulares as Neoliberal Local Membership." *Geopolitics* 12 (2): 299–319.

Verba, S., K. Schlozman, and H. Brady. 1995. *Voice and Equality: Civic Voluntarism in American Politics*. Cambridge, MA: Harvard University Press.

Verdery, C. Stewart. 2003. Statement. *Hearings*, Subcommittee on Immigration, Border Security, and Claims, House Committee on the Judiciary, 108th Congress. Washington, DC: Government Printing Office.

Vertovec, Steven. 1999. "Conceiving and Researching Transnationalism." *Ethnic and Racial Studies* 22 (2): 447–462.

———. 2004. "Cheap Calls: The Social Glue of Migrant Transnationalism." *Global Networks* 4 (2): 219–224.

Wald, Kenneth D. 2008. "Homeland Interests, Hostland Politics: Politicized Ethnic Identity among Middle Eastern Heritage Groups in the United States." *International Migration Review* 42 (2): 273–301.

Waldinger, Roger. 2003. "Foreigners Transformed: International Migration and the Making of a Divided People." *Diaspora* 12 (2): 247–272.

———. 2007a. "Between Here and There: How Attached Are Latino Immigrants to Their Native Country?" Report, Pew Hispanic Center, October 25.

———. 2007b. "Transforming Foreigners into Americans." In *The New Americans*, Mary Waters and Reed Ueda, eds., 137–148. Cambridge, MA: Harvard University Press.

———. 2008. "Immigrant 'Transnationalism' and the Presence of the Past." In *Borders, Boundaries, and Bonds: America and Its Immigrants in Eras of Globalization*, Elliot Barkan et al., eds., 267–285. New York: New York University Press.

Waldinger, Roger, and David Fitzgerald. 2004. "Transnationalism in Question." *American Journal of Sociology* 109 (5): 1177–1195.

Waldinger, Roger, Eric Popkin, and Hector Aquiles Magana. 2007. "Conflict and Contestation in the Cross-Border Community: Hometown Associations Reassessed." *Ethnic and Racial Studies* 31: 1–28.

Waldinger, Roger, and Thomas Soehl. 2013. "The Bounded Polity: The Limits to Mexican Emigrant Political Participation." *Social Forces* 91 (4): 1239–1266.

Waldinger, Roger, Thomas Soehl, and Nelson Lim. 2012. "Emigrants and the Body Politic Left Behind." *Journal of Ethnic and Migration Studies* 38 (5): 711–736.

Wayland, Sarah. 2004. "Ethnonationalist Networks and Transnational Opportunities: The Sri Lankan Tamil Diaspora." *Review of International Studies* 30 (3): 405–426.

Weil, Patrick. 1991. *La France et ses étrangers: L'aventure d'une politique de l'immigration, 1938–1991*. Paris: Calmann-Levy.

Weisser, Michael. 1989. *A Brotherhood of Memory: Jewish Landsmanshaftn in the New World*. Ithaca, NY: Cornell University Press.

Wells, Miriam. 2004. "The Grassroots Reconfiguration of US Immigration Policy." *International Migration Review* 38 (4): 1308–1347.

Wells Fargo. 2001. "Wells Fargo to Accept Matrícula Consular Card as Identification for New Account Openings." Wells Fargo news release, November 9.

———. 2003. "Wells Fargo Matrícula Account Openings Surpass Quarter Million Mark." News Release, October 24.

White, Hugh. 2007. *Looking after Australians Overseas*. Canberra, Australia: Lowy Institute for International Policy.

Wilding, Raelene. 2006. "Virtual Intimacies? Families Communicating Across Transnational Contexts." *Global Networks* 6 (2): 125–142.

Woldenberg, Jose. 2004. "La autoridad electoral federal ante el voto de los Mexicanos en el exterior." In *La puerta que llama: El voto de los mexicanos en el exterior*, Gonzalo Badillo Moreno, ed., 301–310. Mexico City: Senado de la Republica.

Wong, Janelle, et al. 2011. *Asian American Political Participation: Emerging Constituents and Their Participation.* New York: Russell Sage Foundation.

World Bank. 2006. *Global Economic Prospects: Economic Implications of Remittances and Migration.* Washington, DC: World Bank.

Wyman, David. 1993. *Round-Trip to America: The Immigrants Return to Europe, 1880–1920.* Ithaca, NY: Cornell University Press.

Zamudio Grave, Patricia. 1999. *Huejuquillense Immigrants in Chicago: Culture, Gender, and Community in the Shaping of Consciousness.* PhD dissertation: Northwestern University.

Zhang, Kenny. 2007. *Global Canadians: A Survey of the Views of Canadians Abroad.* Vancouver, British Columbia: Asia Pacific Foundation of Canada.

Zolberg, Aristide. 1999. "Matters of State: Theorizing Immigration Policy." In *The Handbook of International Migration: The American Experience,* Charles Hirschmann, Philip Kasinitz, and Josh DeWind, eds., 71–92. New York: Russell Sage.

Zolberg, Aristide, and Long Litt Woon. 1999. "Why Islam Is Like Spanish: Cultural Incorporation in Europe and the United States." *Politics and Society* 27: 5–38.

Zumbansen, Peer. 2006. "Transnational Law." In *Encyclopedia of Comparative Law,* Jan Smits, ed., 738–754. London: Edward Elgar.

# Acknowledgments

The product of more than a decade's work, this book, like any other long-term endeavor, owes much to those who have encouraged, supported, and worked with me along the way. As an intellectual project, the book's origins lie in an article that I co-authored in the early 2000s with David Fitzgerald, then a graduate student at UCLA, now the holder of the Gildred Chair in US-Mexican Relations at UC–San Diego and an influential immigration scholar in his own right. The stimulus needed to move toward a book came from Nancy Green's invitation to present a series of lectures to her immigration seminar at the École des Hautes Études en Sciences Sociales in Paris in 2006. I am delighted to take this opportunity to thank David for initially venturing out with me on this path, Nancy for the invitation that proved so important, and the École des Hautes Études en Sciences Sociales for the visiting professorship that made those lectures possible. As it happens, the last touches on this book were also made in Paris, where a fellowship from the Fondation de la Maison des Sciences de l'Homme allowed me to work on the copy-edited version of this manuscript in style. Grateful thanks to Michel Wieviorka, a distinguished sociologist and administrator of the Maison des Sciences de l'Homme, and Dana Diminescu, the director of the program on *Migrations et numérique,* who made this stay possible.

It is also a great pleasure to express my appreciation to the funders that provided support for the various research projects on which this book is based. I am particularly grateful for a fellowship from the John Simon Guggenheim Foundation as well as grants from the Russell Sage (#88–08–05) and National Science (SES-0751944) Foundations. Needless to say, I am solely responsible for the conclusions reported in these pages.

Portions of two chapters were previously published and I am grateful to Oxford University Press for allowing them to be reprinted here: parts of Chapter 3 were first published in a chapter entitled, "Beyond Transnationalism: An Alternative Perspective on Immigrants' Homeland Connections," in the *Oxford Handbook of the Politics of International Migration,* edited by Marc Rosenblum and Daniel Tichenor; parts of Chapter 5 were published as "Engaging from Abroad: The Sociology of Emigrant Politics," *Migration Studies, doi: 10.1093/migration/mnt003,* first published online: August 14, 2013.

Thanks to Roberto Suro, then director of the Pew Hispanic Center, I was able to collaborate with the center in designing a questionnaire oriented toward many of the questions pursued in this book and that was used by the 2006 Latino National Survey. I am grateful to Roberto for engaging me in that project and for his continuing colleagueship.

Three-quarters of a sabbatical taken in 2009 and 2010 allowed me to take the long breather from normal academic responsibilities needed to devote full attention to this project. Thanks to one-quarter of a sabbatical in 2014, I was finally able to bring this book to completion. I am deeply grateful to my home institution, UCLA—and indirectly, the taxpayers of California—for such generous support.

For the past twenty-three years, I have had the good fortune to be a member of UCLA's Department of Sociology. I wish to thank my colleagues for the uniquely supportive and stimulating intellectual environment that they have provided: without them, and without the marvelous graduate students that they have attracted, this book could not have been written. Collaboration with Renee Reichl Luthra, Hector Aquiles Magaña, and Arpi Miller, then graduate students and now on to other and better things, made this a more fruitful and enjoyable project. A special word of thanks is owed Thomas Soehl for several years of close and very stimulating collaboration; the results of our work together appear at various points in the book, but especially in Chapters 4 and 5.

I am also grateful to Michael Aronson, my editor at Harvard University Press, for his interest in this project. Mike and I worked together almost twenty years ago on a previous project and I am delighted to be reunited with him once again.

And last, a word for my particular homeland: while very good times were had in the writing of this book, the best times were spent with Hilary, Max, Mimi, and Joey. This book is for you.

# Index